New Life Tables for Latin American Populations In the Nineteenth and Twentieth Centuries

EDUARDO E. ARRIAGA

Price—$2.75

Institute of International Studies
University of California, Berkeley

FOREWORD

In 1963 the University of California at Berkeley, in be-
half of its demographic research office, International Population
and Urban Research, received from the Rockefeller Foundation a
generous grant for comparative studies in Latin American demography.
With this support, plus additional funds from the Institute of
International Studies, a program was begun in which studies appear-
ing logically to be prior to other possible investigations were
given priority. Such basic studies had three characteristics--
they had to deal with fundamental rather than peripheral aspects
of demography, to cover as long a period as possible, and to pay
particular attention to methodological problems. The results of
the first of these studies were reported in two monographs on
fertility published by the Institute of International Studies:
O. A. Collver's Birth Rates in Latin America, published in 1965,
and J. R. Rele's Fertility Analysis Through Extension of Stable
Population Concepts, published in 1967. Collver attempted to reconstruct the history of fertility in Latin American countries as
far back as data permitted, and Rele tested and extended some of
the results for recent periods using somewhat different methods.
These two studies were among the first to call attention to the
widespread rise in fertility in the underdeveloped countries in
recent decades--a rise due to the extremely rapid improvement in
health conditions.

Along with the studies of fertility in Latin America, a
companion investigation of historical trends in mortality was
begun. Here, as with the analysis of fertility, a major problem
was that of evaluating, correcting, and utilizing whatever data
existed, especially in the effort to obtain wide geographical
coverage and historical depth. In the absence of wholly reliable
registration data on deaths, it was decided to utilize new methods
that have evolved in recent years out of stable population theory
to construct a set of life tables for as many Latin American countries and for as many dates as possible. Mr. Eduardo Arriaga, a
member of the staff of IPUR, undertook this task, and the present
volume provides the results.

These life tables represent, I believe, the most comprehensive, consistent, and accurate body of information available on
on the course of mortality in the Latin American region. They
are of particular interest in view of the fact that mortality has
apparently fallen faster in Latin American than in any other area
in the world. We therefore have before us the basic data docu-
menting in detail the emergence of the new situation in the world

iii

whereby nonindustrial nations have acquired, almost overnight, the low levels of mortality characteristic of highly industrial nations. The difference between these low levels of mortality and the extremely high and generally rising rates of fertility demonstrated by Collver and Rele gives the underdeveloped countries--and particularly Latin America--an unprecedented rate of population growth that seems to be independent of the rate of economic development.

IPUR plans further comparative studies that will build on these basic findings. The life tables in the present volume, for example, will serve as a necessary preliminary to studies of the causes and correlates of mortality change, and for analyses of the demographic, social, and economic consequences of such change. In publishing the life tables, IPUR hopes that they will be used widely by other investigators as well. The life table compresses into brief space a remarkable amount of information about the mortality of a population; the implications of the present set of tables will require many analyses to explore. The author and his assistants are to be congratulated on the results of the years of labor that have gone into this exacting task.

Kingsley Davis

International Population and Urban Research
Institute of International Studies
University of California, Berkeley

ACKNOWLEDGMENTS

This study was prepared as part of a program of research being carried out at International Population and Urban Research, University of California, Berkeley. I am most grateful to Professor Kingsley Davis, the Director of IPUR, for his suggestions, advice, and encouragement, without which this study would not have been possible.

During a period when he had a visiting appointment at Berkeley, Nathan Keyfitz, now permanently at the University of California, was most helpful with his suggestions regarding the evaluation of life tables. I also wish to thank Mrs. Nancy Wang for her invaluable assistance in processing data, Mrs. Sheila Moses and Mrs. Susan Abbasi of IPUR and Miss Lee Goldberg of the Institute of International Studies for their assistance in editing, and the other staff members of IPUR, who contributed in many ways to the presentation of this study.

My wife, Regina B. de Arriaga, has given me invaluable help and encouragement throughout this study. I should also like to express my deep gratitude to the Rockefeller Foundation for providing the grant which made this research possible.

Berkeley, California   Eduardo E. Arriaga
January, 1968

TABLE OF CONTENTS

INTRODUCTION

Mortality can be measured in different ways. One of the best ways is through the construction of life tables, since the life table is one of the most comprehensive expressions of the mortality level.

In this study, we have constructed life tables for seventeen Latin American countries. For a few of these countries, other life tables have been constructed in recent years; however, these have often been considerably deficient in accuracy because they have been based, for the most part, on registered deaths and on census population figures. Since under-registration of deaths is common, and since census information is generally defective in these areas, life tables based on these sources are unreliable unless careful corrections are made. In cases where life tables have been constructed by calculating survival ratios from censuses, the analysis of incompleteness of the data has often not been made with sufficient rigor.

The objective of the present study is to establish the mortality level in each of the countries considered, not only at the present, but also as far in the past as is possible. Life tables for historical trends have not been previously attempted, due to problems presented by deficiencies in the data. In this study we resolved these problems by using a new method of life table construction. This method, devised by the author for this study,[1] is based on the stable population theory; with it only the proportional age group distribution of the population aged 10-59 and an estimate of the natural growth rate are used. With this method we were able to obtain life tables for some countries such as Brazil, Costa Rica, Guatemala, Mexico, and Paraguay for years previous to 1900.

In the few cases where vital statistics were reliable, any of the usual methods of life table construction could have been used used. Here we used one formulated by Barral Souto and Somoza[2] which gives a good estimation of mortality in the first five years of life. Among the twenty Latin American countries, only three-- Argentina, Cuba, and Uruguay--were not considered. For these particular cases, it was not possible to construct historical life tables, not only because of lack of data, but also because of the effect that migration and declining fertility have had on the age structure of their population.

1

NEW LIFE TABLES FOR LATIN AMERICAN POPULATIONS

TABLE A

EXPECTATION OF LIFE AT BIRTH ($\overset{o}{e}_o$) BY SEX

Country and Sex	1860	1870	1880	1890	1900	1910	1920	1930	1940	1950	1960
BOLIVIA					*	'	'	'	'	*	
Total					25.5	28.5	31.6	34.7	38.8	43.1	
Male					25.2	28.1	31.1	34.1	38.1	42.2	
Female					25.7	28.8	32.1	35.3	39.5	44.0	
BRAZIL		"	'	*	*	'	*	'	*	*	*
Total		27.3	27.6	27.8	29.4	30.6	32.0	34.0	36.7	43.0	55.5
Male		27.1	27.3	27.5	29.1	30.1	31.4	33.4	36.1	42.1	54.0
Female		27.6	27.9	28.2	29.7	31.1	32.5	34.6	37.3	43.9	57.0
CHILE					'	"	*	*	*	"	*
Total					28.7	30.2	30.5	35.2	38.1	48.5	56.5
Male					28.4	29.8	30.1	34.6	37.4	47.0	54.2
Female					29.1	30.6	30.9	35.8	38.7	50.0	58.7
COLOMBIA						'	"	'	"	"	
Total						30.5	32.0	34.2	38.0	48.5	
Male						30.1	31.5	33.6	37.1	47.3	
Female						30.9	32.5	34.8	39.0	49.7	
COSTA RICA	"	'	"	"	'	'	'	"	'	*	"
Total	25.9	27.6	28.6	30.1	31.6	32.6	36.8	41.9	48.7	55.5	61.8
Male	25.6	27.1	28.1	29.7	31.1	32.0	35.7	40.9	47.4	54.0	60.2
Female	26.3	28.0	29.0	30.5	32.0	33.2	37.9	43.0	49.9	57.0	63.5
DOMINICAN REPUBLIC								"	"	*	*
Total								26.1	34.0	43.7	52.2
Male								26.0	33.9	43.6	50.8
Female								26.1	34.0	43.8	53.5
ECUADOR										*	"
Total										47.9	53.8
Male										46.7	52.4
Female										49.0	55.2
EL SALVADOR								*	'	*	"
Total								28.7	37.5	47.2	56.0
Male								28.8	37.1	46.2	54.5
Female								28.5	37.9	48.2	57.5
GUATEMALA				"	'	'	"	'	*	*	"
Total				23.5	24.0	24.6	25.5	26.6	30.4	40.7	49.5
Male				23.3	23.8	24.4	25.2	26.3	29.9	39.9	47.6
Female				23.7	24.2	24.9	25.8	26.9	30.9	41.5	51.4

2

TABLE A (continued)

Country and Sex	1860	1870	1880	1890	1900	1910	1920	1930	1940	1950	1960
HAITI											
Total										39.4*	
Male										38.7	
Female										40.1	
HONDURAS											
Total								34.0*	37.5*	42.7*	52.8"
Male								33.4	36.8	41.8	51.5
Female								34.5	38.1	43.6	54.2
MEXICO											
Total				23.5"	25.3*	27.6*	34.0"	33.9*	38.8*	47.6*	58.0*
Male				23.4	25.0	27.3	33.0	33.0	37.7	46.2	56.4
Female				23.6	25.6	27.9	35.0	34.7	39.8	49.0	59.6
NICARAGUA											
Total							24.3*	28.6'	34.5*	40.1*	49.0"
Male							23.9	28.1	33.9	39.3	47.6
Female							24.7	29.1	35.1	40.8	50.4
PANAMA											
Total								35.9*	42.4*	50.2*	61.5*
Male								35.5	41.5	48.8	59.8
Female								36.2	43.3	51.5	63.2
PARAGUAY											
Total			22.7'	24.1"	26.2"	28.5'	31.0'	34.5'	39.2'	45.8*	54.0"
Male			22.0	23.4	25.5	27.7	30.3	33.6	37.3	44.8	52.6
Female			23.4	24.8	26.9	29.2	31.8	35.1	40.1	46.8	55.4
PERU											
Total									36.5*	39.9'	48.5"
Male									34.6	38.0	46.5
Female									38.3	41.7	50.6
VENEZUELA											
Total							31.3'	32.5"	38.7"	52.6*	62.2"
Male							30.7	31.9	38.0	51.2	60.6
Female							31.9	33.1	39.4	54.0	63.8

* Life table values.

" Interpolated from a near life table value.

' Interpolated between two life table values.

NEW LIFE TABLES FOR LATIN AMERICAN POPULATIONS

Table A, which presents the expectations of life at birth in each country to be considered, gives us an international comparison of mortality levels. For comparative purposes these expectations of life were interpolated to the same years from the values obtained in the life tables.

In Chapter I we give a detailed explanation of the two methods described above. In subsequent chapters we have considered each country separately, and have made a brief analysis of the demographic characteristics and census information of each. Mexico received the most detailed analysis, because the availability of information in that country made possible an evaluation of vital statistics and their use. Two practical examples of the methodology used are given in the appendices.

Life tables constructed by the author's proposed method were tested in order to ascertain whether the tables represent reality. The testing method used is based on stable population theory and is given in Appendix IV. The life tables and testing method were calculated using a Data Control 6400 computer.

NOTES

[1]E. Arriaga, "Método para la Construcción de Tablas de Vida para Poblaciones que Caracen de Estadísticas Vitales," Proceedings of the World Population Conference, Belgrade, 1965 (New York: United Nations, 1967), Vol. III, paper 127.

[2]J. Barral Souto and J. Somoza, "Construcción de una Tabla Abreviada de Mortalidad para la Argentina," Segundo Coloquio de Estadística (Córdoba, Argentina: 1953).

I. METHODS USED IN THE CONSTRUCTION OF LIFE TABLES

As we said in the introduction, it was necessary to make use of two methods in constructing life tables. One is appropriate for the few cases where vital statistics are reliable (called here Method A); the other is a method by which is it possible to obtain life tables without vital statistics (called here Method B). In most cases, we applied the second method, not only because of lack of vital statistics information, but also because under-enumeration in some censuses made the proportional age distribution of the population the only reliable source of information.

METHOD A. CONSTRUCTION OF LIFE TABLES WHEN VITAL STATISTICS ARE SUFFICIENTLY RELIABLE

Method A makes it possible, by using census population information and death statistics, to find the force of mortality and hence the other life table functions.[1] The central mortality rate is defined as:

$$n^m x \quad = \quad \frac{\int_x^{x+n} l_t \, \mu_t \, dt}{\int_x^{x+n} l_t \, dt} \quad ,$$

where the numerator is the theoretical number of deaths between the ages x to x+n, and the denominator is the theoretical survivors between the ages of x to x+n. The limit of $n^m x$, when n tends to zero, gives the force of mortality.

$$\lim_{n \to o} n^m x \quad = \quad \mu_x \quad = \quad \lim_{n \to o} \frac{\int_x^{x+n} l_t \, \mu_t \, dt}{\int_x^{x+n} l_t \, dt} \quad ,$$

and, from μ_x by integrating

$$\int_x^{x+n} \mu_t \, dt \quad = \quad - \int_x^{x+n} d \log_e l_t \, dt \quad = \quad - \log_e n^p x \quad .$$

5

Now, in order to integrate μ_x, it is necessary to formulate an hypothesis about its analytical structure. For the sake of simplicity and because the integral would be used for short intervals, it was assumed that the force of mortality follows Gompertz' law:

$$\mu_x = Bc^x .$$

With this assumption, using logarithms to the base 10, it is possible to state that:

$$\log_{10} {}_np_x = -M \int_x^{x+n} Bc^t\, dt =$$

$$n \cdot M^2 \frac{\frac{\triangle}{n}\mu_x}{\frac{\triangle}{n}\log_{10}\mu_x} \tag{1}$$

where $M = \log_{10}e$.

The relation between l_x and ${}_np_x$ is: $l_{x+n} = l_x \cdot {}_np_x$, or using logarithms,

$$\log_{10}l_{x+n} = \log_{10}l_x + \log_{10}{}_np_x ; \tag{2}$$

then, having $\log_{10} {}_np_x$ (which will be negative) it is possible by addition (in this case being subtraction) to obtain the values of $\log_{10}l_x$. The first value, for age 0, can be fixed arbitrarily in order to get any power of 10 for l_0 (radix of the life table).[2] By taking antilogarithms of $\log_{10}l_x$, we obtain l_x, and therefore any other function of the life table by the usual procedure.

Now, for practical purposes, our problem is how to obtain ${}_nm_x$ and ${}_0m_x$ (or μ_x). To obtain the first, the usual approximation is considered appropriate:

$${}_nm_x = \frac{Dx,\ x+n}{Px,\ x+n}$$

$$= \frac{\text{Death between ages x and x+n}}{\text{Enumerated population between x and x+n}}$$

It is possible to obtain the second (μ_x), by interpolating among

CHAPTER I. METHODS USED IN THE CONSTRUCTION OF LIFE TABLES

several values of $_nm_x$, where the length of the interval n is considered as a variable. In this case, in order to obtain the values of $_nm_x$ when n = 0, the interpolation is made with a third degree function.[3] The coefficients used in this interpolation for ages 15 and over are:

$$_0m_x = \mu_x = \frac{1}{6} \left(-_{-2n}m_x + 4_{-n}m_x + 4_nm_x - _{2n}m_x \right), \quad (3)$$

where in this case n is equal to 5. The coefficients for the interpolation are different for the ages 0, 1, 2, 3, 4, 5, and 10 (because in the interpolation asymmetrical intervals are used) and are given in Table I-1. For the application of this method in a practical case (Costa Rica, 1963), see Appendix I.

TABLE I-1[*]

COEFFICIENTS OF $_nm_x$

$$\mu_0 = 4_1m_0 - 6_2m_0 + 4_3m_0 - _4m_0$$

$$\mu_1 = \frac{1}{4} \left(-_1m_1 + 6_1m_1 - 4_2m_1 + _3m_1 \right)$$

$$\mu_2 = \frac{1}{4} \left(-_1m_2 + 6_1m_2 - 4_2m_2 + _3m_2 \right)$$

$$\mu_3 = \frac{1}{120} \left(35_{-1}m_3 + 140_1m_3 - 56_2m_3 + _7m_3 \right)$$

$$\mu_4 = \frac{1}{140} \left(-35_{-2}m_4 + 120_{-1}m_4 + 56_1m_4 - _6m_4 \right)$$

$$\mu_5 = \frac{1}{56} \left(35_{-3}m_5 - 120_{-2}m_5 + 140_{-1}m_5 + _5m_5 \right)$$

$$\mu_{10} = \frac{1}{4} \left(-_5m_{10} + 6_5m_{10} - 4_{10}m_{10} + _{15}m_{10} \right)$$

[*]Source: J. Barral Souto and J. Somoza, "Construcción de una Tabla Abreviada de Mortalidad para la Argentina," Segundo Coloquio de Estadística (Córdoba, Argentina: 1953).

METHOD B. CONSTRUCTION OF LIFE TABLES WHEN VITAL STATISTICS CANNOT
BE UTILIZED

The method devised for the case when vital statistics cannot be utilized is based on the stable population theory. The principal characteristic of this method is that it does not use death statistics. The basic data used are the proportional five-year age group distribution between ages 10 and 59, and the natural growth rate of the population at the date when the proportional distribution was observed.

One of the advantages of this method is that for accuracy in the life table it only requires that the completeness of enumeration in the census should be relatively the same in all the ten-year age groups between ages 10 and 59. It is not important whether or not there is underenumeration in these ages, as long as the underenumeration is evenly distributed in these ten-year age groups. Thus the completeness of enumeration in the ages under 10, and 60 and over--which is commonly the most troublesome--does not have any effect on the results.[4] We can usually assume that because completeness of the census is similar in each ten-year age group between the ages 10 and 59, census deficiencies do not rule out the use of census statistics. This is not always true, however. Sometimes misdeclaration of age causes the completeness in these ten-year age groups to differ. But by smoothing the population, the hypothesis of equal completeness holds.

The estimated natural growth rate must be as close to the actual rate as possible. It can be quite satisfactorily achieved by using the available information.

The method under consideration has certain limitations. Because it is based on the stable population theory, it can be used only where two conditions hold: (a) almost constant fertility in past years, and (b) relatively insignificant international migration. In some cases, when the population has experienced international migration, the method could be applied with care by using the native population (this is permissable, however, only when the migration has occurred recently, and when the native-born from foreign parents are not yet a significant factor in the native population structure).

Fortunately, both conditions, almost constant fertility in past years and an insignificant number of migrants, exist in nearly all the countries to be considered here. One exception is Mexico after 1920, where there was migration and a change in fertility during the period of the Civil War (1920-1920); however, Method A can be applied for the period after 1920 because statistics begin to be reliable, so this exception does not disrupt our analysis. Brazil in the late years of the last century could be considered another exception to insignificant international

8

migration. The proportion of foreign-born in 1900 reached its maximum at 6.2 percent. After 1900 this proportion declined continuously, until it was 2.1 percent in 1950. Fortunately for our purposes we have census information on the native-born by age for almost all censuses. This information helps in correcting age structure, and made possible the application of Method B.

The complete procedure for applying Method B and a comparison of that method with Method A are given in Appendix II, which uses as an example the case of Honduras in 1940. Reference to this practical application can be made for each step discussed in the following explanation of the method.

In our explanation of Method B, we must keep in mind one of the fundamental equations of the stable population theory:

$$C(x) \quad = \quad b \cdot e^{-rx} p(x) \quad ; \tag{4}$$

where:

$C(x)$ is the proportion of the total population aged x;

b is the intrinsic birth rate of the population;

e is the base for the Naperian logarithms;

r is the intrinsic growth rate of the population;

x is the age; and

$p(x)$ is the probability at birth that a person will reach age x.

Based on this definition, $p(x)$ is equivalent to the function l_x of a life table when the radix is one. Hence in this particular case, l_x could be substituted in Equation 4, which gives

$$C(x) \quad = \quad b \cdot e^{-rx} l_x \quad .$$

The formula is valid when age is exactly x. Transposing and adopting the equation to the use of quinquennial age groups (by integrating using the trapezoid rule), it can be written

$$_5L_x \quad = \quad \frac{1}{b} C(x, x+5) \cdot {}_e r(x+2.5) \quad ; \tag{5}$$

where:

$C(x, x+5)$ is the proportion of the total population in ages x to less than x+5;

x+2.5 is the mean age of the group studied; and

$_5L_x$ is the total number of persons aged x to less than x+5 in a life table where $l_0 = 1$.

It is obvious that $_5L_x$ can be found if $C(x, x+5)$, r, and b are known. The proportion of the total population in each quinquennial age group can be obtained from the census $(C'(x, x+5))$ and the estimates of r at census date by considering intercensal geometric growth rates and existing estimates.[5] The problem is how to obtain an estimate of the intrinsic birth rate which will differ from estimates of the crude birth rates. To estimate the intrinsic birth rate (in agreement with age distribution and growth rate) and also to obtain the smoothed values of $C(x, x+5)$, we employ the following method:

Equation 5, rearranged, and using Naperian logarithms, can be written as

$$\ln \frac{C(x, x+5)}{_5L_x} = \ln b - r(x+2.5) .$$ (6)

This equation shows that the distribution of the logarithms of the quotients $\frac{C(x, x+5)}{_5L_x}$ is, in theory, a straight line of which the slope is the intrinsic growth rate of the population and the constant term is the Naperian logarithm of the intrinsic birth rate. However, there are two problems which remain to be solved. First, because data of the proportional age group distribution from censuses have some irregularities and because the populations are not perfectly stable (although almost), the logarithms of the quotients mentioned are not in a straight line (even if as recommended in Appendix III, a smoothing of census population has previously been made). Also, the $_5L_x$ values are not available. These $_5L_x$ values can be taken from a life table constructed for another country with similar demographic characteristics. Unfortunately such tables are not always available, particularly for the earliest years, but the United Nations Model Life Tables provide a good substitute for them.[6] Once the tables described above are

CHAPTER I. METHODS USED IN THE CONSTRUCTION OF LIFE TABLES

accepted, the quotients (Eq. 6) can be obtained. The straight line is obtained by making an adjustment by the least square method. The selection of the set of values of $_5L_x$ to be used (in order to obtain b) is made on the condition that the slope of the adjusted straight line should be the closest value to the estimated intrinsic growth rate for the population at the time considered. The quotient values on which the adjustment is based are those which pertain only to the quinquennial age groups 10-59.

       Once the parameters of the straight line are determined, the value of b is obtained and, in addition, the values for all the quinquennial age groups 0-84. Then, by using antilogarithms and multiplying the values by the same $_5L_x$ used previously, the smoothed values of C(x, x+5) are obtained. At this point, Equation 5 can be applied by using C(x, x+5) and the estimates of r and b.[7] In this way, the values of $_5L_x$ for the population considered were determined, except for the open age group 85 and over.

       In order to determine the l_x function, we obtain certain convenient values for L_x by individual age by using Beer's multipliers.[8] We find values of l_1 and l_5 by interpolation with third degree function values of L_x.[9] We obtain the l_x for ages 10-80 by interpolating with third degree function values of $_5L_x$.[10] The probabilities of survival are calculated by

$$_5P_x = \frac{1x + 5}{1x} \quad .$$

Because l_{85} is not available $_5P_{80}$ is calculated by extrapolation with a fourth degree function and then, $l_{85} = l_{80} \cdot {}_5P_{80}$.[11] The value L_{85+} is estimated as

$$L_{85+} = l_{85} (\log_{10} l_{85}) \quad .$$

All the other functions are calculated in the usual manner.

       The results obtained with Method B will be affected by the life table model used in Equation 6. For this reason it is important to use in that equation life tables which we would expect to have approximately the same mortality pattern as that assumed in the population. The problem is that mortality patterns of countries where vital statistics are not reliable cannot be known. In those cases we used the United Nations Model Life Tables, which were the only ones available at the time of our study.[12]

The results obtained with Method B were tested using a procedure based on the stable population theory (Appendix IV) and were also checked against those life tables obtained with Method A. There were few differences between life tables constructed by the two methods (see Appendix II); hence we can accept the levels of mortality obtained with Method B as being reasonable estimates of the actual mortality levels.

We would like to note here that Method B is very sensitive to high growth rates when these are over 35, and to mortality when the level exceeds a life expectancy of 60. Fortunately, when countries approach this level of mortality, they generally already have reliable statistics which would make possible the use of any of the methods based on death and population. The principal usefulness of Method B is that it can be applied in cases where practically no statistics exist (a fact usually correlated with high mortality) and where no highly accurate method can be used.

NOTES

[1] J. Barral Souto and J. Somoza, "Construcción de una Tabla Abreviada de Mortalidad para la Argentina," Segundo Coloquio de Estadística (Córdoba, Argentina: 1953).

[2] For example, if $\log_{10} l_0 = 5$, $l_0 = 100,000$.

[3] A graphical interpretation of these values is:

$$_0 m_x$$

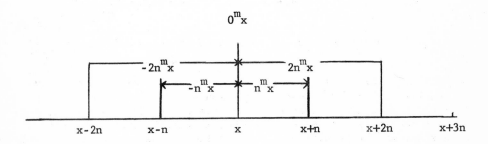

CHAPTER I. METHODS USED IN THE CONSTRUCTION OF LIFE TABLES

[4]The same life table will be obtained no matter what conditions prevail in the population under 10 and 60 and over (even assuming that this population is nil). The completeness of the population enumeration in these ages can affect, as can be shown analytically, the value of constant b (birth rate). Because for each table b is constant and perfectly determined, it does not affect the functions of the life table.

[5]O. Andrew Collver, Birth Rates in Latin America: New Estimates of Historical Trends and Fluctuations (Berkeley: Institute of International Studies, University of California, 1965) [Research Series No. 7].

[6]United Nations, Department of Economic and Social Affairs, Methods for Population Projections by Sex and Age, Manual III, (ST/SOA/Series A, Population Studies No. 25) (New York, 1956), pp. 78-79.

[7]When a life table is constructed for both sexes combined, the growth rate used in the exponent of $e^{r(x+2.5)}$ to obtain the values of $_5L_x$ (Eq. 5), is the one estimated for the total population. When life tables are constructed for each sex separately, we use a different growth rate for each sex rather than that for the total population. We calculated the growth rates for each sex by considering the difference between the slopes of the lines of adjustment (found by the least square method, Eq. 6). The same relation of these slopes to their average is maintained between the estimated growth rates for each sex and that rate which will be used in the above-mentioned exponent of Equation 5. In symbols, if b_1 and b_2 are the slopes of the adjusted lines for males and females respectively (Eq. 6), and r is the estimated growth for the total population, r_1 and r_2 (growth rates for males and females to be applied in Eq. 5) can be obtained by:

$$r_1 = a_1 r \quad \text{and} \quad r_2 = a_2 r ,$$

where

$$a_1 = \frac{2 b_1}{b_1 + b_2} \quad \text{and} \quad a_2 = \frac{2 b_2}{b_1 + b_2} .$$

[8]H. S. Beers, "Six-Term Formulas for Routine Actuarial Interpolation," Record of the American Institute of Actuaries, Vol. 34
(June, 1945), p 60.

[9]

$$l_1 = .3125 \, L_0 + .9375 \, L_1 - .3125 \, L_2 + .0625 \, L_3$$

$$l_5 = -.0625 \, L_3 + .5625 \, L_4 + .5625 \, L_5 - .0625 \, L_6 \quad .$$

[10]For ages 15-75 we used the following:

$$l_x = -.0125 \, _5L_{x-10} + .1125 \, _5L_{x-5} + .1125 \, _5L_x - .0125 \, _5L_{x+5}$$

and

$$l_{10} = .0625 \, _5L_5 + .1875 \, _5L_{10} - .0625 \, _5L_{15} + .0125 \, _5L_{20}$$

$$l_{80} = .0125 \, _5L_{65} - .0625 \, _5L_{70} + .1875 \, _5L_{75} + .0625 \, _5L_{80} \quad .$$

[11]

$$_5P_{80} = \, _5P_{55} - \, ^5_5P_{60} + 10 \, _5P_{65} - 10 \, _5P_{70} + \, ^5_5P_{75}$$

[12]The book by A. Coale and P. Demeny, Regional Model Life
Tables and Stable Population (Princeton, New Jersey: 1966), was
not available to us at the time of our study. The use of Coale
and Demeny's model life tables would have given us the opportunity

to examine a greater variety mortality patterns, with the possibility in some cases of choosing better life tables than those
provided by the United Nations.

II. BOLIVIA

Seven censuses have been taken in Bolivia, two in the present century, in 1900 and in 1950. Information on population by age group is available only for these two censuses. The long intercensal period makes a cohort comparison of the two censuses impossible. Vital statistics are not complete, and the use of death registration for the construction of life tables is not advisable. Therefore, life tables were constructed using Method B. The conditions required for the use of this method exist in the Bolivian population: fertility has not changed significantly in past years, and international migration has not been of great magnitude.[1]

PROPORTIONAL AGE GROUP DISTRIBUTION OF THE POPULATION

In the case of Bolivia only a very rough graphical analysis by cohort can be made because of the fifty-year interval between censuses. However, irregularities in enumeration can be observed (Fig. II-1). For example, underenumeration in ages under 25 years is obvious in the 1900 census. Underenumeration also occurs in the 1950 census in the age group 10-19.

In 1900 age group distribution was presented in an unusual way, with age groups of 0-6, 7-13, 14-17, 18-25, 26-30, 31-40, 41-99, and 100 and over. Therefore, we regrouped these age groups in the usual way[2] (in ten-year age groups), and corrected them for the irregularities already mentioned in ages under 30.[3]

Some brief corrections were made for the 1950 census, principally in female age distribution.[4] Then, the age group distributions for both years were smoothed (according to the procedure explained in Appendix III), and the proportional five-year age group distributions for ages 10-59 found for the two years (Table II-1).

ESTIMATION OF NATURAL GROWTH RATES

The annual average geometric growth rate for the fifty-year period between 1900 and 1950 is 10 per thousand. This value does not help significantly in the establishment of the natural growth rates for census years, but it at least gives a maximum limit for the growth rate in 1900. The natural growth rate for 1950 was estimated at 23 per thousand.[5]

16

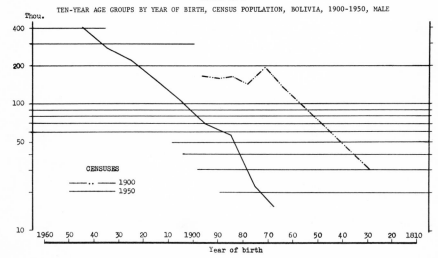

FIGURE II-1

TEN-YEAR AGE GROUPS BY YEAR OF BIRTH, CENSUS POPULATION, BOLIVIA, 1900-1950, MALE

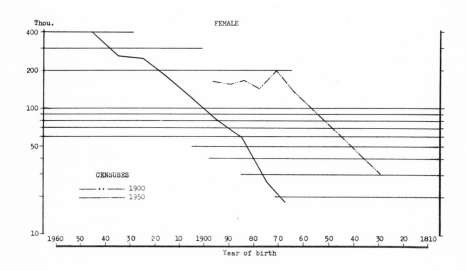

FEMALE

TABLE II-1

SMOOTHED PROPORTIONAL DISTRIBUTION OF THE POPULATION BY SEX
AND FIVE-YEAR AGE GROUPS, AGES 10-59, BOLIVIA, CENSUS YEARS

Age Groups	1900		1950	
	Male	Female	Male	Female
Total	1.000000	1.000000	1.000000	1.000000
10-59	.649369	.655876	.624696	.642349
10-14	.115088	.114603	.117194	.116678
15-19	.101687	.101963	.101401	.102225
20-24	.088617	.089554	.086161	.088147
25-29	.077208	.078305	.073684	.075939
30-34	.066298	.067264	.062115	.063973
35-39	.056547	.057455	.052244	.054269
40-44	.046769	.047620	.042451	.045005
45-49	.039062	.039821	.035433	.037935
50-54	.031896	.032562	.029411	.031713
55-59	.026197	.026729	.024602	.026465

18

CHAPTER II. BOLIVIA

Lack of information makes uncertain an accurate estimation of the natural growth rate for 1900. We estimated this growth rate by considering the estimate of the 1950 growth rate and the average geometric growth rate for the entire fifty-year period. As a result, a growth rate of 8 per thousand was accepted for 1900.

CONSTRUCTION OF LIFE TABLES

Life tables were constructed by using Method B, the proportional age group distribution of Table II-1, and by considering the estimates of natural growth rates of 8 and 23 per thousand for 1900 and 1950 respectively. The United Nations set of $_5L_x$ values used in the quotient $\dfrac{C'(x,\ x+5)}{_5L_x}$ were levels 10 and 45 for 1900 and 1950 respectively. The slopes of the straight lines of adjustment and the growth rates used for each sex in the exponent of e (Eq. 5, Chap. I) can be seen in Table II-2. The life tables obtained are given in Tables II-3 and II-4,[6] and a summary of life expectancy is presented in table II-5.

TABLE II-2

GROWTH RATES USED IN THE CONSTRUCTION OF LIFE TABLES FOR BOLIVIA

				Slopes of the Straight Lines of Adjustment of the $\log_e \dfrac{C'(x,\ x+5)}{_nL_5}$		
		Growth Rates				
Year	Total	Male	Female	Male	Female	Average
1900	.0080	.00786	.00814	.007225	.007477	.007351
1950	.0230	.02349	.02251	.023090	.022125	.022608

19

TABLE II-3

ABRIDGED LIFE TABLE, BOLIVIA, 1900
MALE

Age x n	l_x	$_nd_x$	$_np_x$	$_nq_x$	$_nL_x$	T_x	e_x
0 1	100,000	28,501	.71499	.28501	73,531	2,516,781	25.17
1 4	71,499	12,872	.81998	.18002	258,071	2,443,250	34.17
0 5	100,000	41,373	.58627	.41373	331,602	2,516,781	25.17
5 5	58,627	5,661	.90344	.09656	272,768	2,185,179	37.27
10 5	52,966	2,536	.95212	.04788	258,191	1,912,411	36.11
15 5	⁵0,430	2,695	.94656	.05344	246,014	1,654,220	32.80
20 5	47,735	3,320	.93044	.06956	230,662	1,408,206	29.50
25 5	44,415	3,651	.91780	.08220	213,056	1,177,544	26.51
30 5	40,764	3,904	.90423	.09577	194,246	964,488	23.66
35 5	36,860	4,256	.88453	.11547	173,925	770,242	20.90
40 5	32,604	4,639	.85771	.14229	151,663	596,317	18.29
45 5	27,965	4,854	.82644	.17356	127,730	444,654	15.90
50 5	23,111	4,811	.79184	.20816	103,429	316,924	13.71
55 5	18,300	4,570	.75029	.24971	79,872	213,495	11.67
60 5	13,731	4,149	.69779	.30221	57,955	133,623	9.73
65 5	9,581	3,585	.62580	.37420	38,566	75,668	7.90
70 5	5,996	2,836	.52706	.47294	22,330	37,102	6.19
75 5	3,160	1,895	.40034	.59966	10,439	14,772	4.67
80 5	1,265	948	.25038	.74962	3,541	4,333	3.42
85 +	317	317	0.00000	1.00000	792	792	2.50

TABLE II-3 (continued)

ABRIDGED LIFE TABLE, BOLIVIA, 1900
FEMALE

Age x n	l_x	$_nd_x$	$_np_x$	$_nq_x$	$_nL_x$	T_x	e_x
0 1	100,000	26,536	.73464	.26536	75,550	2,569,643	25.70
1 4	73,464	13,287	.81913	.18087	265,080	2,494,093	33.95
0 5	100,000	39,824	.60176	.39824	340,630	2,569,643	25.70
5 5	60,176	6,000	.90029	.09971	279,521	2,229,013	37.04
10 5	54,176	2,896	.94655	.05345	263,394	1,949,492	35.98
15 5	51,281	3,099	.93957	.06043	249,253	1,686,098	32.88
20 5	48,182	3,748	.92221	.07779	231,855	1,436,845	29.82
25 5	44,434	4,100	.90774	.09226	212,039	1,204,990	27.12
30 5	40,334	4,254	.89452	.10548	191,099	992,951	24.62
35 5	36,080	4,280	.88137	.11863	169,661	801,852	22.22
40 5	31,800	4,194	.86812	.13188	148,426	632,191	19.88
45 5	27,606	4,120	.85077	.14923	127,720	483,765	17.52
50 5	23,486	4,100	.82545	.17455	107,174	356,045	15.16
55 5	19,387	4,089	.78910	.21090	86,716	248,871	12.84
60 5	15,298	4,039	.73600	.26400	66,348	162,156	10.60
65 5	11,259	3,812	.66145	.33855	46,549	95,807	8.51
70 5	7,447	3,271	.56084	.43916	28,608	49,258	6.61
75 5	4,177	2,386	.42867	.57133	14,264	20,651	4.94
80 5	1,790	1,328	.25854	.74146	5,152	6,386	3.57
85 +	463	463	0.00000	1.00000	1,234	1,234	2.67

TABLE II-4

ABRIDGED LIFE TABLE, BOLIVIA, 1950
MALE

Age x n	l_x	$_n d_x$	$_n p_x$	$_n q_x$	$_n L_x$	T_x	e_x
0 1	100,000	17,677	.82323	.17677	83,405	4,219,784	42.20
1 4	82,323	6,822	.91713	.08287	314,475	4,136,379	50.25
0 5	100,000	24,499	.75501	.24499	397,880	4,219,784	42.20
5 5	75,501	3,037	.95978	.04022	366,693	3,821,904	50.62
10 5	72,464	1,521	.97900	.02100	358,490	3,455,211	47.68
15 5	70,943	1,935	.97272	.02728	350,505	3,096,721	43.65
20 5	69,007	2,586	.96253	.03747	338,844	2,746,216	39.80
25 5	66,421	2,812	.95766	.04234	325,056	2,407,372	36.24
30 5	63,609	2,906	.95431	.04569	310,877	2,082,316	32.74
35 5	60,703	3,175	.94769	.05231	295,806	1,771,439	29.18
40 5	57,528	3,662	.93634	.06366	278,863	1,475,633	25.65
45 5	53,865	4,356	.91914	.08086	258,931	1,196,770	22.22
50 5	49,510	5,207	.89483	.10517	235,111	937,839	18.94
55 5	44,303	6,160	.86096	.13904	206,739	702,728	15.86
60 5	38,143	7,142	.81276	.18724	173,494	495,989	13.00
65 5	31,001	7,964	.74309	.25691	135,563	322,496	10.40
70 5	23,036	8,106	.64814	.35186	94,699	186,933	8.11
75 5	14,931	7,055	.52748	.47252	55,946	92,234	6.18
80 5	7,876	4,851	.38401	.61599	25,761	36,288	4.61
85 +	3,024	3,024	0.00000	1.00000	10,527	10,527	3.48

TABLE II-4 (continued)

ABRIDGED LIFE TABLE, BOLIVIA, 1950
FEMALE

Age x n	l_x	$_nd_x$	$_np_x$	$_nq_x$	$_nL_x$	T_x	e_x
0 1	100,000	15,828	.84172	.15828	85,246	4,400,139	44.00
1 4	84,172	6,829	.91886	.08114	321,898	4,314,893	51.26
0 5	100,000	22,657	.77343	.22657	407,145	4,400,139	44.00
5 5	77,343	3,151	.95926	.04074	375,643	3,992,995	51.63
10 5	74,192	1,719	.97683	.02317	366,672	3,617,352	48.76
15 5	72,473	2,135	.97053	.02947	357,606	3,250,679	44.85
20 5	70,337	2,764	.96070	.03930	345,058	2,893,073	41.13
25 5	67,573	3,022	.95528	.04472	330,334	2,548,015	37.71
30 5	64,551	3,076	.95234	.04766	315,078	2,217,681	34.36
35 5	61,474	3,134	.94902	.05098	299,576	1,902,603	30.95
40 5	58,340	3,308	.94331	.05669	283,595	1,603,027	27.48
45 5	55,033	3,712	.93255	.06745	266,224	1,319,432	23.98
50 5	51,321	4,360	.91505	.08495	246,166	1,053,208	20.52
55 5	46,961	5,306	.88700	.11300	222,261	807,042	17.19
60 5	41,655	6,573	.84219	.15781	192,743	584,781	14.04
65 5	35,081	7,897	.77490	.22510	156,503	392,039	11.18
70 5	27,184	8,704	.67981	.32019	114,448	235,536	8.66
75 5	18,480	8,187	.55697	.44303	71,061	121,088	6.55
80 5	10,293	6,055	.41177	.58823	34,653	50,027	4.86
85 +	4,238	4,238	0.00000	1.00000	15,373	15,373	3.63

TABLE II-5

LIFE EXPECTANCY, BOLIVIA
CENSUS YEARS

Year	Total*	Male	Female
1900	25.5	25.2	25.7
1950	43.1	42.2	44.0

*Simple arithmetic average of male and female.

NOTES

[1]The emigration from Bolivia to Argentina, Chile, and Peru is known, but the total amount of this migration is in part compensated for by the immigration of Peruvians, Chileans, Brazilians, Argentinians, and Germans (in descending order of magnitude). In any case, Bolivia has a negative balance of immigration, which can be considered to have a negligible effect on the age group distribution between ages 10 and 59. In both censuses the irregularities in the age structure due to misdeclaration of age are a more perturbing factor than the effects of migration and emigration.

[2]We needed to estimate ages 18-19 in the age group 18-25, age 30 in the age group 26-30; age 40 in the age group 31-40, and ages 41-49 and 50-59 in the age group 41-99. For this purpose we used the information by individual age given in the 1950 census, assuming that the relative errors of age declaration in each age group in 1950 were similar to those in 1900.

[3]In both sexes, the age groups 10-19 and 20-29 were increased and the age group 30-39 diminished.

[4]For both sexes, the age group 10-19 was increased. In addition, for females, the age groups 20-29 and 30-39 were slightly diminished.

[5]In our calculations we consulted various other estimates. See Benjamin Franco, "Estimaciones de Tasas de Natalidad de Crecimento y de Mortalidad en la Rep. de Bolivia Alrededor de 1950, CELADE (Santiago, Chile, 1959), B.59.1/7.1; O. Andrew Collver, Birth Rates in Latin America: New Estimates of Historical Trends and Fluctuations (Berkeley: Institute of International Studies, University of California, 1965) [Research Series No. 7] p. 74; and United Nations, The Population of South America 1950-1980 (ST/SOA/Series A, Population Studies, No. 21) (New York, 1954), p. 47.

[6]A practical example of life table construction using Method B is given in Appendix II.

III. BRAZIL

Demographically Brazil--the largest and most populated country in Latin America--presents a special case. Censuses have been taken frequently, but a national vital statistics registration does not exist. Death information is available only for certain regions and cities, and, of course, its completeness is questionable. Thus, we cannot construct life tables for Brazil using Method A. We will, then, consider using Method B. To use Method B we would have to face the problem of international migration. Around 1900, the country received a significant migratory influx relative to the population size at that time. Fortunately, however, constant fertility during past years, the other requirement for the application of Method B, has been observed in Brazil. Information on the foreign-born population, which is available for most years, will permit us to correct in some way the distortion of the age structure due to international migration.

PROPORTIONAL AGE GROUP DISTRIBUTION OF THE POPULATION

Information on population by age group and sex is available in the seven censuses taken in Brazil.[1] A graphical cohort analysis of this information can be made using Figure III-1. If we accept the 1960 census as not having been overenumerated, we can conclude that previous censuses were underenumerated, principally the 1900 census and those prior to that date.[2] Because the degree of underenumeration seems practically the same in all age groups, the proportional age group distribution is not affected, except when some irregularities pertain exclusively to certain age groups. One of these irregularities, obviously due to poor enumeration, can be observed in the population enumerated as under 20 years of age in 1872.

Before making any correction of census information, and in order to avoid the effect of international migration, we considered the age distribution of native-born persons.[3] Then in most of the cases we modified census information by ten-year age groups slightly, by taking into consideration the irregularities detected in the graph.[4] Finally, we smoothed the population distribution by age groups according to the procedure explained in Appendix III. The proportional age group distribution for each sex and for all census years is given in Table III-1.

ESTIMATION OF NATURAL GROWTH RATES

We estimated natural growth rates by considering intercensal geometric growth rates for total and native populations,

FIGURE III-1

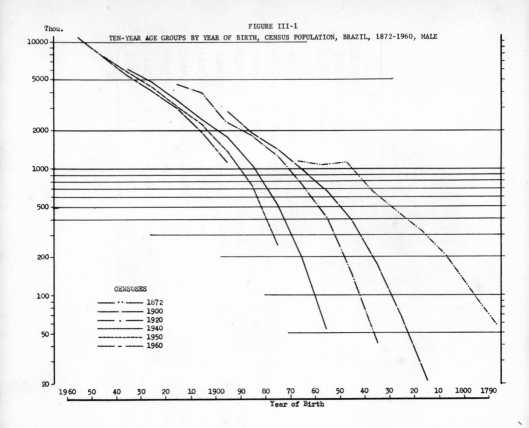

TEN-YEAR AGE GROUPS BY YEAR OF BIRTH, CENSUS POPULATION, BRAZIL, 1872-1960, MALE

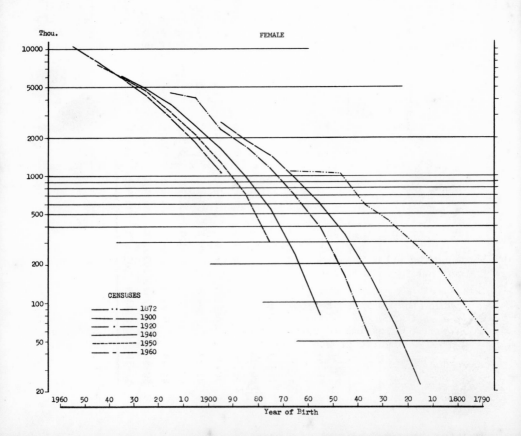

FEMALE

TABLE III-1

SMOOTHED PROPORTIONAL DISTRIBUTION OF THE POPULATION BY SEX AND FIVE-YEAR AGE GROUPS, AGES 10-59
BRAZIL, CENSUS YEARS

Age Groups	1872 Male	1872 Female	1890 Total	1900 Male	1900 Female	1920 Male	1920 Female	1940 Male	1940 Female	1950 Male	1950 Female	1960 Male	1960 Female
Total	1.000000	1.000000	1.000000	1.000000	1.000000	1.000000	1.000000	1.000000	1.000000	1.000000	1.000000	1.000000	1.000000
10-59	.663085	.658127	.648420	.650781	.643057	.648454	.654379	.656049	.661321	.655182	.663252	.639521	.648720
10-14	.118509	.116119	.122354	.121505	.118615	.123812	.125059	.127676	.128706	.123012	.125844	.126042	.126249
15-19	.106550	.105031	.107124	.106906	.104753	.107184	.108240	.109513	.110029	.107347	.109078	.106016	.106784
20-24	.094060	.093043	.091897	.092057	.090640	.091118	.091924	.092052	.092139	.092112	.092854	.090044	.090747
25-29	.079422	.078517	.078034	.078648	.077761	.077852	.078126	.078087	.078179	.079019	.079344	.076057	.076636
30-34	.068202	.067662	.065745	.065442	.064871	.065489	.064528	.065232	.065652	.066448	.066588	.062099	.063844
35-39	.056426	.056446	.054612	.054623	.053888	.054900	.054364	.054648	.055119	.055742	.055916	.052160	.052633
40-44	.047855	.048028	.044110	.045417	.045539	.045053	.046125	.045198	.045545	.045649	.046041	.042425	.044810
45-49	.038424	.038950	.035498	.036473	.036905	.036088	.037368	.036305	.036808	.036777	.037274	.035181	.035680
50-54	.030248	.030728	.027516	.028549	.028554	.027541	.028655	.027764	.028506	.028439	.029024	.027959	.028866
55-59	.023389	.023603	.021530	.021161	.021531	.019417	.019990	.019574	.020638	.020637	.021289	.021538	.022471

and for intercensal periods of different lengths.[5] Intercensal growth rates were calculated once by taking the population enumerated in each census, and a second time once the populations had been corrected for omission. We calculated intercensal growth rates and considered their trends in order to estimate the natural growth rate for each census year. The rates are: 12.6, 16.3, 16.7, 20.5, 24.2, 27.1, and 32.0 per thousand for the years 1872, 1890, 1900, 1920, 1940, 1950, and 1960 respectively.

CONSTRUCTION OF LIFE TABLES

Life tables were constructed using Method B, the proportional age group distribution (Table III-1), and the natural growth rates estimated above. The values of $_5L_x$ chosen from the United Nations Model Life Tables used in quotient $\dfrac{C'(x,\ x+5)}{_5L_x}$ were those of levels 15, 15, 20, 25, 35, 45, and 70 for the years 1872, 1890, 1900, 1920, 1940, 1950, and 1960 respectively. The slopes of the straight lines of adjustment and the growth rates used in the exponent of e (Eq. 5, Chap. I) for each sex are given in Table III-2 The life tables are given in Tables III-3 to III-9.[6] A summary of the life expectancy at birth for each sex and year is presented in Table III-10.

TABLE III-2

GROWTH RATES USED IN THE CONSTRUCTION OF LIFE TABLES FOR BRAZIL

	Growth Rates			Slopes of the Straight Lines of Adjustment of the $\log_e \dfrac{C'((x,\ x+5)}{_nL_5}$		
Year	Total	Male	Female	Male	Female	Average
1872	.0126	.02169	.01251	.012898	.012735	.012817
1890	.0163					.015886
1900	.0167	.01677	.01653	.017422	.017332	.017377
1920	.0205	.02043	.02057	.020985	.021133	.021059
1940	.0242	.02425	.02415	.025019	.024917	.024968
1950	.0271	.02677	.02743	.026477	.027137	.026807
1960	.0320	.03193	.03201	.031697	.031771	.031734

CHAPTER III. BRAZIL

TABLE III-3

ABRIDGED LIFE TABLE, BRAZIL, 1879
MALE

Age x n	l_x	$_nd_x$	$_np_x$	$_nq_x$	$_nL_x$	T_x	e_x
0 1	100,000	26,702	.73298	.26702	75,178	2,707,635	27.08
1 4	73,298	11,942	.83708	.16292	267,312	2,632,456	35.91
0 5	100,000	38,644	.61356	.38644	342,490	2,707,635	27.08
5 5	61,356	5,424	.91159	.08841	287,569	2,365,145	38.55
10 5	55,931	2,592	.95365	.04635	272,919	2,077,576	37.15
15 5	53,339	2,798	.94754	.05246	260,313	1,804,656	33.83
20 5	50,541	3,425	.93224	.06776	244,415	1,544,343	30.56
25 5	47,116	3,714	.92118	.07882	226,363	1,299,928	27.59
30 5	43,402	3,906	.91002	.08998	207,393	1,073,565	24.74
35 5	39,497	4,208	.89346	.10654	187,202	866,171	21.93
40 5	35,289	4,582	.87016	.12984	165,243	678,969	19.24
45 5	30,707	4,856	.84187	.15813	141,500	513,726	16.73
50 5	25,851	4,937	.80904	.19096	116,911	372,226	14.40
55 5	20,915	4,848	.76819	.23181	92,349	255,315	12.21
60 5	16,066	4,573	.71540	.28460	68,662	162,966	10.14
65 5	11,494	4,107	.64266	.35734	46,869	94,305	8.20
70 5	7,387	3,371	.54368	.45632	27,921	47,435	6.42
75 5	4,016	2,340	.41732	.58268	13,518	19,514	4.86
80 5	1,676	1,227	.26762	.73238	4,807	5,996	3.58
85 +	449	449	0.00000	1.00000	1,189	1,189	2.65

TABLE III-3 (continued)

ABRIDGED LIFE TABLE, BRAZIL, 1872
FEMALE

Age x n	l_x	$_n d_x$	$_n p_x$	$_n q_x$	$_n L_x$	T_x	e_x
0 1	100,000	24,860	.75140	.24860	77,066	2,760,531	27.61
1 4	75,140	12,303	.83627	.16373	273,948	2,683,466	35.71
0 5	100,000	37,163	.62837	.37163	351,013	2,760,531	27.61
5 5	62,837	5,737	.90870	.09130	294,071	2,409,518	38.35
10 5	57,100	2,943	.94846	.05154	277,942	2,115,446	37.05
15 5	54,157	3,198	.94095	.05905	263,399	1,837,504	33.93
20 5	50,958	3,848	.92449	.07551	245,474	1,574,105	30.89
25 5	47,111	4,154	.91182	.08818	225,242	1,328,631	28.20
30 5	42,956	4,249	.90108	.09892	204,189	1,103,389	25.69
35 5	38,707	4,240	.89047	.10953	182,888	899,200	23.23
40 5	34,468	4,161	.87928	.12072	161,870	716,311	20.78
45 5	30,307	4,141	.86336	.13664	141,218	554,442	18.29
50 5	26,166	4,210	.83910	.16090	120,360	413,224	15.79
55 5	21,956	4,316	.80341	.19659	99,075	292,864	13.34
60 5	17,639	4,399	.75059	.24941	77,241	193,789	10.99
65 5	13,240	4,288	.67613	.32387	55,325	116,548	8.80
70 5	8,952	3,798	.57568	.42432	34,817	61,223	6.84
75 5	5,153	2,863	.44446	.55554	17,887	26,406	5.12
80 5	2,291	1,656	.27719	.72281	6,739	8,518	3.72
85 +	635	635	0.00000	1.00000	1,779	1,779	2.80

TABLE III-4

ABRIDGED LIFE TABLE, BRAZIL, 1890
TOTAL

Age x n	l_x	$_nd_x$	$_np_x$	$_nq_x$	$_nL_x$	T_x	e_x
0 1	100,000	25,722	.74278	.25722	76,165	2,781,322	27.81
1 4	74,278	11,989	.83859	.16141	271,134	2,705,157	36.42
0 5	100,000	37,711	.62289	.37711	347,299	2,781,322	27.81
5 5	62,289	5,416	.91304	.08696	292,199	2,434,023	39.08
10 5	56,872	2,614	.95404	.04596	277,611	2,141,824	37.66
15 5	54,259	2,865	.94719	.05281	264,761	1,864,213	34.36
20 5	51,394	3,532	.93128	.06872	248,445	1,599,452	31.12
25 5	47,862	3,858	.91939	.08061	229,752	1,351,007	28.23
30 5	44,004	4,029	.90843	.09157	210,051	1,121,255	25.48
35 5	39,974	4,205	.89480	.10520	189,472	911,204	22.79
40 5	35,769	4,384	.87743	.12257	167,998	721,732	20.18
45 5	31,385	4,543	.85524	.14476	145,656	553,734	17.64
50 5	26,842	4,650	.82677	.17323	122,630	408,078	15.20
55 5	22,192	4,689	.78872	.21128	99,248	285,448	12.86
60 5	17,503	4,618	.73614	.26386	75,886	186,201	10.64
65 5	12,885	4,346	.66267	.33733	53,321	110,314	8.56
70 5	8,538	3,731	.56300	.43700	32,839	56,993	6.67
75 5	4,807	2,721	.43399	.56601	16,491	24,154	5.02
80 5	2,086	1,513	.27471	.72529	6,082	7,663	3.67
85 +	573	573	0.00000	1.00000	1,581	1,581	2.76

TABLE III-5

ABRIDGED LIFE TABLE, BRAZIL, 1900
MALE

Age x n	l_x	$_nd_x$	$_np_x$	$_nq_x$	$_nL_x$	T_x	e_x
0 1	100,000	25,091	.74909	.25091	76,649	2,904,899	29.05
1 4	74,909	11,069	.85223	.14777	275,668	2,828,250	37.76
0 5	100,000	36,160	.63840	.36160	352,316	2,904,899	29.05
5 5	63,840	5,133	.91960	.08040	301,204	2,552,583	39.98
10 5	58,707	2,570	.95622	.04378	286,907	2,251,379	38.35
15 5	56,137	2,829	.94961	.05039	274,238	1,964,472	34.99
20 5	53,308	3,460	.93509	.06491	258,153	1,690,234	31.71
25 5	49,848	3,716	.92546	.07454	239,978	1,432,081	28.73
30 5	46,132	3,861	.91630	.08370	221,129	1,192,103	25.84
35 5	42,271	4,135	.90218	.09782	201,241	970,973	22.97
40 5	38,136	4,509	.88175	.11825	179,672	769,732	20.18
45 5	33,627	4,842	.85600	.14400	156,192	590,061	17.55
50 5	28,784	5,046	.82470	.17530	131,399	433,869	15.07
55 5	23,739	5,113	.78462	.21538	105,909	302,469	12.74
60 5	18,626	4,994	.73188	.26812	80,504	196,560	10.55
65 5	13,632	4,651	.65881	.34119	56,261	116,057	8.51
70 5	8,981	3,952	.55998	.44002	34,428	59,796	6.66
75 5	5,029	2,846	.43412	.56588	17,237	25,367	5.04
80 5	2,183	1,563	.28412	.71588	6,398	8,131	3.72
85 +	620	620	0.00000	1.00000	1,732	1,732	2.79

TABLE III-5 (continued)

ABRIDGED LIFE TABLE, BRAZIL, 1900
FEMALE

Age x n	l_x	$_nd_x$	$_np_x$	$_nq_x$	$_nL_x$	T_x	e_x
0 1	100,000	23,163	.76837	.23163	78,613	2,972,664	29.73
1 4	76,837	11,373	.85198	.14802	282,775	2,894,051	37.66
0 5	100,000	34,536	.65464	.34536	361,388	2,972,664	29.73
5 5	65,464	5,447	.91679	.08321	308,459	2,611,276	39.89
10 5	60,017	2,931	.95117	.04883	292,600	2,302,817	38.37
15 5	57,086	3,218	.94363	.05637	277,991	2,010,217	35.21
20 5	53,868	3,858	.92837	.07163	259,984	1,732,226	32.16
25 5	50,009	4,139	.91723	.08277	239,749	1,472,242	29.44
30 5	45,870	4,201	.90842	.09158	218,856	1,232,494	26.87
35 5	41,669	4,174	.89983	.10017	197,859	1,013,638	24.33
40 5	37,495	4,117	.89021	.10979	177,146	815,779	21.76
45 5	33,378	4,154	.87555	.12445	156,588	638,633	19.13
50 5	29,224	4,306	.85265	.14735	135,472	482,045	16.49
55 5	24,918	4,530	.81819	.18181	113,441	346,573	13.91
60 5	20,388	4,763	.76639	.23361	90,177	233,132	11.43
65 5	15,625	4,802	.69269	.30731	66,060	142,955	9.15
70 5	10,823	4,409	.59261	.40739	42,685	76,895	7.10
75 5	6,414	3,448	.46236	.53764	22,662	34,211	5.33
80 5	2,966	2,079	.29883	.70117	8,937	11,549	3.89
85 +	886	886	0.00000	1.00000	2,612	2,612	2.95

TABLE III-6

ABRIDGED LIFE TABLE, BRAZIL, 1920
MALE

Age x n	l_x	$_nd_x$	$_np_x$	$_nq_x$	$_nL_x$	T_x	e_x
0 1	100,000	23,545	.76455	.23545	78,049	3,144,336	31.44
1 4	76,455	10,136	.86742	.13258	283,868	3,066,287	40.11
0 5	100,000	33,682	.66318	.33682	361,916	3,144,336	31.44
5 5	66,318	4,715	.92890	.07110	315,096	2,782,419	41.96
10 5	61,603	2,405	.96096	.03904	301,849	2,467,324	40.05
15 5	59,198	2,721	.95403	.04597	289,836	2,165,475	36.58
20 5	56,477	3,374	.94026	.05974	274,216	1,875,639	33.21
25 5	53,103	3,615	.93193	.06807	256,483	1,601,422	30.16
30 5	49,488	3,736	.92451	.07549	238,212	1,344,939	27.18
35 5	45,752	4,004	.91248	.08752	218,975	1,106,727	24.19
40 5	41,748	4,405	.89449	.10551	198,019	887,752	21.26
45 5	37,343	4,820	.87092	.12908	174,903	689,733	18.47
50 5	32,523	5,169	.84107	.15893	149,893	514,830	15.83
55 5	27,354	5,420	.80186	.19814	123,340	364,937	13.34
60 5	21,934	5,498	.74934	.25066	95,913	241,597	11.01
65 5	16,436	5,323	.67615	.32385	68,693	145,684	8.86
70 5	11,113	4,693	.57770	.42230	43,240	76,991	6.93
75 5	6,420	3,513	.45278	.54722	22,429	33,752	5.26
80 5	2,907	2,024	.30355	.69645	8,723	11,322	3.90
85 +	882	882	0.00000	1.00000	2,599	2,599	2.95

TABLE III-6 (continued)

ABRIDGED LIFE TABLE, BRAZIL, 1920
FEMALE

Age x n	l_x	$_n d_x$	$_n p_x$	$_n q_x$	$_n L_x$	T_x	e_x
0 1	100,000	21,495	.78505	.21495	80,118	3,254,280	32.54
1 4	78,505	10,326	.86847	.13153	291,708	3,174,162	40.43
0 5	100,000	31,821	.68179	.31821	371,826	3,254,280	32.54
5 5	68,179	4,949	.92741	.07259	323,775	2,882,454	42.28
10 5	63,230	2,702	.95727	.04273	309,288	2,558,679	40.47
15 5	60,528	3,039	.94978	.05022	295,658	2,249,391	37.16
20 5	57,488	3,698	.93567	.06433	278,498	1,953,734	33.98
25 5	53,790	3,986	.92589	.07411	259,033	1,675,236	31.14
30 5	49,804	4,047	.91874	.08126	238,906	1,416,203	28.44
35 5	45,757	4,034	.91184	.08816	218,662	1,177,296	25.73
40 5	41,723	4,026	.90351	.09649	198,557	958,634	22.98
45 5	37,697	4,151	.88988	.11012	178,251	760,077	20.16
50 5	33,546	4,421	.86821	.13179	156,872	581,826	17.34
55 5	29,124	4,806	.83497	.16503	133,902	424,954	14.59
60 5	24,318	5,247	.78424	.21576	108,763	291,052	11.97
65 5	19,071	5,506	.71127	.28873	81,672	182,289	9.56
70 5	13,565	5,268	.61161	.38839	54,309	100,618	7.42
75 5	8,296	4,292	.48268	.51732	29,887	46,308	5.58
80 5	4,005	2,708	.32371	.67629	12,386	16,421	4.10
85 +	1,296	1,296	0.00000	1.00000	4,035	4,035	3.11

TABLE III-7

ABRIDGED LIFE TABLE, BRAZIL, 1940
MALE

Age x n	l_x	$_nd_x$	$_np_x$	$_nq_x$	$_nL_x$	T_x	e_x
0 1	100,000	20,459	.79541	.20459	80,883	3,606,148	36.06
1 4	79,541	8,542	.89261	.10739	299,678	3,525,265	44.32
0 5	100,000	29,001	.70999	.29001	380,561	3,606,148	36.06
5 5	70,999	4,063	.94278	.05722	340,943	3,225,587	45.43
10 5	66,937	2,181	.96742	.03258	329,143	2,884,644	43.10
15 5	64,756	2,545	.96070	.03930	318,053	2,555,501	39.46
20 5	62,211	3,186	.94879	.05121	303,351	2,237,448	35.97
25 5	59,025	3,398	.94244	.05756	286,606	1,934,098	32.77
30 5	55,628	3,477	.93749	.06251	269,531	1,647,491	29.62
35 5	52,151	3,721	.92865	.07135	251,665	1,377,961	26.42
40 5	48,429	4,148	.91435	.08565	232,107	1,126,296	23.26
45 5	44,281	4,679	.89434	.10566	210,055	894,189	20.19
50 5	39,603	5,242	.86764	.13236	185,275	684,133	17.27
55 5	34,361	5,799	.83123	.16877	157,651	498,858	14.52
60 5	28,562	6,260	.78083	.21917	127,415	341,208	11.95
65 5	22,302	6,485	.70920	.29080	95,371	213,793	9.59
70 5	15,817	6,133	.61222	.38778	63,272	118,422	7.49
75 5	9,683	4,945	.48937	.51063	35,050	55,150	5.70
80 5	4,739	3,110	.34377	.65623	14,868	20,101	4.24
85 +	1,629	1,629	0.00000	1.00000	5,232	5,232	3.21

TABLE III-7 (continued)

ABRIDGED LIFE TABLE, BRAZIL, 1940
FEMALE

Age x n	1_x	$d_{n\,x}$	$_np_x$	$_nq_x$	$L_{n\,x}$	T_x	e_x
0 1	100,000	18,660	.81340	.18660	82,691	3,725,462	37.25
1 4	81,340	8,656	.89359	.10641	306,670	3,642,771	44.78
1 5	100,000	27,315	.72685	.27315	389,361	3,725,462	37.25
5 5	72,685	4,240	.94167	.05833	348,915	3,336,101	45.90
10 5	68,445	2,428	.96453	.03547	336,112	2,987,186	43.64
15 5	66,017	2,818	.95731	.04269	323,654	2,651,074	40.16
20 5	63,199	3,473	.94505	.05495	307,607	2,327,420	36.83
25 5	59,726	3,730	.93754	.06246	289,321	2,019,812	33.82
30 5	55,996	3,757	.93291	.06709	270,580	1,730,492	30.90
35 5	52,239	3,748	.92824	.07176	251,807	1,459,911	27.95
40 5	48,491	3,798	.92167	.07833	233,021	1,208,104	24.91
45 5	44,692	4,035	.90972	.09028	213,604	975,083	21.82
50 5	40,658	4,468	.89010	.10990	192,431	761,479	18.73
55 5	36,189	5,093	.85927	.14073	168,689	569,048	15.72
60 5	31,096	5,872	.81115	.18885	141,340	400,359	12.87
65 5	25,224	6,542	.74066	.25934	110,126	259,019	10.27
70 5	18,682	6,666	.64317	.35683	76,605	148,893	7.97
75 5	12,016	5,801	.51722	.48278	44,665	72,288	6.02
80 5	6,215	3,950	.36447	.63553	20,024	27,624	4.44
85 +	2,265	2,265	0.00000	1.00000	7,600	7,600	3.36

TABLE III-8

ABRIDGED LIFE TABLE, BRAZIL, 1950
MALE

Age x n	l_x	$_nd_x$	$_np_x$	$_nq_x$	$_nL_x$	T_x	e_x
0 1	100,000	17,687	.82313	.17687	83,398	4,205,391	42.05
1 4	82,313	6,852	.91676	.08324	314,375	4,121,992	50.08
0 5	100,000	24,539	.75461	.24539	397,773	4,205,391	42.05
5 5	75,461	3,074	.95926	.04074	366,399	3,807,618	50.46
10 5	72,387	1,558	.97848	.02152	358,011	3,441,218	47.54
15 5	70,829	1,969	.97220	.02780	349,839	3,083,208	43.53
20 5	68,860	2,616	.96201	.03799	338,029	2,733,358	39.69
25 5	66,244	2,839	.95715	.04285	324,101	2,395,329	36.16
30 5	63,406	2,930	.95380	.04620	309,798	2,071,228	32.67
35 5	60,476	3,194	.94718	.05282	294,621	1,761,430	29.13
40 5	57,282	3,675	.93584	.06416	277,597	1,466,809	25.61
45 5	53,607	4,361	.91865	.08135	257,619	1,189,211	22.18
50 5	49,246	5,203	.89435	.10565	233,794	931,593	18.92
55 5	44,043	6,144	.86050	.13950	205,471	697,799	15.84
60 5	37,899	7,113	.81233	.18767	172,337	492,328	12.99
65 5	30,786	7,921	.74269	.25731	134,588	319,991	10.39
70 5	22,865	8,053	.64780	.35220	93,967	185,403	8.11
75 5	14,812	7,003	.52719	.47281	55,484	91,436	6.17
80 5	7,809	4,812	.38375	.61625	25,535	35,953	4.60
85 +	2,997	2,997	0.00000	1.00000	10,418	10,418	3.48

TABLE III-8 (continued)

ABRIDGED LIFE TABLE, BRAZIL, 1950
FEMALE

Age x n	l_x	$_nd_x$	$_np_x$	$_nq_x$	$_nL_x$	T_x	e_x
0 1	100,000	15,836	.84164	.15836	85,241	4,386,905	43.87
1 4	84,164	6,856	.91854	.08146	321,810	4,301,664	51.11
0 5	100,000	22,692	.77308	.22692	407,051	4,386,905	43.87
5 5	77,308	3,184	.95881	.04119	375,384	3,979,854	51.48
10 5	74,123	1,751	.97638	.02362	366,251	3,604,470	48.63
15 5	72,373	2,165	.97009	.02991	357,031	3,238,219	44.74
20 5	70,208	2,790	.96026	.03974	344,345	2,881,188	41.04
25 5	67,418	3,045	.95484	.04516	329,499	2,536,843	37.63
30 5	64,373	3,096	.95190	.04810	314,137	2,207,344	34.29
35 5	61,277	3,151	.94858	.05142	298,544	1,893,207	30.90
40 5	58,126	3,321	.94287	.05713	282,488	1,594,663	27.43
45 5	54,805	3,720	.93212	.06788	265,063	1,312,175	23.94
50 5	51,085	4,361	.91463	.08537	244,980	1,047,111	20.50
55 5	46,724	5,299	.88660	.11340	221,089	802,132	17.17
60 5	41,425	6,553	.84181	.15819	191,637	581,043	14.03
65 5	34,872	7,862	.77455	.22545	155,534	389,406	11.17
70 5	27,010	8,657	.67950	.32050	113,688	233,872	8.66
75 5	18,353	8,136	.55671	.44329	70,556	120,184	6.55
80 5	10,217	6,013	.41153	.58847	34,391	49,628	4.86
85 +	4,205	4,205	0.00000	1.00000	15,237	15,237	3.62

TABLE III-9

ABRIDGED LIFE TABLE, BRAZIL, 1960
MALE

Age x n	l_x	$_n d_x$	$_n p_x$	$_n q_x$	$_n L_x$	T_x	e_x
0 1	100,000	11,363	.88637	.11363	89,251	5,402,720	54.03
1 4	88,637	3,862	.95643	.04357	346,156	5,313,469	59.95
0 5	100,000	15,225	.84775	.15225	435,407	5,402,720	54.03
5 5	84,775	1,715	.97977	.02023	417,771	4,967,313	58.59
10 5	83,060	914	.98900	.01100	413,053	4,549,542	54.77
15 5	82,146	1,264	.98461	.01539	408,028	4,136,489	50.36
20 5	80,882	1,732	.97859	.02141	400,268	3,728,460	46.10
25 5	79,150	1,875	.97631	.02369	391,030	3,328,192	42.05
30 5	77,276	1,930	.97503	.02497	381,621	2,937,163	38.01
35 5	75,346	2,157	.97137	.02863	371,540	2,555,542	33.92
40 5	73,189	2,630	.96406	.03594	359,745	2,184,002	29.84
45 5	70,558	3,413	.95163	.04837	344,856	1,824,257	25.85
50 5	67,145	4,527	.93258	.06742	325,204	1,479,401	22.03
55 5	62,618	5,983	.90445	.09555	299,163	1,154,198	18.43
60 5	56,635	7,785	.86255	.13745	264,973	855,034	15.10
65 5	48,851	9,740	.80062	.19938	221,190	590,062	12.08
70 5	39,111	11,193	.71380	.28620	168,246	368,872	9.43
75 5	27,918	11,141	.60093	.39907	111,068	200,626	7.19
80 5	16,776	8,983	.46456	.53544	59,228	89,558	5.34
85 +	7,794	7,794	0.00000	1.00000	30,331	30,331	3.89

TABLE III-9 (continued)

ABRIDGED LIFE TABLE, BRAZIL, 1960
FEMALE

Age x n	l_x	$_nd_x$	$_np_x$	$_nq_x$	$_nL_x$	T_x	e_x
0 1	100,000	9,649	.90351	.09649	90,930	5,704,320	57.04
1 4	90,351	3,680	.95927	.04073	353,431	5,613,390	62.13
0 5	100,000	13,329	.86671	.13329	444,361	5,704,320	57.04
5 5	86,671	1,697	.98042	.01958	427,397	5,259,959	60.69
10 5	84,974	960	.98870	.01130	422,510	4,832,561	56.87
15 5	84,014	1,256	.98506	.01494	417,304	4,410,051	52.49
20 5	82,758	1,662	.97992	.02008	409,818	3,992,747	48.25
25 5	81,097	1,834	.97738	.02262	400,918	3,582,929	44.18
30 5	79,262	1,901	.97602	.02398	391,600	3,182,011	40.15
35 5	77,361	2,017	.97392	.02608	381,852	2,790,411	36.07
40 5	75,344	2,286	.96965	.03035	371,237	2,408,559	31.97
45 5	73,058	2,818	.96143	.03857	358,669	2,037,322	27.89
50 5	70,240	3,642	.94815	.05185	342,681	1,678,653	23.90
55 5	66,597	4,870	.92688	.07312	321,733	1,335,972	20.06
60 5	61,728	6,703	.89141	.10859	293,263	1,014,239	16.43
65 5	55,025	9,123	.83420	.16580	254,054	720,976	13.10
70 5	45,901	11,531	.74880	.25120	202,151	466,922	10.17
75 5	34,371	12,509	.63606	.36394	140,458	264,772	7.70
80 5	21,862	10,839	.50420	.49580	79,757	124,314	5.69
85 +	11,023	11,023	0.00000	1.00000	44,557	44,557	4.04

TABLE III-10

LIFE EXPECTANCY, BRAZIL
CENSUS YEARS

Year	Total*	Male	Female
1872	27.4	27.1	27.6
1890	27.8		
1900	29.4	29.1	29.7
1920	32.0	31.4	32.5
1940	36.7	36.1	37.3
1950	43.0	42.1	43.9
1960	55.5	54.0	57.0

*Simple arithmetic average of male and
female.

NOTES

[1] The exception is the 1890 census which only published age
group distribution for both sexes combined.

[2] We reached our conclusions by comparing differences in the
cohorts (persons who have died) between 1900 and 1920, and between 1920 and 1940. We would expect the relative differences
between the 1900 and 1920 censuses to be greater than the relative differences between the 1920 and 1940 censuses, because we
would expect higher mortality during the period 1900-1920 than
during the period of the next twenty years. Nevertheless, the
census information shows the opposite.

[3] The distributions of foreign-born by age for 1890 and 1920
were estimated on the basis of 1900 census information for 1890,
and 1940 and 1950 census information for 1920.

[4] Most of our modifications were made for those years where
irregularities due to misdeclaration of age were obvious, such
as 1872, 1890, and 1920. For other years, very slight modifications were made: for 1940, 1950, and 1960 we made a small reduction in the total population enumerated in older age groups,
because the age distribution of the foreign population was
available for 1940 and 1950.

[5] We considered, for example, the years 1920-1940, 1920-1950,
1940-1950, 1940-1960, and so forth.

[6] An example of life table construction using Method B is
given in Appendix II.

IV. CHILE

Thirteen censuses have been taken in Chile, six in the present century and seven in the nineteenth century. Census information useful for life tables exists only after 1907, when the eighth census was taken. Vital statistics are available for the early census dates, but except for recent decades their completeness is questionable.

A graphical cohort analysis of the census information is presented in Figure IV-1. We can see that all censuses previous to the 1960 census have an obvious underenumeration of population in the age group 0-9, but all other age groups seem to be similarly complete throughout the censuses. Only the 1952 census seems to be less complete than previous censuses. This census also presents some irregularities in both sexes, in the age group 10-19. The 1960 census seems more complete than all previous censuses and can be considered the best in regard to enumeration. Death statistics from the earlier censuses are considered complete, but statistics on birth registration are not.[1]

After considering the available information, we decided to use Method B to construct life tables for the period before 1960, and to use Method A for the year 1960.

The Chilean population satisfies the necessary requirements for the use of Method B. International migration has not been significant in the past; in addition, fertility has been almost constant with a very slight tendency to decline since 1907. Of course, when applying Method B, it would have been preferable to have had constant fertility in the past, but a very slow decline over several decades does not significantly affect the proportional age distribution of the population. Therefore we decided to use Method B for census years from 1907 to 1952.

LIFE TABLES FOR 1907, 1920, 1930, 1940, AND 1952; CONSTRUCTION BY METHOD B

Proportional Age Group Distribution of the Population

The age distribution from 10-59 for the years 1907, 1920, 1930, and 1940 seems to be without differential enumeration among ten-year age groups. Therefore, we accepted the proportional age group distribution for the first four censuses. Because of irregularities in the 1952 age distribution (see Fig. IV-1) some age

FIGURE IV-1

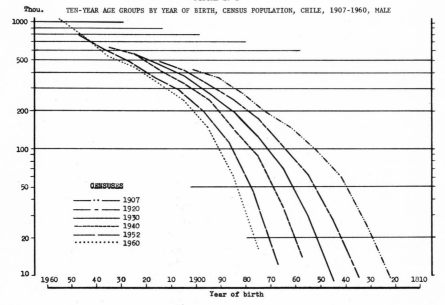

TEN-YEAR AGE GROUPS BY YEAR OF BIRTH, CENSUS POPULATION, CHILE, 1907-1960, MALE

CENSUSES
———··——— 1907
———·—— 1920
————— 1930
---------- 1940
— — — 1952
············ 1960

Year of birth

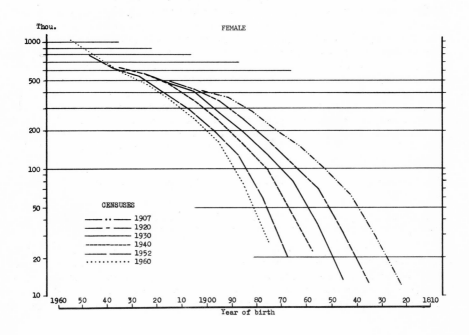

FEMALE

CENSUSES
———··——— 1907
———·—— 1920
————— 1930
---------- 1940
— — — 1952
············ 1960

Year of birth

groups were modified. For males, the age groups 10-19 and 30-39 were increased, and the age group 40-49 was decreased. For females the age group 10-19 was increased and the 20-29 age group decreased. After these corrections were made, all the census age group distributions were smoothed, according to the procedure explained in Appendix III. The proportional age group distributions for each year--which are used to construct the life tables--are presented in Table IV-1.

Estimation of Natural Growth Rates

After modifying the total population for underenumeration, principally in 1952, natural growth rates for each census year were estimated by considering existing estimates[2] and intercensal geometric growth rates. The natural growth rates for census years are: 11.7, 12.2, 14.2, 17.0, and 21.5 per thousand for the years 1907, 1920, 1930, 1940, and 1952 respectively.

Construction of Life Tables for Census Years through 1952

Life tables were constructed using Method B, the proportional age group distribution of Table IV-1, and the natural growth rates estimated above.

The set of United Nations values used in the quotient $\frac{C'(x, x+5)}{5^L_x}$ were levels 20, 20, 25, 35, and 65 for the years 1907, 1920, 1930, 1940, and 1952 respectively. The slopes of the straight lines of adjustment and the growth rates used for each sex are shown in Table IV-2. Finally, the life tables themselves are presented in Tables IV-3 to IV-7.[3]

LIFE TABLE FOR 1959-1961; CONSTRUCTION BY METHOD A

The life table for 1959-1961 was constructed using death statistics and census population information, both of which will be analyzed below.

Analysis of Death Statistics

Death registration in Chile has long been considered complete. After our analysis, we accepted its completeness.[4] Therefore, we made a weighted average of deaths registered in 1959, 1960, and 1961 in order to obtain the age group distribution of deaths at the census date[5] (Table IV-8). Cohort deaths from those born between 1951 and 1960 were needed in order to evaluate the birth register and the enumerated population in age group 0-4; a Lexis' diagram[6] was used for this purpose. The cohort deaths obtained are given in Table IV-9. Death separation factors for ages under one year were calculated in the usual way (Table IV-10).

TABLE IV-1

SMOOTHED PROPORTIONAL DISTRIBUTION OF THE POPULATION BY SEX AND FIVE-YEAR AGE GROUPS
AGES 10-59, CHILE, CENSUS YEARS

Age Groups	1907 Male	1907 Female	1920 Male	1920 Female	1930 Male	1930 Female	1940 Male	1940 Female	1952 Male	1952 Female
Total 10-59	1.000000	1.000000	1.000000	1.000000	1.000000	1.000000	1.000000	1.000000	1.000000	1.000000
	.676130	.677917	.679456	.680849	.680699	.680522	.690631	.691711	.676130	.678919
10-14	.117272	.114152	.115074	.113692	.114602	.112837	.118642	.114635	.116838	.112898
15-19	.104882	.104213	.103725	.103940	.103868	.103929	.105125	.104660	.101693	.100868
20-24	.092598	.094063	.092390	.093944	.093134	.094711	.092035	.094582	.089249	.089847
25-29	.080842	.082849	.081683	.083201	.082397	.083939	.081067	.083988	.078565	.080570
30-34	.068585	.070388	.070900	.071530	.071323	.071895	.070945	.072823	.067948	.069947
35-39	.058682	.059974	.061070	.061113	.061257	.061188	.061682	.062549	.059166	.060026
40-44	.049363	.049629	.051254	.050351	.051223	.050144	.052905	.052016	.051564	.051815
45-49	.041569	.041523	.042591	.041840	.042444	.041484	.044386	.043315	.044305	.044840
50-54	.034417	.034238	.033857	.033837	.033784	.033473	.035617	.034986	.037026	.037440
55-59	.027920	.027888	.026912	.027401	.026667	.026922	.028227	.028157	.029776	.030668

TABLE IV-2

GROWTH RATES USED IN THE CONSTRUCTION OF LIFE TABLES FOR CHILE

Year	Growth Rates			Slopes of the Straight Lines of Adjustment of the $\log_e \frac{C(x, x+5)}{_nL_5}$		
	Total	Male	Female	Male	Female	Average
1907	.0117	.01138	.01202	.011273	.011903	.011588
1920	.0122	.01186	.01254	.011245	.012035	.011640
1930	.0142	.01367	.01473	.013540	.014592	.014066
1940	.0170	.01651	.01749	.016064	.017023	.016544
1952	.0215	.02143	.02157	.021653	.021801	.021727

Analysis of Census Population

The census taken in 1960 was, in general, accurate and complete but, in any case, we made an analysis of the completeness of age group 0-4. In this analysis we used cohort deaths from Table IV-9 and registered births for 1951-1960.[7] Assuming complete registration of death and accuracy in the census enumeration of ages 3-8, we obtained an estimate of under-registration of births between 1954 and 1957 (see Table IV-11).[8] We estimated the under-registration of births between 1958 and 1960 by considering the trend of completeness for the years 1952-1953 and 1954-1957. Then, we estimated the population by individual ages from 0-4 (a) by subtracting the cohort deaths from the corrected annual births for 1956-1960; (b) by shifting the previous result to the census date; and (c) by increasing males until we had obtained the same sex ratio as the census (Table IV-12). The total population by sex and five-year age groups is presented in Table IV-13.

Construction of the Life Table for 1959-1961

The life table for 1959-1961 was constructed using Method A, deaths from Table IV-8, and population from Table IV-13. Only values of μ_x were graphically smoothed slightly.[9] The life table is given in Table IV-14, and a summary of life expectancy is presented in Table IV-15.

TABLE IV-3

ABRIDGED LIFE TABLE, CHILE, 1907
MALE

Age x n	l_x	$_nd_x$	$_np_x$	$_nq_x$	$_nL_x$	T_x	e_x
0 1	100,000	25,020	.74980	.25020	76,699	2,966,630	29.67
1 4	74,980	10,901	.85462	.14538	276,286	2,889,931	38.54
0 5	100,000	35,921	.64079	.35921	352,985	2,966,630	29.67
5 5	64,079	4,925	.92314	.07686	302,923	2,613,645	40.79
10 5	59,154	2,374	.95987	.04013	289,642	2,310,722	39.06
15 5	56,780	2,657	.95321	.04679	277,905	2,021,080	35.59
20 5	54,123	3,321	.93864	.06136	262,599	1,743,175	32.21
25 5	50,802	3,608	.92898	.07102	245,040	1,480,575	29.14
30 5	47,195	3,786	.91979	.08021	226,652	1,235,535	26.18
35 5	43,409	4,097	.90561	.09439	207,051	1,008,883	23.24
40 5	39,312	4,517	.88510	.11490	185,562	801,832	20.40
45 5	34,795	4,897	.85925	.14075	161,926	616,270	17.71
50 5	29,898	5,147	.82784	.17216	136,741	454,345	15.20
55 5	24,750	5,257	.78760	.21240	110,634	317,604	12.83
60 5	19,493	5,172	.73466	.26534	84,415	206,970	10.62
65 5	14,321	4,850	.66131	.33869	59,218	122,555	8.56
70 5	9,471	4,147	.56211	.43789	36,376	63,337	6.69
75 5	5,324	3,003	.43583	.56417	18,281	26,961	5.06
80 5	2,320	1,658	.28543	.71457	6,812	8,680	3.74
85 +	662	662	0.00000	1.00000	1,868	1,868	2.82

TABLE IV-3 (continued)

ABRIDGED LIFE TABLE, CHILE, 1907
FEMALE

Age x n	l_x	$_nd_x$	$_np_x$	$_nq_x$	$_nL_x$	T_x	e_x
0 1	100,000	23,075	.76925	.23075	78,675	3,050,678	30.51
1 4	76,925	11,164	.85487	.14513	283,544	2,972,004	38.64
0 5	100,000	34,239	.65761	.34239	362,219	3,050,678	30.51
5 5	65,761	5,191	.92107	.07893	310,592	2,688,460	40.88
10 5	60,570	2,691	.95557	.04443	295,981	2,377,867	39.26
15 5	57,879	3,012	.94796	.05204	282,498	2,081,887	35.97
20 5	54,867	3,695	.93265	.06735	265,416	1,799,389	32.80
25 5	51,171	4,019	.92145	.07855	245,885	1,533,973	29.98
30 5	47,152	4,121	.91260	.08740	225,491	1,288,088	27.32
35 5	43,031	4,132	.90397	.09603	204,797	1,062,597	24.69
40 5	38,899	4,111	.89431	.10569	184,202	857,801	22.05
45 5	34,788	4,189	.87958	.12042	163,575	673,599	19.36
50 5	30,599	4,389	.85658	.14342	142,169	510,024	16.67
55 5	26,210	4,667	.82196	.17804	119,597	367,856	14.03
60 5	21,544	4,957	.76992	.23008	95,508	248,259	11.52
65 5	16,587	5,045	.69587	.30413	70,288	152,751	9.21
70 5	11,542	4,671	.59533	.40467	45,625	82,463	7.14
75 5	6,871	3,679	.46458	.53542	24,335	36,838	5.36
80 5	3,192	2,232	.30069	.69931	9,641	12,503	3.92
85 +	960	960	0.00000	1.00000	2,863	2,863	2.98

TABLE IV-4

ABRIDGED LIFE TABLE, CHILE, 1920
MALE

Age x n	l_x	$_nd_x$	$_np_x$	$_nq_x$	$_nL_x$	T_x	e_x
0 1	100,000	24,973	.75027	.24973	76,733	3,009,039	30.09
1 4	75,027	10,788	.85621	.14379	276,701	2,932,306	39.08
0 5	100,000	35,761	.64239	.35761	353,434	3,009,039	30.09
5 5	64,239	4,785	.92552	.07448	304,079	2,655,605	41.34
10 5	59,455	2,240	.96232	.03768	291,487	2,351,526	39.55
15 5	57,215	2,539	.95563	.04437	280,386	2,060,038	36.01
20 5	54,676	3,224	.94103	.05897	265,618	1,779,652	32.55
25 5	51,452	3,532	.93135	.06865	248,487	1,514,034	29.43
30 5	47,919	3,732	.92213	.07787	230,425	1,265,546	26.41
35 5	44,188	4,069	.90791	.09209	211,033	1,035,122	23.43
40 5	40,119	4,519	.88735	.11265	189,612	824,088	20.54
45 5	35,600	4,933	.86143	.13857	165,881	634,477	17.82
50 5	30,667	5,215	.82994	.17006	140,437	468,596	15.28
55 5	25,452	5,355	.78960	.21040	113,913	328,159	12.89
60 5	20,097	5,295	.73653	.26347	87,138	214,246	10.66
65 5	14,802	4,988	.66299	.33701	61,284	127,108	8.59
70 5	9,813	4,283	.56354	.43646	37,741	65,824	6.71
75 5	5,530	3,114	.43697	.56303	19,015	28,084	5.08
80 5	2,417	1,725	.28632	.71368	7,103	9,068	3.75
85 +	692	692	0.00000	1.00000	1,965	1,965	2.84

TABLE IV-4 (continued)

ABRIDGED LIFE TABLE, CHILE, 1920
FEMALE

Age x n	l_x	$_nd_x$	$_np_x$	$_nq_x$	$_nL_x$	T_x	e_x
0 1	100,000	23,038	.76962	.23038	78,701	3,084,536	30.85
1 4	76,962	11,076	.85609	.14391	283,870	3,005,835	39.06
0 5	100,000	34,114	.65886	.34114	362,570	3,084,536	30.85
5 5	65,886	5,081	.92288	.07712	311,498	2,721,966	41.31
10 5	60,805	2,588	.95743	.04257	297,420	2,410,468	39.64
15 5	58,217	2,922	.94980	.05020	284,423	2,113,049	36.30
20 5	55,294	3,624	.93446	.06554	267,743	1,828,626	33.07
25 5	51,670	3,966	.92324	.07676	248,523	1,560,883	30.21
30 5	47,704	4,085	.91438	.08562	228,352	1,312,361	27.51
35 5	43,620	4,112	.90573	.09427	207,798	1,084,008	24.85
40 5	39,507	4,107	.89605	.10395	187,264	876,210	22.18
45 5	35,401	4,202	.88129	.11871	166,617	688,946	19.46
50 5	31,198	4,423	.85824	.14176	145,094	522,329	16.74
55 5	26,775	4,724	.82355	.17645	122,295	377,234	14.09
60 5	22,051	5,041	.77141	.22859	97,852	254,939	11.56
65 5	17,010	5,150	.69722	.30278	72,153	157,087	9.23
70 5	11,860	4,786	.59648	.40352	46,927	84,934	7.16
75 5	7,074	3,781	.46552	.53448	25,078	38,007	5.37
80 5	3,293	2,300	.30148	.69852	9,954	12,930	3.93
85 +	993	993	0.00000	1.00000	2,975	2,975	3.00

TABLE IV-5

ABRIDGED LIFE TABLE, CHILE, 1930
MALE

Age x n	l_x	$_nd_x$	$_np_x$	$_nq_x$	$_nL_x$	T_x	e_x
0 1	100,000	21,909	.78091	.21909	79,531	3,455,352	34.55
1 4	78,091	9,125	.88315	.11685	292,575	3,375,821	43.23
0 5	100,000	31,034	.68966	.31034	372,106	3,455,352	34.55
5 5	68,966	4,141	.93996	.06004	330,190	3,083,246	44.71
10 5	64,825	2,063	.96818	.03182	318,858	2,753,056	42.47
15 5	62,762	2,430	.96128	.03872	308,399	2,434,199	38.78
20 5	60,332	3,108	.94848	.05152	294,171	2,125,800	35.24
25 5	57,224	3,364	.94122	.05878	277,716	1,831,629	32.01
30 5	53,860	3,494	.93513	.06487	260,684	1,553,913	28.85
35 5	50,366	3,787	.92481	.07519	242,610	1,293,229	25.68
40 5	46,580	4,248	.90879	.09121	222,622	1,050,619	22.56
45 5	42,331	4,781	.88707	.11293	200,036	827,997	19.56
50 5	37,551	5,305	.85873	.14127	174,821	627,961	16.72
55 5	32,246	5,781	.82071	.17929	147,055	453,140	14.05
60 5	26,464	6,115	.76893	.23107	117,193	306,084	11.57
65 5	20,349	6,184	.69610	.30390	86,256	188,891	9.28
70 5	14,165	5,697	.59785	.40215	56,034	102,636	7.25
75 5	8,469	4,459	.47342	.52658	30,198	46,602	5.50
80 5	4,009	2,704	.32562	.67438	12,337	16,404	4.09
85 +	1,305	1,305	0.00000	1.00000	4,068	4,068	3.12

TABLE IV-5 (continued)

ABRIDGED LIFE TABLE, CHILE, 1930
FEMALE

Age x n	l_x	$_nd_x$	$_np_x$	$_nq_x$	$_nL_x$	T_x	e_x
0 1	100,000	19,987	.80013	.19987	81,466	3,575,475	35.75
1 4	80,013	9,265	.88420	.11580	300,006	3,494,009	43.67
0 5	100,000	29,252	.70748	.29252	381,473	3,575,475	35.75
5 5	70,748	4,336	.93871	.06129	338,588	3,194,002	45.15
10 5	66,412	2,329	.96493	.03507	326,177	2,855,414	43.00
15 5	64,083	2,723	.95751	.04249	314,246	2,529,237	39.47
20 5	61,360	3,414	.94435	.05565	298,584	2,214,991	36.10
25 5	57,946	3,721	.93579	.06421	280,477	1,916,407	33.07
30 5	54,225	3,796	.92999	.07001	261,651	1,635,930	30.17
35 5	50,429	3,816	.92433	.07567	242,594	1,374,279	27.25
40 5	46,613	3,871	.91696	.08304	223,445	1,131,685	24.28
45 5	42,742	4,095	.90419	.09581	203,691	908,240	21.25
50 5	38,647	4,503	.88348	.11652	182,271	704,549	18.23
55 5	34,144	5,078	.85127	.14873	158,457	522,278	15.30
60 5	29,066	5,768	.80156	.19844	131,376	363,821	12.52
65 5	23,298	6,304	.72941	.27059	100,991	232,445	9.98
70 5	16,994	6,282	.63031	.36969	69,027	131,453	7.74
75 5	10,711	5,330	.50238	.49762	39,298	62,426	5.83
80 5	5,381	3,517	.34636	.65364	17,033	23,128	4.30
85 +	1,864	1,864	0.00000	1.00000	6,095	6,095	3.27

TABLE IV-6

ABRIDGED LIFE TABLE, CHILE, 1940
MALE

Age x n	l_x	$_nd_x$	$_np_x$	$_nq_x$	$_nL_x$	T_x	e_x
0 1	100,000	20,345	.79655	.20345	80,958	3,741,143	37.41
1 4	79,655	8,228	.89671	.10329	300,760	3,660,184	45.95
0 5	100,000	28,573	.71427	.28573	381,718	3,741,143	37.41
5 5	71,427	3,673	.94858	.05142	344,064	3,359,424	47.03
10 5	67,754	1,807	.97333	.02667	334,180	3,015,360	44.50
15 5	65,947	2,206	.96655	.03345	324,888	2,681,180	40.66
20 5	63,741	2,896	.95457	.04543	311,758	2,356,293	36.97
25 5	60,846	3,153	.94818	.05182	296,344	2,044,535	33.60
30 5	57,693	3,277	.94321	.05679	280,387	1,748,190	30.30
35 5	54,416	3,575	.93431	.06569	263,397	1,467,803	26.97
40 5	50,841	4,071	.91992	.08008	244,407	1,204,407	23.69
45 5	46,770	4,687	.89979	.10021	222,535	960,000	20.53
50 5	42,083	5,348	.87292	.12708	197,478	737,465	17.52
55 5	36,735	6,014	.83630	.16370	169,058	539,986	14.70
60 5	30,722	6,587	.78558	.21442	137,467	370,928	12.07
65 5	24,134	6,914	.71351	.28649	103,522	233,461	9.67
70 5	17,220	6,614	.61594	.38406	69,099	129,939	7.55
75 5	10,607	5,383	.49246	.50754	38,510	60,840	5.74
80 5	5,223	3,414	.34642	.65358	16,436	22,330	4.28
85 +	1,809	1,809	0.00000	1.00000	5,894	5,894	3.26

TABLE IV-6 (continued)

ABRIDGED LIFE TABLE, CHILE, 1940
FEMALE

Age x n	l_x	$_nd_x$	$_np_x$	$_nq_x$	$_nL_x$	T_x	e_x
0 1	100,000	18,541	.81459	.18541	82,768	3,870,241	38.70
1 4	81,459	8,329	.89776	.10224	307,795	3,787,472	46.50
0 5	100,000	26,870	.73130	.26870	390,564	3,870,241	38.70
5 5	73,130	3,836	.94755	.05245	352,159	3,479,677	47.58
10 5	69,294	2,043	.97052	.02948	341,337	3,127,518	45.13
15 5	67,251	2,473	.96323	.03677	330,720	2,786,181	41.43
20 5	64,778	3,181	.95090	.04910	316,268	2,455,461	37.91
25 5	61,598	3,490	.94335	.05665	299,307	2,139,194	34.73
30 5	58,108	3,563	.93868	.06132	281,653	1,839,886	31.66
35 5	54,545	3,600	.93399	.06601	263,733	1,558,234	28.57
40 5	50,945	3,700	.92737	.07263	245,568	1,294,500	25.41
45 5	47,244	3,999	.91535	.08465	226,499	1,048,932	22.20
50 5	43,245	4,515	.89561	.10439	205,310	822,433	19.02
55 5	38,731	5,245	.86458	.13542	181,093	617,123	15.93
60 5	33,486	6,156	.81616	.18384	152,672	436,030	13.02
65 5	27,330	6,963	.74523	.25477	119,692	283,358	10.37
70 5	20,367	7,187	.64713	.35287	83,774	163,666	8.04
75 5	13,180	6,319	.52055	.47945	49,147	79,892	6.06
80 5	6,861	4,340	.36744	.63256	22,170	30,745	4.48
85 +	2,521	2,521	0.00000	1.00000	8,575	8,575	3.40

TABLE IV-7

ABRIDGED LIFE TABLE, CHILE, 1952
MALE

Age x n	l_x	$_nd_x$	$_np_x$	$_nq_x$	$_nL_x$	T_x	e_x
0 1	100,000	12,651	.87349	.12651	88,068	5,080,349	50.80
1 4	87,349	4,558	.94782	.05218	339,519	4,992,281	57.15
0 5	100,000	17,209	.82791	.17209	427,587	5,080,349	50.80
5 5	82,791	2,144	.97410	.02590	406,518	4,652,762	56.20
10 5	80,647	1,213	.98496	.01504	400,231	4,246,245	52.65
15 5	79,434	1,577	.98015	.01985	393,719	3,846,014	48.42
20 5	77,857	2,075	.97335	.02665	384,297	3,452,295	44.34
25 5	75,782	2,225	.97064	.02936	373,312	3,067,998	40.48
30 5	73,558	2,272	.96911	.03089	362,168	2,694,687	36.63
35 5	71,286	2,485	.96514	.03486	350,407	2,332,519	32.72
40 5	68,800	2,949	.95714	.04286	337,011	1,982,112	28.81
45 5	65,852	3,700	.94381	.05619	320,568	1,645,101	24.98
50 5	62,152	4,720	.92406	.07594	299,671	1,324,533	21.31
55 5	57,432	6,028	.89505	.10495	273,017	1,024,862	17.84
60 5	51,404	7,613	.85190	.14810	239,080	751,845	14.63
65 5	43,791	9,259	.78857	.21143	196,866	512,765	11.71
70 5	34,532	10,345	.70042	.29958	147,222	315,899	9.15
75 5	24,187	10,006	.58630	.41370	95,132	168,677	6.97
80 5	14,181	7,819	.44860	.55140	49,349	73,545	5.19
85 +	6,362	6,362	0.00000	1.00000	24,196	24,196	3.80

TABLE IV-7 (continued)

ABRIDGED LIFE TABLE, CHILE, 1952
FEMALE

Age x n	l_x	$_nd_x$	$_np_x$	$_nq_x$	$_nL_x$	T_x	e_x
0 1	100,000	10,882	.89118	.10882	89,811	5,352,599	53.53
1 4	89,118	4,434	.95024	.04976	346,894	5,262,788	59.05
0 5	100,000	15,316	.84684	.15316	436,705	5,352,599	53.53
5 5	84,684	2,166	.97442	.02558	416,007	4,915,895	58.05
10 5	82,518	1,296	.98430	.01570	409,384	4,499,888	54.53
15 5	81,222	1,611	.98017	.01983	402,495	4,090,504	50.36
20 5	79,612	2,051	.97424	.02576	393,123	3,688,009	46.33
25 5	77,560	2,225	.97132	.02868	382,249	3,294,886	42.48
30 5	75,336	2,274	.96982	.03018	371,022	2,912,637	38.66
35 5	73,062	2,366	.96761	.03239	359,465	2,541,615	34.79
40 5	70,696	2,603	.96318	.03682	347,180	2,182,150	30.87
45 5	68,092	3,094	.95457	.04543	333,125	1,834,970	26.95
50 5	64,999	3,864	.94056	.05944	315,886	1,501,846	23.11
55 5	61,135	5,005	.91812	.08188	294,017	1,185,960	19.40
60 5	56,129	6,679	.88101	.11899	265,203	891,943	15.89
65 5	49,451	8,809	.82186	.17814	226,735	626,740	12.67
70 5	40,641	10,790	.73452	.26548	177,382	400,005	9.84
75 5	29,852	11,345	.61994	.38006	120,547	222,623	7.46
80 5	18,506	9,508	.48621	.51379	66,496	102,075	5.52
85 +	8,998	8,998	0.00000	1.00000	35,579	35,579	3.95

TABLE IV-8

DEATHS BY SEX AND AGE GROUP
USED IN THE CONSTRUCTION OF THE LIFE TABLE
CHILE, 1959-1961

Age Group	Male	Female
Total	50,346	43,068
0	17,604	14,821
1	2,361	2,365
2	780	766
3	426	382
4	282	264
0-4	21,453	18,598
5-9	827	674
10-14	528	412
15-19	732	593
20-24	975	750
25-29	1,103	848
30-34	1,333	1,004
35-39	1,381	1,008
40-44	1,654	1,060
45-49	1,947	1,246
50-54	2,237	1,424
55-59	2,460	1,708
60-64	2,836	2,115
65-69	2,853	2,279
70-74	2,875	2,549
75-79	2,333	2,442
80-84	1,578	2,006
85 +	1,241	2,352

TABLE IV-9

COHORT DEATHS IN THE POPULATION
BORN 1951-1960, CHILE

Year of Birth	Up to the end of 1960	
	Male	Female
1951	18,696	16,684
1952	18,231	15,972
1953	18,441	16,286
1954	19,204	16,899
1955	19,249	16,984
1956	19,223	17,074
1957	20,268	17,735
1958	20,256	17,382
1959	19,129	16,226
1960	13,409	11,148

TABLE IV-10

SEPARATION FACTOR FOR DEATHS
UNDER AGE ONE, CHILE, 1950-1961

Year	Male	Female
1950	.2524	.2645
1951	.2786	.2862
1952	.2553	.2702
1953	.2525	.2580
1954	.2686	.2779
1955	.2699	.2812
1956	.2747	.2849
1957	.2783	.2923
1958	.2853	.2982
1959	.2826	.2938
1960	.2800	.2895
1961	.2774	.2852

TABLE IV-11

EVALUATION OF BIRTH REGISTRATION, CHILE, 1952-1957

Age Groups	1960 Census Population	Population at 1-1-61	Cohort Deaths 1952-1960	Year Interval of Births	Expected Births	Registered Births	(6)/(7)
(1)	(2)	(3)	(4)	(5)	(6)	(7)	(8)
Male							
3-6	435,167	436,038	77,944	1954-57	513,982	482,095	1.066
7-8	197,804	198,200	36,672	1952-53	234,872	206,840	1.136
Female							
3-6	431,703	432,566	68,692	1954-57	501,258	465,432	1.077
7-8	196,406	196,799	32,258	1952-53	229,057	200,438	1.143

TABLE IV-12

ESTIMATION OF POPULATION, AGES 0-4, AT CENSUS DATE, CHILE, 1960

Year of Birth	Registered Births	Omission of Births Estimated Percent	Corrected Births (2)x[1+(3)]	Cohort Death	Age of the Population	Estimated Population at 1-1-61	Estimated Population at Census Date (7)x0.998
(1)	(2)	(3)	(4)	(5)	(6)	(7)	(8)
				Male			
1960	132,518	5.2	139,409	13,409	0	126,000	125,748
1959	129,289	5.4	136,271	19,129	1	117,142	116,908
1958	127,432	5.7	134,696	20,259	2	114,437	114,208
1957	127,389	6.2	135,287	20,268	3	115,019	114,789
1956	120,260	6.4	127,957	19,223	4	108,734	108,517
				Female			
1960	128,135	6.2	136,079	11,148	0	124,931	124,681
1959	124,985	6.4	132,984	16,226	1	116,758	116,524
1958	122,815	6.7	131,044	17,382	2	113,662	113,435
1957	122,220	7.0	130,775	17,735	3	113,040	112,814
1956	117,008	7.4	125,667	17,074	4	108,593	108,376

TABLE IV-13

POPULATION BY SEX AND AGE GROUPS
USED IN THE CONSTRUCTION OF LIFE TABLE
CHILE, 1960

Age Groups	Population	
	Male	Female
Total	3,639,979	3,787,214
0	126,139	124,681
1	117,272	116,524
2	114,557	113,435
3	115,146	112,814
4	108,854	108,376
0-4	581,968	575,830
5-9	492,442	489,047
10-14	420,881	415,428
15-19	354,554	370,253
20-24	287,637	310,762
25-29	251,833	275,172
30-34	246,879	260,273
35-39	199,965	215,448
40-44	178,478	185,401
45-49	157,143	167,091
50-54	137,561	141,015
55-59	103,319	109,013
60-64	86,342	96,713
65-69	60,615	67,605
70-74	38,032	46,423
75-79	22,740	28,965
80-84	12,116	18,685
85 +	7,474	14,090

TABLE IV-14

ABRIDGED LIFE TABLE, CHILE, 1960
MALE

Age x n	l_x	$_nd_x$	$_np_x$	$_nq_x$	$_nL_x$	T_x	e_x
0 1	100,000	11,458	.88542	.11458	91,750	5,417,863	54.18
1 1	88,542	2,171	.97548	.02452	87,261	5,326,113	60.15
2 1	86,371	649	.99249	.00751	86,027	5,238,852	60.66
3 1	85,722	331	.99614	.00386	85,550	5,152,825	60.11
4 1	85,391	232	.99728	.00272	85,270	5,067,275	59.34
0 5	100,000	14,841	.85159	.14841	435,858	5,417,863	54.18
5 5	85,159	740	.99131	.00869	423,945	4,982,005	58.50
10 5	84,419	570	.99325	.00675	420,670	4,558,060	53.99
15 5	83,849	862	.98972	.01028	417,090	4,137,390	49.34
20 5	82,987	1,334	.98393	.01607	411,600	3,720,300	44.83
25 5	81,653	1,747	.97860	.02140	403,898	3,308,700	40.52
30 5	79,906	2,144	.97317	.02683	394,170	2,904,802	36.35
35 5	77,762	2,636	.96610	.03390	382,220	2,510,632	32.29
40 5	75,126	3,332	.95565	.04435	367,300	2,128,412	28.33
45 5	71,794	4,237	.94098	.05902	348,378	1,761,112	24.53
50 5	67,557	5,419	.91979	.08021	324,238	1,412,734	20.91
55 5	62,138	6,862	.88957	.11043	293,535	1,088,496	17.52
60 5	55,276	8,456	.84702	.15298	255,240	794,961	14.38
65 5	46,820	10,127	.78370	.21630	208,783	539,721	11.53
70 5	36,693	11,311	.69174	.30826	155,188	330,938	9.02
75 5	25,382	10,925	.56958	.43042	99,598	175,750	6.92
80 5	14,457	8,337	.42332	.57668	51,443	76,152	5.27
85 5	6,120	4,474	.26895	.73105	19,415	24,709	4.04
90 +	1,646	1,646	0.00000	1.00000	5,294	5,294	3.22

TABLE IV-14 (continued)

ABRIDGED LIFE TABLE, CHILE, 1960
FEMALE

Age x n	l_x	$_nd_x$	$_np_x$	$_nq_x$	$_nL_x$	T_x	e_x
0 1	100,000	10,121	.89879	.10121	92,814	5,871,048	58.71
1 1	89,879	2,855	.96824	.03176	88,195	5,778,234	64.29
2 1	87,024	641	.99263	.00737	86,684	5,690,039	65.38
3 1	86,383	311	.99640	.00360	86,221	5,603,355	64.87
4 1	86,072	214	.99751	.00249	85,961	5,517,134	64.10
0 5	100,000	14,142	.85858	.14142	439,875	5,871,048	58.71
5 5	85,858	642	.99252	.00748	427,685	5,431,173	63.26
10 5	85,216	454	.99467	.00533	424,945	5,003,488	58.72
15 5	84,762	663	.99218	.00782	422,153	4,578,543	54.02
20 5	84,099	988	.98825	.01175	418,025	4,156,390	49.42
25 5	83,111	1,278	.98462	.01538	412,360	3,738,365	44.98
30 5	81,833	1,558	.98096	.01904	405,270	3,326,005	40.64
35 5	80,275	1,856	.97688	.02312	396,735	2,920,735	36.38
40 5	78,419	2,234	.97151	.02849	386,510	2,524,000	32.19
45 5	76,185	2,825	.96292	.03708	373,863	2,137,490	28.06
50 5	73,360	3,765	.94868	.05132	357,388	1,763,627	24.04
55 5	69,595	5,067	.92719	.07281	335,308	1,406,239	20.21
60 5	64,528	6,813	.89442	.10558	305,608	1,070,931	16.60
65 5	57,715	9,213	.84037	.15963	265,543	765,323	13.26
70 5	48,502	11,816	.75638	.24362	212,970	499,780	10.30
75 5	36,686	13,286	.63785	.36215	150,215	286,810	7.82
80 5	23,400	12,056	.48479	.51521	86,860	136,595	5.84
85 5	11,344	7,810	.31153	.68847	37,195	49,735	4.38
90 +	3,534	3,534	0.00000	1.00000	12,540	12,540	3.55

TABLE IV-15

LIFE EXPECTANCY, CHILE
CENSUS YEARS

Year	Total*	Male	Female
1907	30.1	29.7	30.5
1920	30.5	30.1	30.9
1930	35.2	34.6	35.8
1940	38.1	37.4	38.7
1952	50.2	50.8	53.5
1960	56.5	54.2	58.7

*Simple arithmetic average of male and female.

NOTES

[1] At the present time statistics on birth registration are still not complete.

[2] O. Andrew Collver, Birth Rates in Latin America: New Estimates of Historical Trends and Fluctuations (Berkeley: Institute of International Studies, University of California, 1965) [Research Series No. 7], p. 82.

[3] A practical example of life table construction using Method B is given in Appendix II.

[4] Our analysis was mainly of deaths under one year. Information about these deaths is given by ages in days and months since 1936. We observed a very strange pattern of the ratio -1 day/-1 year: it did not increase; rather, in the case of Chile this ratio has decreased since 1943-1945. After a detailed analysis of deaths under one year old by ages in months, we concluded that the trend of the quotient could be due to the fact that deaths were registered as having occurred at a later age than they actually did. (This phenomenon of "shifting" makes deaths at 1-5 months old appear to be over-registered.) This fact of shifting is supported by the trend of infant mortality--deaths under one year old per thousand births--which has remained almost constant since 1952. If there were under-registration of deaths (as the ratio -1 day/ -1 year would indicate) the infant mortality rate--assuming declining mortality--would decline (if the registration of birth is complete or if it has the same degree of completeness through time).

[5]The weights were   .241, .333, and .426 for 1959, 1960, and 1961 respectively.

[6]See Roland Pressat, L'Analyse Démographique (Paris: Presses Universitaires de France, 1961), Chapters 2 and 3.

[7]Births registered no more than two years late during a year. See Dirección General de Estadística. Boletín No. 12, Diciembre Sinopsis 1962, Santiago, Chile, p. 341.

[8]Late registration of births in Chile, as in other Latin American countries, is very high. The Dirección de Estadística, Boletín No. 12 (Dic. 1962, p. 341), classifies births registered more or less than two years late. For the period 1951-1960, 15% of the registered births during one year were registered two years late (with a maximum of 22.2% for 1954 and a minimum of 9.5% in 1959). The same statistics office has published (in Demografia) an estimate of the actual births occurring during a year. (In this estimate those births which have been registered less than two years late during the years 1931-1951 are increased by 9.5%. After 1951, the actual number of births during a year are considered to be the number of births which occurred during a year and registered between January 1 and March 31 of the following year, increased by 5%.) We do not consider these estimates in this study.

[9]We did not smooth either population or death registration.

V. COLOMBIA

Thirteen censuses have been taken in Colombia between 1825 and 1964, but age group distribution information is available only for three, those of 1918, 1938, and 1951.[1] Vital statistics, principally information on death, are not complete. Therefore, life tables cannot be constructed using Method A.

Previous estimates show that in the past, the fertility level in Colombia has been practically constant at a high level.[2] In addition, international migration has not been significant.[3] Therefore, the requirements for fertility and migration necessary to apply Method B are present. To use this method, we must find the proportional five-year age group distribution for ages 10-59 and the natural growth rates for census years.

PROPORTIONAL AGE GROUP DISTRIBUTION OF THE POPULATION

A graphical cohort analysis (Fig. V-1) shows that the last two censuses are comparable in completeness. We made a similar graphical analysis for total population in order to compare the 1918 census, which presents a higher underenumeration than the two later censuses, principally in ages under 30 years. Thus, only the 1918 census was modified, by slightly increasing the population enumerated in ages under 30. After this correction was made, the age group distributions of population for all censuses were smoothed according to the procedure explained in Appendix III (see Table V-1).

ESTIMATION OF NATURAL GROWTH RATES

Growth rates for census years were estimated by considering the intercensal annual geometric growth rates for the periods 1918-1938, 1938-1951, and 1951-1964.[4] The estimated rates were 17, 21, and 26.7 per thousand for 1918, 1938, and 1951 respectively.

CONSTRUCTION OF LIFE TABLES

Life tables were constructed using Method B, the age group distribution of Table V-1, and the natural growth rates estimated above. The set of United Nations $_5L_x$ values used in the quotient $\dfrac{C'(x,\ x+5)}{_5L_x}$ were 25, 35, and 60 for the years 1918, 1938, and 1951 respectively. The slopes of the straight lines of adjustment and the growth rates used in the exponent of e (Eq. 5, Chap. I) are shown in Table V-2. Life tables for Colombia are presented in Tables V-3, V-4, and V-5, and a summary of the life expectancy found is given in Table V-6.[5]

FIGURE V-1

TEN-YEAR AGE GROUPS BY YEAR OF BIRTH, CENSUS POPULATION,

COLOMBIA, 1938-1951, MALE

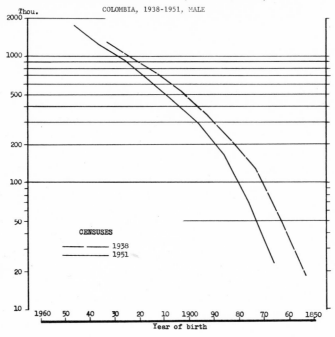

FEMALE

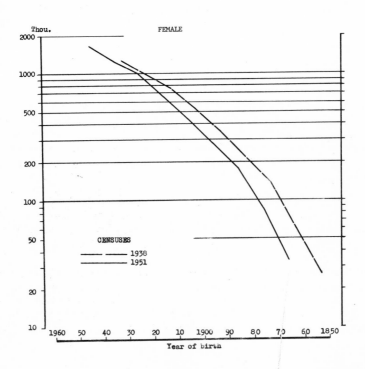

TABLE V-1

SMOOTHED PROPORTIONAL DISTRIBUTION OF THE POPULATION BY SEX
AND FIVE-YEAR AGE GROUPS, AGES 10-59, COLOMBIA, CENSUS YEARS

Age Groups	1918 Total	1938 Male	1938 Female	1951 Male	1951 Female
Total	1.000000	1.000000	1.000000	1.000000	1.000000
10-59	.649984	.651503	.654233	.639201	.646139
10-14	.117713	.117506	.118299	.115383	.116387
15-19	.103609	.104397	.105442	.102434	.103247
20-24	.089891	.091450	.092643	.089624	.090751
25-29	.078096	.079306	.080132	.077508	.078575
30-34	.067103	.067067	.067084	.065060	.066197
35-39	.056782	.056408	.056109	.054719	.055076
40-44	.046272	.045844	.045256	.044665	.044742
45-49	.037742	.037324	.036877	.036743	.037173
50-54	.029479	.029256	.029195	.029548	.029969
55-59	.023297	.022945	.023196	.023517	.024022

TABLE V-2

GROWTH RATES USED IN THE CONSTRUCTION OF LIFE TABLES FOR COLOMBIA

	Growth Rates			Slopes of the Straight Lines of Adjustment of the $\log_e \dfrac{C'(x,\ x+5)}{{}_nL_5}$		
Year	Total	Male	Female	Male	Female	Average
1918	.0170					.017564
1938	.0210	.02053	.02147	.021323	.022297	.021810
1951	.0267	.02629	.02711	.026788	.027619	.027204

TABLE V-3

ABRIDGED LIFE TABLE, COLOMBIA, 1918
TOTAL

Age x n	l_x	$_nd_x$	$_np_x$	$_nq_x$	$_nL_x$	T_x	e_x
0 1	100,000	22,520	.77480	.22520	79,083	3,198,855	31.99
1 4	77,480	10,232	.86794	.13206	287,784	3,119,772	40.27
0 5	100,000	32,753	.67247	.32753	366,867	3,198,855	31.99
5 5	67,247	4,834	.92812	.07188	319,424	2,831,988	42.11
10 5	62,413	2,555	.95907	.04093	305,549	2,512,564	40.26
15 5	59,859	2,882	.95186	.04814	292,722	2,207,015	36.87
20 5	56,977	3,537	.93792	.06208	276,326	1,914,293	33.60
25 5	53,440	3,801	.92887	.07113	257,724	1,637,967	30.65
30 5	49,639	3,892	.92159	.07841	238,521	1,380,243	27.81
35 5	45,746	4,020	.91213	.08787	218,778	1,141,723	24.96
40 5	41,727	4,216	.89897	.10103	198,246	922,945	22.12
45 5	37,511	4,485	.88043	.11957	176,536	724,700	19.32
50 5	33,026	4,795	.85483	.14517	153,344	548,164	16.60
55 5	28,231	5,112	.81891	.18109	128,586	394,820	13.99
60 5	23,119	5,371	.76768	.23232	102,307	266,235	11.52
65 5	17,748	5,413	.69500	.30500	75,159	163,927	9.24
70 5	12,335	4,979	.59634	.40366	48,759	88,769	7.20
75 5	7,356	3,901	.46964	.53036	26,150	40,010	5.44
80 5	3,455	2,365	.31536	.68464	10,551	13,860	4.01
85 +	1,089	1,089	0.00000	1.00000	3,309	3,309	3.04

TABLE V-4

ABRIDGED LIFE TABLE, COLOMBIA, 1938
MALE

Age x n	l_x	$_nd_x$	$_np_x$	$_nq_x$	$_nL_x$	T_x	e_x
0 1	100,000	20,461	.79539	.20461	80,881	3,603,553	36.04
1 4	79,539	8,548	.89253	.10747	299,657	3,522,672	44.29
0 5	100,000	29,009	.70991	.29009	380,538	3,603,553	36.04
5 5	70,991	4,070	.94267	.05733	340,882	3,223,015	45.40
10 5	66,921	2,188	.96730	.03270	329,044	2,882,134	43.07
15 5	64,733	2,551	.96059	.03941	317,919	2,553,089	39.44
20 5	62,181	3,191	.94868	.05132	303,187	2,235,170	35.95
25 5	58,990	3,402	.94232	.05768	286,417	1,931,983	32.75
30 5	55,588	3,481	.93738	.06262	269,321	1,645,566	29.60
35 5	52,107	3,724	.92854	.07146	251,439	1,376,245	26.41
40 5	48,383	4,149	.91424	.08576	231,870	1,124,807	23.25
45 5	44,234	4,679	.89423	.10577	209,816	892,936	20.19
50 5	39,555	5,240	.86753	.13247	185,042	683,120	17.27
55 5	34,315	5,795	.83113	.16887	157,433	498,079	14.51
60 5	28,521	6,254	.78073	.21927	127,224	340,646	11.94
65 5	22,267	6,477	.70912	.29088	95,216	213,422	9.58
70 5	15,790	6,124	.61215	.38785	63,162	118,206	7.49
75 5	9,666	4,936	.48931	.51069	34,984	55,043	5.69
80 5	4,730	3,104	.34372	.65628	14,839	20,059	4.24
85 +	1,626	1,626	0.00000	1.00000	5,220	5,220	3.21

TABLE V-4 (continued)

ABRIDGED LIFE TABLE, COLOMBIA, 1938
FEMALE

Age x n	l_x	$_nd_x$	$_np_x$	$_nq_x$	$_nL_x$	T_x	e_x
0 1	100,000	18,665	.81335	.18665	82,687	3,718,625	37.19
1 4	81,335	8,672	.89338	.10662	306,615	3,635,938	44.70
0 5	100,000	27,337	.72663	.27337	389,302	3,718,625	37.19
5 5	72,663	4,259	.94138	.05862	348,758	3,329,323	45.82
10 5	68,404	2,446	.96424	.03576	335,860	2,980,565	43.57
15 5	65,958	2,835	.95703	.04297	323,315	2,644,705	40.10
20 5	63,123	3,486	.94477	.05523	307,192	2,321,390	36.78
25 5	59,637	3,741	.93726	.06274	288,844	2,014,197	33.77
30 5	55,895	3,766	.93263	.06737	270,053	1,725,354	30.87
35 5	52,130	3,755	.92797	.07203	251,241	1,455,300	27.92
40 5	48,375	3,803	.92139	.07861	232,427	1,204,059	24.89
45 5	44,572	4,036	.90945	.09055	212,996	971,632	21.80
50 5	40,536	4,466	.88983	.11017	191,826	758,635	18.72
55 5	36,070	5,085	.85901	.14099	168,108	566,809	15.71
60 5	30,984	5,859	.81091	.18909	140,810	398,701	12.87
65 5	25,126	6,522	.74044	.25956	109,681	257,891	10.26
70 5	18,604	6,642	.64298	.35702	76,272	148,210	7.97
75 5	11,962	5,777	.51706	.48294	44,457	71,938	6.01
80 5	6,185	3,932	.36432	.63568	19,925	27,480	4.44
85 +	2,253	2,253	0.00000	1.00000	7,555	7,555	3.35

CHAPTER V. COLOMBIA

TABLE V-5

ABRIDGED LIFE TABLE, COLOMBIA, 1951
MALE

Age x n	l_x	$_nd_x$	$_np_x$	$_nq_x$	$_nL_x$	T_x	e_x
0 1	100,000	13,950	.86050	.13950	86,872	4,793,323	47.93
1 4	86,050	5,228	.93924	.06076	332,881	4,706,452	54.69
0 5	100,000	19,179	.80821	.19179	419,753	4,793,323	47.93
5 5	80,821	2,515	.96888	.03112	395,468	4,373,570	54.11
10 5	78,307	1,444	.98157	.01843	387,940	3,978,102	50.80
15 5	76,863	1,822	.97629	.02371	380,286	3,590,163	46.71
20 5	75,041	2,355	.96862	.03138	369,524	3,209,876	42.78
25 5	72,686	2,506	.96552	.03448	357,114	2,840,352	39.08
30 5	70,179	2,544	.96374	.03626	344,592	2,483,238	35.38
35 5	67,635	2,753	.95930	.04070	331,483	2,138,646	31.62
40 5	64,882	3,203	.95063	.04937	316,772	1,807,163	27.85
45 5	61,679	3,916	.93652	.06348	299,132	1,490,391	24.16
50 5	57,764	4,864	.91579	.08421	277,319	1,191,259	20.62
55 5	52,899	6,051	.88562	.11438	250,200	913,940	17.28
60 5	46,849	7,440	.84120	.15880	216,588	663,740	14.17
65 5	39,409	8,811	.77642	.22358	175,875	447,152	11.35
70 5	30,598	9,584	.68678	.31322	129,243	271,277	8.87
75 5	21,014	9,012	.57115	.42885	81,659	142,034	6.76
80 5	12,002	6,820	.43174	.56826	41,127	60,375	5.03
85 +	5,182	5,182	0.00000	1.00000	19,248	19,248	3.71

TABLE V-5 (continued)

ABRIDGED LIFE TABLE, COLOMBIA, 1951
FEMALE

Age x n	l_x	$_n d_x$	$_n p_x$	$_n q_x$	$_n L_x$	T_x	e_x
0 1	100,000	12,117	.87883	.12117	88,682	5,043,782	50.44
1 4	87,883	5,130	.94162	.05838	340,463	4,955,099	56.38
0 5	100,000	17,247	.82753	.17247	429,146	5,043,782	50.44
5 5	82,753	2,563	.96903	.03097	405,079	4,614,636	55.76
10 5	80,190	1,557	.98059	.01941	397,085	4,209,557	52.49
15 5	78,634	1,890	.97597	.02403	388,890	3,812,472	48.48
20 5	76,744	2,366	.96917	.03083	378,014	3,423,581	44.61
25 5	74,378	2,547	.96576	.03424	365,528	3,045,567	40.95
30 5	71,832	2,584	.96403	.03597	352,717	2,680,040	37.31
35 5	69,248	2,656	.96165	.03835	339,657	2,327,323	33.61
40 5	66,592	2,864	.95699	.04301	325,989	1,987,667	29.85
45 5	63,728	3,318	.94794	.05206	310,721	1,661,677	26.07
50 5	60,410	4,039	.93315	.06685	292,471	1,350,957	22.36
55 5	56,372	5,099	.90954	.09046	269,906	1,058,485	18.78
60 5	51,272	6,625	.87079	.12921	240,934	788,580	15.38
65 5	44,648	8,499	.80965	.19035	203,294	547,646	12.27
70 5	36,149	10,110	.72034	.27966	156,343	344,352	9.53
75 5	26,039	10,313	.60393	.39607	103,888	188,009	7.22
80 5	15,726	8,360	.46838	.53162	55,636	84,121	5.35
85 +	7,366	7,366	0.00000	1.00000	28,485	28,485	3.87

TABLE V-6

LIFE EXPECTANCY, COLOMBIA
CENSUS YEARS

Year	Total*	Male	Female
1918	32.0		
1938	36.6	36.0	37.2
1951	49.2	47.9	50.4

*Simple arithmetic average of male and
female.

NOTES

[1]For 1918, only age distribution for both sexes combined has
been published.

[2]O. Andrew Collver, Birth Rates in Latin America: New Estimates
of Historical Trends and Fluctuations (Berkeley: Institute of
International Studies, University of California, 1965) [Research
Series No. 7], p. 90.

[3]In the 1951 census, approximately 45,000 foreign-born inhabitants were enumerated, less than 5 per thousand in relation to the
total population. In addition, in the 1950 Venezuelan census,
41,000 Colombians were enumerated.

[4]We considered that the 1918 census probably had more omission
than the subsequent ones.

[5]An example of life table construction using Method B is given
in Appendix II.

VI. COSTA RICA

Six national censuses have been taken in Costa Rica, in 1864, 1883, 1892, 1927, 1950, and 1963. The age group distribution of the population by sex is available for each census. Death statistics by age are not available for early census years, and only the very recent figures are reliable. It would be impossible, therefore, to use Method A to construct life tables for the early census years. However, Costa Rica meets the requirements needed for the application of Method B--fertility has been practically constant (at high levels) in the past, and net international migration can be considered negligible, as the available estimates show.[1] Thus in constructing life tables for Costa Rica, we have used Method B for all census years except 1963, in which the statistics necessary for the application of Method A were available.

LIFE TABLES FOR 1864, 1883, 1892, 1927, AND 1950; CONSTRUCTION BY METHOD B

Proportional Age Group Distribution of the Population

To construct life tables for these years, first the proportional five-year age group distribution of the population between 10 and 59, and the natural growth rates for each census year were required. The 1950 census provided the age group distribution for the 1950 and previous censuses.[2]

Then we made a graphical cohort analysis with the census distributions of the population by ten-year age groups (Fig. VI-1). From this analysis it appears that differential underenumeration in the ten-year age groups between ages 10 and 59 has not been important; underenumeration has been evenly distributed throughout all age groups for some years, such as 1864, 1883, and 1950. Therefore, we smoothed the census information according to the procedure explained in Appendix III. The proportional five-year age group distribution for ages 10-59 is presented in Table VI-1.

Estimation of Natural Growth Rates

We made an estimate of the natural growth rates for years in which censuses were taken by considering existing estimates of growth rates[3] and the annual geometric growth rates for the intercensal periods. To obtain the latter, we considered the total

FIGURE VI-1

TEN-YEAR AGE GROUPS BY YEAR OF BIRTH, CENSUS POPULATION, COSTA RICA, 1864-1963, MALE

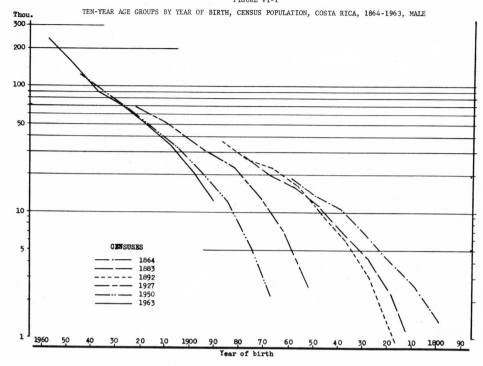

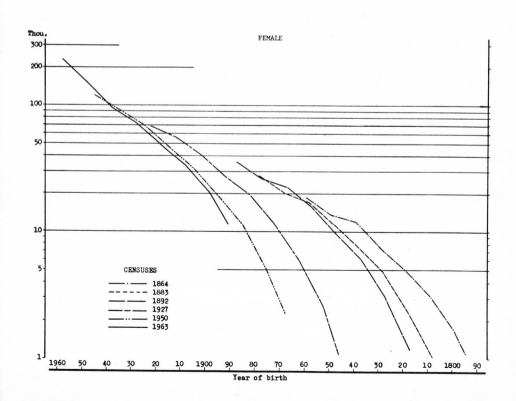

FEMALE

TABLE VI-1

SMOOTHED PROPORTIONAL DISTRIBUTION OF THE POPULATION BY SEX AND FIVE-YEAR AGE GROUPS,
AGES 10-59, COSTA RICA, CENSUS YEARS

Age Groups	1864 Male	1864 Female	1883 Male	1883 Female	1892 Male	1892 Female	1927 Male	1927 Female	1950 Male	1950 Female
Total 10-59	1.000000 .648294	1.000000 .663200	1.000000 .656562	1.000000 .661774	1.000000 .665889	1.000000 .667060	1.000000 .668344	1.000000 .668238	1.000000 .640476	1.000000 .652753
10-14	.125537	.119755	.122488	.118319	.115015	.114632	.120394	.124753	.121478	.122424
15-19	.109889	.107558	.107794	.105658	.104118	.104200	.105222	.109511	.104796	.107176
20-24	.094467	.095270	.093374	.093102	.093087	.093540	.090562	.094537	.088727	.092255
25-29	.080167	.082526	.080326	.081069	.082345	.082632	.078461	.080900	.075718	.078966
30-34	.065692	.068944	.067565	.068969	.071744	.071341	.067032	.066988	.063691	.065801
35-39	.053538	.057143	.056136	.057904	.060641	.060238	.057677	.056040	.053619	.054878
40-44	.041302	.044963	.044494	.046471	.048172	.048014	.049489	.046048	.044129	.044350
45-49	.032700	.036172	.035634	.037658	.038633	.038795	.041246	.037495	.036317	.036065
50-54	.025450	.028606	.027789	.029782	.029958	.030501	.033127	.029565	.029205	.028671
55-59	.019552	.022263	.020962	.022842	.022176	.023167	.025134	.022339	.022796	.022167

78

population given in each census and also took into account the probable omission of the 1950, 1883, and 1864 censuses.[4] Estimates of the natural growth rates for every census year are 16.0, 16.0, 16.0, 22.6, and 31.0 per thousand for the years 1864, 1883, 1892, 1927, and 1950 respectively.

Construction of Life Tables for Census Years through 1950

Life tables for the first five census years were constructed by using Method B, the proportional five-year age group distribution of the population (Table VI-1) and the natural growth rates estimated above. The United Nations set of $_5L_x$ values used in the quotient $\dfrac{C'(x,\ x+5)}{_5L_x}$ were levels 15, 20, 40, and 70 for the years 1864, 1883, 1892, 1927, and 1950, respectively. The slopes of the straight lines of adjustment and the growth rates used for each sex in the exponent of e (Eq. 5, Chap. I) are presented in Table VI-2. The life tables obtained are presented in Tables VI-3 to VI-7.[5]

LIFE TABLE FOR 1963; CONSTRUCTION BY METHOD A

The life table for 1963 was constructed using death statistics for 1962-1964 and 1963 census population information. Population and death statistics were accepted as published,[6] except for deaths in ages one and under one year and population under five years old, for which estimates were made.

Analysis of Death Statistics

The intercensal period of 12.5 years between 1950 and 1963 and the underenumeration of the 1950 census make a good cohort analysis evaluating the completeness of death registration impossible. Age group distribution of deaths was accepted as published, except for ages one and under one year. Under-registration of deaths is usually higher for these ages than others, especially in rural areas. (This is true of most Latin American countries.) In order to have an idea of the underenumeration of deaths for ages one and under one year, it was necessary to make an assumption relating under-registration of deaths to under-registered births.[7] The omission in death registration for these ages was estimated, as shown in Tables VI-8 and VI-9. Probably, there is under-registration of deaths for other age groups, but because the census population probably also contains some omission, we preferred to make no further changes.[8] The same omission estimated for all deaths was assumed for each sex. Once deaths for ages one and under one year were corrected and the category of unknown spread proportionately, we obtained the age group distribution of deaths used in the life tables by making

TABLE VI-2

GROWTH RATES USED IN THE CONSTRUCTION OF LIFE TABLES
FOR COSTA RICA

	Growth Rates			Slopes of the Straight Lines of Adjustment of the $\log_e \frac{C'(x,\ x+5)}{_nL_5}$		
Year	Total	Male	Female	Male	Female	Average
1864	.0160	.01754	.01446	.018800	.015538	.017169
1883	.0160	.01684	.01516	.018297	.016479	.017388
1892	.0160	.01601	.01599	.015336	.015452	.015394
1927	.0226	.02008	.02512	.020100	.025060	.022580
1950	.0310	.02996	.03204	.029763	.031839	.030801

a weighted average of the distributions for 1962, 1963, and 1964 (Table VI-10).[9]

In order to correct the census population aged 0-4 by individual ages, cohort deaths from population born since 1958 were needed. We estimated these cohort deaths by using the registered deaths which had been corrected for omissions, and a Lexis' diagram.[10] The death separation factors used were .28 for deaths occurring under one year and .50 for other ages (see Table VI-11).

Analysis of Census Population

We accepted the age group distribution of the population given in the 1963 census,[11] except for the individual ages in the group 0-4. We estimated the population aged 0-4 on the basis of births and cohort deaths during 1958-1963. Information on births is available by year of registration and by year of occurrence. In order to estimate the population of the individual ages 0-4, we found it preferable to use the births which occurred rather than those registered in each year. Unfortunately, the period of time we are considering is so close to the present date that not all births which occurred are available for study, because they will be registered in subsequent years. However, the Statistics Office publishes an estimate of births for each year, and after an analysis, we accepted these as estimates of actual births. Except for the year 1958, these estimates are given by sex. For that year births were separated into sex groups by using the sex ratio of those registered in the same year.[12]

We estimated the individual ages 0-4 by using births and their cohort deaths (Table VI-11) as shown in Table VI-12. We then made two estimates of the population for the beginning of 1963 and 1964. In order to obtain the population at census date, a weighted average was made from the two estimates.[13] The estimated population for individual ages 0-4, and the five-year age groups from the census (the unknown being spread proportionately among the enumerated population in each age group) are presented in Table VI-13.

Construction of Life Tables

The basic information needed for the construction of the life tables by Method A was derived from the age distribution of the population (Table VI-13) and age distribution of deaths (Table VI-10) presented in the two preceding sections. In this case, population and death values were not smoothed. However, the calculated values of μ_x were very slightly smoothed. The life table for 1963 is presented in Table VI-14.[14] A summary of the estimates of life expectancy for all census years is presented in Table VI-15.

TABLE VI-3

ABRIDGED LIFE TABLE, COSTA RICA, 1864
MALE

Age x n	l_x	$_nd_x$	$_np_x$	$_nq_x$	$_nL_x$	T_x	e_x
0 1	100,000	26,801	.73199	.26801	75,107	2,632,743	26.33
1 4	73,199	12,160	.83388	.16612	266,483	2,557,636	34.94
0 5	100,000	38,961	.61039	.38961	341,590	2,632,743	26.33
5 5	61,039	5,692	.90674	.09326	285,309	2,291,152	37.54
10 5	55,347	2,843	.94862	.05138	269,354	2,005,843	36.24
15 5	52,503	3,014	.94258	.05742	255,564	1,736,489	33.07
20 5	49,489	3,595	.92735	.07265	238,698	1,480,925	29.92
25 5	45,893	3,839	.91634	.08366	219,909	1,242,227	27.07
30 5	42,054	3,985	.90524	.09476	200,422	1,022,318	24.31
35 5	38,069	4,234	.88877	.11123	179,961	821,896	21.59
40 5	33,835	4,547	.86560	.13440	158,017	641,935	18.97
45 5	29,287	4,761	.83745	.16255	134,603	483,918	16.52
50 5	24,527	4,788	.80479	.19521	110,629	349,315	14.24
55 5	19,739	4,655	.76416	.23584	86,928	238,685	12.09
60 5	15,084	4,349	.71164	.28836	64,292	151,757	10.06
65 5	10,734	3,872	.63930	.36070	43,657	87,465	8.15
70 5	6,862	3,151	.54083	.45917	25,870	43,808	6.38
75 5	3,711	2,171	.41507	.58493	12,460	17,938	4.83
80 5	1,540	1,131	.26600	.73400	4,407	5,478	3.56
85 +	410	410	0.00000	1.00000	1,071	1,071	2.61

TABLE VI-3 (continued)

ABRIDGED LIFE TABLE, COSTA RICA, 1864
FEMALE

Age x n	l_x	$_nd_x$	$_np_x$	$_nq_x$	$_nL_x$	T_x	e_x
0 1	100,000	24,942	.75058	.24942	77,006	2,697,503	26.98
1 4	75,058	12,484	.83367	.16633	273,259	2,620,497	34.91
0 5	100,000	37,426	.62574	.37426	350,266	2,697,503	26.98
5 5	62,574	5,958	.90478	.09522	292,196	2,347,237	37.51
10 5	56,615	3,148	.94440	.05560	274,994	2,055,041	36.30
15 5	53,468	3,371	.93695	.06305	259,496	1,780,047	33.29
20 5	50,097	3,980	.92056	.07944	240,808	1,520,551	30.35
25 5	46,117	4,246	.90794	.09206	220,020	1,279,743	27.75
30 5	41,871	4,302	.89725	.10275	198,606	1,059,723	25.31
35 5	37,569	4,257	.88668	.11332	177,131	861,117	22.92
40 5	33,311	4,146	.87554	.12446	156,107	683,986	20.53
45 5	29,165	4,092	.85969	.14031	135,610	527,879	18.10
50 5	25,073	4,124	.83553	.16447	115,089	392,269	15.64
55 5	20,949	4,190	.80000	.20000	94,333	277,180	13.23
60 5	16,759	4,233	.74740	.25260	73,231	182,848	10.91
65 5	12,526	4,093	.67325	.32675	52,230	109,617	8.75
70 5	8,433	3,599	.57324	.42676	32,729	57,387	6.80
75 5	4,834	2,695	.44250	.55750	16,743	24,657	5.10
80 5	2,139	1,550	.27562	.72438	6,281	7,914	3.70
85 +	590	590	0.00000	1.00000	1,634	1,634	2.77

TABLE VI-4

ABRIDGED LIFE TABLE, COSTA RICA, 1883
MALE

Age x n	l_x	$_nd_x$	$_np_x$	$_nq_x$	$_nL_x$	T_x	e_x
0 1	100,000	25,166	.74834	.25166	76,595	2,841,491	28.41
1 4	74,834	11,246	.84972	.15028	275,013	2,764,896	36.95
0 5	100,000	36,413	.63587	.36413	351,608	2,841,491	28.41
5 5	63,587	5,350	.91586	.08414	299,390	2,489,883	39.16
10 5	58,237	2,775	.95236	.04764	284,035	2,190,493	37.61
15 5	55,463	3,006	.94580	.05420	270,402	1,906,458	34.37
20 5	52,457	3,602	.93133	.06867	253,519	1,636,056	31.19
25 5	48,855	3,823	.92174	.07826	234,724	1,382,537	28.30
30 5	45,031	3,935	.91262	.08738	215,419	1,147,813	25.49
35 5	41,097	4,169	.89856	.10144	195,257	932,394	22.69
40 5	36,928	4,497	.87821	.12179	173,629	737,137	19.96
45 5	32,430	4,782	.85256	.14744	150,332	563,508	17.38
50 5	27,649	4,938	.82139	.17861	125,962	413,176	14.94
55 5	22,710	4,963	.78147	.21853	101,119	287,214	12.65
60 5	17,748	4,811	.72894	.27106	76,554	186,096	10.49
65 5	12,937	4,448	.65617	.34383	53,285	109,542	8.47
70 5	8,489	3,754	.55774	.44226	32,477	56,257	6.63
75 5	4,735	2,688	.43233	.56767	16,194	23,780	5.02
80 5	2,047	1,468	.28275	.71725	5,987	7,586	3.71
85 +	579	579	0.00000	1.00000	1,599	1,599	2.76

TABLE VI-4 (continued)

ABRIDGED LIFE TABLE, COSTA RICA, 1883
FEMALE

Age x n	l_x	$_nd_x$	$_np_x$	$_nq_x$	$_nL_x$	T_x	e_x
0 1	100,000	23,212	.76788	.23212	78,578	2,930,081	29.30
1 4	76,788	11,491	.85036	.14964	282,343	2,851,504	37.13
0 5	100,000	34,703	.65297	.34703	360,921	2,930,081	29.30
5 5	65,297	5,590	.91440	.08560	307,265	2,569,160	39.35
10 5	59,707	3,063	.94870	.05130	290,715	2,261,895	37.88
15 5	56,645	3,331	.94120	.05880	275,487	1,971,180	34.80
20 5	53,314	3,947	.92598	.07402	256,977	1,695,693	31.81
25 5	49,367	4,203	.91486	.08514	236,364	1,438,716	29.14
30 5	45,164	4,242	.90608	.09392	215,209	1,202,352	26.62
35 5	40,922	4,194	.89750	.10250	194,060	987,143	24.12
40 5	36,728	4,117	.88791	.11209	173,296	793,083	21.59
45 5	32,611	4,132	.87329	.12671	152,789	619,787	19.01
50 5	28,479	4,259	.85045	.14955	131,845	466,998	16.40
55 5	24,220	4,454	.81608	.18392	110,118	335,153	13.84
60 5	19,765	4,656	.76442	.23558	87,309	225,034	11.39
65 5	15,109	4,670	.69090	.30910	63,795	137,725	9.12
70 5	10,439	4,269	.59109	.40891	41,114	73,930	7.08
75 5	6,170	3,325	.46112	.53888	21,772	32,816	5.32
80 5	2,845	1,998	.29779	.70221	8,564	11,044	3.88
85 +	847	847	0.00000	1.00000	2,481	2,481	2.93

TABLE VI-5

ABRIDGED LIFE TABLE, COSTA RICA, 1892
MALE

Age x n	l_x	$_nd_x$	$_np_x$	$_nq_x$	$_nL_x$	T_x	e_x
0 1	100,000	24,967	.75033	.24967	76,737	3,014,022	30.14
1 4	75,033	10,775	.85640	.14360	276,750	2,937,286	39.15
0 5	100,000	35,742	.64258	.35742	353,486	3,014,022	30.14
5 5	64,258	4,768	.92580	.07420	304,214	2,660,536	41.40
10 5	59,490	2,225	.96260	.03740	291,702	2,356,322	39.61
15 5	57,265	2,525	.95591	.04409	280,676	2,064,620	36.05
20 5	54,740	3,213	.94131	.05869	265,971	1,783,944	32.59
25 5	51,528	3,523	.93162	.06838	248,891	1,517,973	29.46
30 5	48,004	3,725	.92240	.07760	230,867	1,269,082	26.44
35 5	44,279	4,066	.90818	.09182	211,501	1,038,215	23.45
40 5	40,214	4,519	.88762	.11238	190,088	826,714	20.56
45 5	35,694	4,937	.86169	.13831	166,346	636,626	17.84
50 5	30,757	5,223	.83019	.16981	140,873	470,280	15.29
55 5	25,534	5,366	.78984	.21016	114,300	329,408	12.90
60 5	20,168	5,309	.73675	.26325	87,460	215,108	10.67
65 5	14,859	5,005	.66318	.33682	61,529	127,648	8.59
70 5	9,854	4,299	.56370	.43630	37,903	66,119	6.71
75 5	5,555	3,127	.43710	.56290	19,102	28,217	5.08
80 5	2,428	1,733	.28642	.71358	7,138	9,115	3.75
85 +	695	695	0.00000	1.00000	1,977	1,977	2.84

TABLE VI-5 (continued)

ABRIDGED LIFE TABLE, COSTA RICA, 1892
FEMALE

Age x n	l_x	$_nd_x$	$_np_x$	$_nq_x$	$_nL_x$	T_x	e_x
0 1	100,000	23,035	.76965	.23035	78,703	3,087,442	30.87
1 4	76,965	11,068	.85619	.14381	283,897	3,008,739	39.09
0 5	100,000	34,103	.65897	.34103	362,600	3,087,442	30.87
5 5	65,897	5,072	.92303	.07697	311,575	2,724,841	41.35
10 5	60,825	2,580	.95759	.04241	297,542	2,413,267	39.68
15 5	58,246	2,915	.94996	.05004	284,587	2,115,724	36.32
20 5	55,331	3,618	.93461	.06539	267,942	1,831,138	33.09
25 5	51,713	3,961	.92340	.07660	248,748	1,563,196	30.23
30 5	47,751	4,081	.91453	.08547	228,597	1,314,448	27.53
35 5	43,670	4,110	.90588	.09412	208,055	1,085,850	24.86
40 5	39,560	4,106	.89620	.10380	187,527	877,795	22.19
45 5	35,453	4,204	.88143	.11857	166,879	690,268	19.47
50 5	31,250	4,425	.85838	.14162	145,346	523,389	16.75
55 5	26,824	4,729	.82369	.17631	122,527	378,043	14.09
60 5	22,095	5,048	.77154	.22846	98,054	255,516	11.56
65 5	17,047	5,160	.69733	.30267	72,314	157,462	9.24
70 5	11,887	4,796	.59658	.40342	47,039	85,148	7.16
75 5	7,092	3,790	.46560	.53440	25,142	38,108	5.37
80 5	3,302	2,306	.30155	.69845	9,981	12,966	3.93
85 +	996	996	0.00000	1.00000	2,985	2,985	3.00

TABLE VI-6

ABRIDGED LIFE TABLE, COSTA RICA, 1927
MALE

Age x n	l_x	$_nd_x$	$_np_x$	$_nq_x$	$_nL_x$	T_x	e_x
0 1	100,000	19,043	.80957	.19043	82,164	3,922,811	39.23
1 4	80,957	7,643	.90559	.09441	307,254	3,840,647	47.44
0 5	100,000	26,686	.73314	.26686	389,418	3,922,811	39.23
5 5	73,314	3,505	.95219	.04781	354,252	3,533,393	48.20
10 5	69,809	1,811	.97405	.02595	344,462	3,179,142	45.54
15 5	67,998	2,208	.96753	.03247	335,108	2,834,680	41.69
20 5	65,790	2,862	.95650	.04350	322,065	2,499,572	37.99
25 5	62,928	3,087	.95094	.04906	306,903	2,177,507	34.60
30 5	59,841	3,181	.94684	.05316	291,349	1,870,604	31.26
35 5	56,660	3,446	.93918	.06082	274,914	1,579,255	27.87
40 5	53,214	3,915	.92643	.07357	256,647	1,304,342	24.51
45 5	49,299	4,539	.90793	.09207	235,574	1,047,695	21.25
50 5	44,760	5,260	.88249	.11751	211,136	812,121	18.14
55 5	39,501	6,032	.84729	.15271	182,920	600,985	15.21
60 5	33,469	6,765	.79788	.20212	150,879	418,065	12.49
65 5	26,704	7,287	.72711	.27289	115,569	267,186	10.01
70 5	19,417	7,164	.63103	.36897	78,806	151,617	7.81
75 5	12,252	6,014	.50918	.49082	45,168	72,811	5.94
80 5	6,239	3,964	.36463	.63537	20,007	27,643	4.43
85 +	2,275	2,275	0.00000	1.00000	7,636	7,636	3.36

TABLE VI-6 (continued)

ABRIDGED LIFE TABLE, COSTA RICA, 1927
FEMALE

Age x n	l_x	$_nd_x$	$_np_x$	$_nq_x$	$_nL_x$	T_x	e_x
0 1	100,000	17,215	.82785	.17215	83,988	4,083,170	40.83
1 4	82,785	7,677	.90727	.09273	314,530	3,999,182	48.31
0 5	100,000	24,892	.75108	.24892	398,519	4,083,170	40.83
5 5	75,108	3,620	.95180	.04820	362,943	3,684,651	49.06
10 5	71,488	2,006	.97194	.02806	352,416	3,321,708	46.47
15 5	69,482	2,419	.96518	.03482	341,969	2,969,292	42.73
20 5	67,063	3,072	.95419	.04581	327,930	2,627,323	39.18
25 5	63,991	3,343	.94776	.05224	311,624	2,299,393	35.93
30 5	60,648	3,394	.94403	.05597	294,764	1,987,769	32.78
35 5	57,254	3,430	.94010	.05990	277,712	1,693,005	29.57
40 5	53,824	3,553	.93399	.06601	260,358	1,415,292	26.29
45 5	50,271	3,887	.92267	.07733	241,934	1,154,934	22.97
50 5	46,384	4,447	.90412	.09588	221,204	913,001	19.68
55 5	41,937	5,257	.87465	.12535	197,157	691,797	16.50
60 5	36,680	6,305	.82812	.17188	168,375	494,640	13.49
65 5	30,375	7,317	.75911	.24089	134,190	326,265	10.74
70 5	23,058	7,779	.66266	.33734	95,906	192,075	8.33
75 5	15,280	7,057	.53812	.46188	57,836	96,168	6.29
80 5	8,222	5,022	.38917	.61083	27,116	38,332	4.66
85 +	3,200	3,200	0.00000	1.00000	11,216	11,216	3.51

TABLE VI-7

ABRIDGED LIFE TABLE, COSTA RICA, 1950
MALE

Age x n	l_x	$_nd_x$	$_np_x$	$_nq_x$	$_nL_x$	T_x	e_x
0 1	100,000	11,366	.88634	.11366	89,249	5,395,935	53.96
1 4	88,634	3,874	.95629	.04371	346,118	5,306,686	59.87
0 5	100,000	15,240	.84760	.15240	435,367	5,395,935	53.96
5 5	84,760	1,730	.97959	.02041	417,659	4,960,567	58.53
10 5	83,030	928	.98882	.01118	412,867	4,542,909	54.71
15 5	82,102	1,278	.98444	.01556	407,771	4,130,041	50.30
20 5	80,824	1,745	.97841	.02159	399,944	3,722,270	46.05
25 5	79,079	1,887	.97614	.02386	390,643	3,322,326	42.01
30 5	77,192	1,941	.97485	.02515	381,175	2,931,683	37.98
35 5	75,251	2,168	.97119	.02881	371,039	2,550,509	33.89
40 5	73,083	2,639	.96389	.03611	359,195	2,179,470	29.82
45 5	70,444	3,419	.95146	.04854	344,266	1,820,275	25.84
50 5	67,025	4,530	.93241	.06759	324,590	1,476,008	22.02
55 5	62,495	5,981	.90429	.09571	298,545	1,151,419	18.42
60 5	56,513	7,777	.86239	.13761	264,377	852,874	15.09
65 5	48,736	9,724	.80048	.19952	220,653	588,497	12.08
70 5	39,013	11,170	.71368	.28632	167,808	367,844	9.43
75 5	27,842	11,114	.60081	.39919	110,758	200,036	7.18
80 5	16,728	8,959	.46446	.53554	59,052	89,278	5.34
85 +	7,769	7,769	0.00000	1.00000	30,226	30,226	3.89

TABLE VI-7 (continued)

ABRIDGED LIFE TABLE, COSTA RICA, 1950
FEMALE

Age x n	l_x	$_nd_x$	$_np_x$	$_nq_x$	$_nL_x$	T_x	e_x
0 1	100,000	9,653	.90347	.09653	90,928	5,696,525	56.97
1 4	90,347	3,693	.95913	.04087	353,391	5,605,596	62.05
0 5	100,000	13,345	.86655	.13345	444,319	5,696,525	56.97
5 5	86,655	1,713	.98024	.01976	427,276	5,252,205	60.61
10 5	84,942	976	.98851	.01149	422,310	4,824,930	56.80
15 5	83,966	1,271	.98487	.01513	417,026	4,402,620	52.43
20 5	82,695	1,676	.97973	.02027	409,468	3,985,594	48.20
25 5	81,020	1,847	.97720	.02280	400,500	3,576,126	44.14
30 5	79,172	1,914	.97583	.02417	391,117	3,175,626	40.11
35 5	77,259	2,029	.97374	.02626	381,308	2,784,510	36.04
40 5	75,230	2,297	.96947	.03053	370,638	2,403,201	31.94
45 5	72,933	2,826	.96125	.03875	358,022	2,032,564	27.87
50 5	70,106	3,648	.94796	.05204	341,998	1,674,542	23.89
55 5	66,458	4,871	.92670	.07330	321,031	1,332,544	20.05
60 5	61,587	6,698	.89124	.10876	292,567	1,011,513	16.42
65 5	54,889	9,109	.83404	.16596	253,403	718,945	13.10
70 5	45,780	11,507	.74865	.25135	201,594	465,543	10.17
75 5	34,273	12,478	.63594	.36406	140,045	263,948	7.70
80 5	21,795	10,809	.50408	.49592	79,508	123,904	5.68
85 +	10,987	10,987	0.00000	1.00000	44,396	44,396	4.04

TABLE VI-8

UNDER-REGISTRATION OF DEATHS UNDER AGE ONE YEAR, COSTA RICA, 1958-1964

		1958	1959	1960	1961	1962	1963	1964
(1)	Birth occurred in the indicated year, registered in the next year	6.537	5.271	5.449	4.515	4.124	2.745	
(2)	Estimated infant mortality rates	.100	.097	.095	.092	.090	.087	
(3)	Expected deaths not registered (1) x (2)	654	511	518	415	371	239	
(4)	Registered deaths	3.711	3.904	4.034	3.803	4.121	4.456	4.869
(5)	Under-registration estimated (3) ÷ (4) (percent)	17.6	13.1	12.8	10.9	9.0	5.4	6.0

TABLE VI-9

UNDER-REGISTRATION OF DEATHS, AGE ONE YEAR, COSTA RICA, 1958-1964

	1958	1959	1960	1961	1962	1963	1964
(1) Birth occurred in the indicated year, registered two years later	1.035	799	674	528	452		
(2) Expected death from (1) *	26	20	17	13	11	10	10
(3) Registered deaths	722	702	762	611	886	850	838
(4) Under-registration estimated (2) ÷ (3) (percent)	3.6	2.8	2.2	2.1	1.2	1.2	1.2

*With an estimated mortality rate of .025

TABLE VI-10

DEATHS BY SEX AND AGE GROUPS USED IN THE
CONSTRUCTION OF THE LIFE TABLE, COSTA RICA, 1962-1964

Age Groups	Male	Female
Total	6,334	5,404
0	2,699	2,110
1	440	442
2	164	177
3	99	98
4	71	64
0-4	3,473	2,891
5-9	172	145
10-14	77	56
15-19	83	54
20-24	107	68
25-29	90	72
30-34	91	82
35-39	106	97
40-44	123	101
45-49	133	118
50-54	177	139
55-59	181	141
60-64	245	219
65-69	256	211
70-74	301	251
75 +	719	759

TABLE VI-11

COHORT DEATHS IN THE POPULATION BORN
1958-1963, COSTA RICA

Year of Birth	Up to the Beginning of 1963		Up to the End of 1963	
	Male	Female	Male	Female
1958	2,999	2,557	--	--
1959	3,047	2,613	3,117	2,693
1960	3,037	2,542	3,158	2,674
1961	2,666	2,133	2,959	2,439
1962	1,830	1,441	2,795	2,238
1963	--	--	1,934	1,480

TABLE VI-12

ESTIMATED POPULATION, AGES 0-4, COSTA RICA, 1963

Year of Birth	Birth	Cohort Deaths		Survivors		Age at Census Date	Survivors at Census Date
		Up to the Beginning of 1963	Up to the End of 1963	At the Beginning of 1963	At the End of 1963		
				Male			
1963	32,742		1,934		30,808	0	30,227
1962	31,866	1,830	2,795	30,036	29,071	1	28,948
1961	31,573	2,666	2,959	28,907	28,614	2	27,268
1960	29,863	3,037	3,158	26,826	26,705	3	25,906
1959	28,692	3,047	3,117	25,645	25,575	4	24,755
1958	27,485	2,999		24,486			
				Female			
1963	31,056		1,480		29,576	0	29,381
1962	30,758	1,441	2,238	29,317	28,520	1	28,098
1961	30,093	2,133	2,439	27,960	27,654	2	26,695
1960	28,922	2,542	2,674	26,380	26,248	3	25,108
1959	27,347	2,613	2,693	24,734	24,654	4	23,694
1958	25,936	2,557		23,379			

TABLE VI-13

POPULATION BY SEX AND AGE GROUPS
USED IN THE CONSTRUCTION OF THE LIFE TABLE
COSTA RICA, 1963

| Age Groups | Population | |
	Male	Female
Total	679,505	677,511
0	30,227	29,381
1	28,948	28,098
2	27,268	26,695
3	25,906	25,108
4	24,755	23,694
5-9	110,493	107,124
10-14	86,185	84,525
15-19	64,014	66,109
20-24	50,578	53,017
25-29	41,371	43,596
30-34	38,547	38,667
35-39	33,370	34,301
40-44	26,929	26,710
45-49	22,792	22,504
50-54	21,006	20,514
55-59	13,404	13,337
60-64	12,883	12,643
65-69	7,362	7,853
70-74	6,073	5,800
75 +	7,394	7,835

TABLE VI-14

ABRIDGED LIFE TABLE, COSTA RICA, 1963
MALE

Age x n	l_x	$_nd_x$	$_np_x$	$_nq_x$	$_nL_x$	T_x	e_x
0 1	100,000	8,061	.91939	.08061	94,196	6,215,110	62.15
1 1	91,939	1,784	.98060	.01940	90,886	6,120,914	66.58
2 1	90,155	592	.99343	.00657	89,841	6,030,028	66.89
3 1	89,563	346	.99614	.00386	89,383	5,940,187	66.32
4 1	89,217	260	.99709	.00291	89,082	5,850,804	65.58
0 5	100,000	11,043	.88957	.11043	453,388	6,215,110	62.15
5 5	88,957	755	.99151	.00849	442,898	5,761,722	64.77
10 5	88,202	427	.99516	.00484	439,943	5,318,824	60.30
15 5	87,775	534	.99392	.00608	437,540	4,878,881	55.58
20 5	87,241	766	.99122	.00878	434,290	4,441,341	50.91
25 5	86,475	939	.98914	.01086	430,028	4,007,051	46.34
30 5	85,536	1,123	.98687	.01313	424,873	3,577,023	41.82
35 5	84,413	1,394	.98349	.01651	418,580	3,152,150	37.34
40 5	83,019	1,809	.97821	.02179	410,573	2,733,570	32.93
45 5	81,210	2,406	.97037	.02963	400,035	2,322,997	28.60
50 5	78,804	3,317	.95791	.04209	385,728	1,922,962	24.40
55 5	75,487	4,722	.93745	.06255	365,630	1,537,234	20.36
60 5	70,765	6,925	.90214	.09786	336,513	1,171,604	16.56
65 5	63,840	10,027	.84294	.15706	294,133	835,091	13.08
70 5	53,813	13,282	.75318	.24682	235,860	540,958	10.05
75 5	40,531	15,205	.62486	.37514	164,643	305,098	7.53
80 5	25,326	13,718	.45834	.54166	92,335	140,455	5.55
85 5	11,608	8,426	.27412	.72588	36,975	48,120	4.15
90 +	3,182	3,182	0.00000	1.00000	11,145	11,145	3.50

TABLE VI-14 (continued)

ABRIDGED LIFE TABLE, COSTA RICA, 1963
FEMALE

Age x n	l_x	$_nd_x$	$_np_x$	$_nq_x$	$_nL_x$	T_x	e_x
0 1	100,000	6,625	.93375	.06625	95,230	6,503,151	65.03
1 1	93,375	1,744	.98132	.01868	92,346	6,407,921	68.63
2 1	91,631	646	.99295	.00705	91,289	6,315,575	68.92
3 1	90,985	357	.99608	.00392	90,799	6,224,286	68.41
4 1	90,628	251	.99723	.00277	90,497	6,133,487	67.68
0 5	100,000	9,623	.90377	.09623	460,161	6,503,151	65.03
5 5	90,377	656	.99274	.00726	450,223	6,042,990	66.86
10 5	89,712	345	.99615	.00385	447,720	5,592,767	62.34
15 5	89,376	388	.99566	.00434	445,910	5,145,047	57.57
20 5	88,988	599	.99327	.00673	443,443	4,699,137	52.81
25 5	88,389	661	.99252	.00748	440,293	4,255,694	48.15
30 5	87,728	928	.98942	.01058	436,320	3,815,401	43.49
35 5	86,800	1,220	.98594	.01406	430,950	3,379,081	38.93
40 5	85,580	1,630	.98095	.01905	423,825	2,948,131	34.45
45 5	83,950	2,179	.97404	.02596	414,303	2,524,306	30.07
50 5	81,771	2,996	.96336	.03664	401,365	2,110,003	25.80
55 5	78,775	4,288	.94557	.05443	383,155	1,708,638	21.69
60 5	74,487	6,335	.91495	.08505	356,598	1,325,483	17.79
65 5	68,152	9,265	.86405	.13595	317,598	968,885	14.22
70 5	58,887	12,575	.78646	.21354	262,998	651,287	11.06
75 5	46,312	15,114	.67365	.32635	193,775	388,289	8.38
80 5	31,198	14,899	.52244	.47756	118,743	194,514	6.23
85 5	16,299	10,694	.34389	.65611	54,760	75,771	4.65
90 +	5,605	5,605	0.00000	1.00000	21,011	21,011	3.75

TABLE VI-15

LIFE EXPECTANCY, COSTA RICA
CENSUS YEARS

Year	Total*	Male	Female
1864	26.7	26.3	27.0
1883	28.9	28.4	29.3
1892	30.5	30.1	30.9
1927	40.0	39.2	40.8
1950	55.5	54.0	57.0
1963	63.6	62.2	65.0

*Simple arithmetic average of male and female.

NOTES

[1] O. Andrew Collver, Birth Rates in Latin America: New Estimates of Historical Trends and Fluctuations (Berkeley: Institute of International Studies, University of California, 1965) [Research Series, No. 7], p. 100.

[2] Costa Rica, Ministerio de Economía y Hacienda, Dirección General de Estadística y Censos, Censo de Poblacíon de Costa Rica, 1950, San José, 1953, pp. 14 and 21.

[3] Collver, op. cit., p. 101.

[4] This omission can be noted in Figure VI-1. For example, in both sexes and for practically all the cohorts, the enumerated survivors in 1963 indicate a very slight decrease from the same cohorts enumerated in 1950. In other words, the census figures give the impression that almost no one died during the 12.5 years of the intercensal period (net international migration during the 1950-1963 period was not significant). If the 1963 census was not overenumerated (and according to the Ministerio de Economía y Hacienda, Dirección General de Estadística y Censos, Evaluación Censos Población Vivienda y Agropecuario, San José, Marzo, 1965, an underenumeration of 1.6% was estimated), then the 1950 census must have been underenumerated. We can use the same reasoning when analyzing the 1883 and 1892 censuses. Obviously, the 1883 census presents some underenumeration with respect to the 1892 census. However, if the 1883 census contained omissions, the 1864 census also contained omissions, perhaps to an even greater degree than that of 1883. The difference between the enumerated

population cohort of 1864 and 1883 seems to be smaller than expected, if we consider that there was between those years a period of high mortality. We must take into account that this impression of underenumeration in the first two censuses could perhaps, in part, be due to the assimilation of the forest population.

[5]A practical example of life table construction using Method B is given in Appendix II.

[6]See Costa Rica, Ministerio de Hacienda, Dirección General de Estadística y Censos, Principales Hechos Vitales Ocurridos en Costa Rica, for years 1958-1963, and Estadística Vital, 1964.

[7]Our assumption here is that those who were not registered as births were not registered as deaths either. (Actually, some of the deaths of children who were not registered as births might have been registered, principally in the cities.) Hence, using this assumption, the proportion of the population living in urban areas, and the proportion of all births that are registered one year later, we found the number of unregistered deaths by multiplying the infant mortality rate for a given year by the number of births that occurred in that year but were registered during the next. (These births represent only a part of those births not registered during the first year of life.) The same assumption was made in order to estimate under-registration of deaths at age one. In this case, mortality rates for age one of a given year and births occurring in that year but registered two years late were considered.

[8]See note 4.

[9]With the weights we obtained the average at the date of the 1963 census. The weights were .38889, .33333, and .27778 for 1962, 1963 and 1964 respectively.

[10]For the Lexis' diagram see Roland Pressat, L'Analyse Démographique (Paris: Presses Universitaires de France, 1961), pp. 16-58.

[11]Costa Rica, Ministerio de Industria y Comercio, Dirección General de Estadística y Censos, Censo de Población 1963, San José, Abril, 1966, p. 380.

[12]The official estimate of births for 1958 was 53,421 and the registered number was 53,899. The sex ratio was 1.05972.

[13]The weights were .753 and .247 for 1963 and 1964 respectively.

[14]For a practical example of life table construction using Method A, see Appendix I.

VII. DOMINICAN REPUBLIC

The Dominican Republic has taken four national censuses, in 1920, 1935, 1950, and 1960, but information by age group is available only for the last three. Vital statistics are not complete. Therefore, the use of Method A is not recommended for the construction of life tables. However, the conditions of constant fertility and insignificant international migration exist in the Dominican Republic, making possible the use of Method B for the construction of life tables.[1] To apply this method, the proportional age group distribution of population aged 10-59 and the natural growth rates for census years are required.

PROPORTIONAL AGE GROUP DISTRIBUTION OF THE POPULATION

A graphical cohort analysis of the ten-year age group distributions of the last three censuses (Fig. VII-1) shows that there have been no disturbing irregularities in age distribution except in the ages under 10. The 1950 and 1935 censuses are less complete than the 1960 census, but each census has practically the same relative completeness for all age groups between 10 and 59.[2] Thus we obtained the smoothed proportional five-year age group distribution of population by sex for ages 10-59 according to the procedure explained in Appendix III. The final results are given in Table VII-1.

ESTIMATION OF NATURAL GROWTH RATES

Estimates of the natural growth rates for census years were made on the basis of the intercensal geometric growth rates, which had been calculated from the 1935 and 1950 censuses (previously corrected for omission in relation to the 1960 census). The estimated rates were 20.7 and 28.7 per thousand for the periods 1935-1950 and 1950-1960 respectively. (The same rates from published data are 23.8 and 35.5 respectively.) Natural growth rates for census years were estimated at 16.0, 25.5, and 32.0 per thousand for 1935, 1950, and 1960 respectively.

CONSTRUCTION OF LIFE TABLES

Life tables were constructed using the proportional age group distribution of Table VII-1 and by taking into account the

102

FIGURE VII-1

TEN-YEAR AGE GROUPS BY YEAR OF BIRTH, CENSUS POPULATION,

DOMINICAN REPUBLIC, 1935-1960, MALE

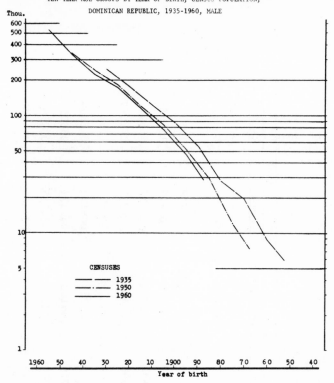

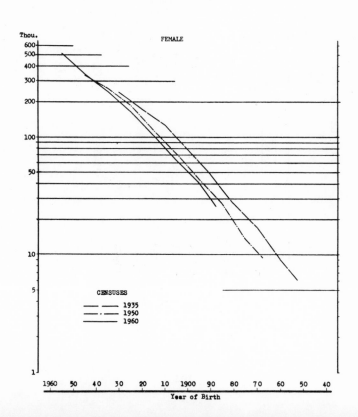

TABLE VII-1

SMOOTHED PROPORTIONAL DISTRIBUTION OF THE POPULATION
BY SEX AND FIVE-YEAR AGE GROUPS, AGES 10-59
DOMINICAN REPUBLIC, CENSUS YEARS

Age Groups	1935		1950		1960	
	Male	Female	Male	Female	Male	Female
Total	1.000000	1.000000	1.000000	1.000000	1.000000	1.000000
10-59	.624154	.624956	.636843	.639116	.604101	.609284
10-14	.112473	.114643	.115295	.120295	.121748	.125323
15-19	.099181	.101997	.101468	.106418	.100929	.105428
20-24	.085487	.088702	.087534	.092170	.081387	.086441
25-29	.074551	.076662	.075736	.078708	.068224	.071989
30-34	.064274	.063851	.064023	.064095	.058003	.059273
35-39	.054895	.053286	.054467	.052844	.049163	.048604
40-44	.045144	.042341	.045276	.041886	.041171	.038357
45-49	.037029	.034430	.037762	.033976	.034178	.030786
50-54	.029247	.027463	.030810	.027171	.027665	.024271
55-59	.021873	.021581	.024472	.021553	.021633	.018812

natural growth rates estimated above. The United Nations set of $_5L_x$ values used to obtain the quotient $\dfrac{C'(x,\ x+5)}{_5L_x}$ were levels 20 and 65 for 1935 and 1960 respectively, and levels 50 for males and 45 for females in 1950. The slopes of the straight lines of adjustment and the growth rates used for each sex and for each year are presented in Table VII-2. The life tables obtained are given in Tables VII-3, VII-4, and VII-5.[3] A summary of the life expectancy established is presented in Table VII-6.

TABLE VII-2

GROWTH RATES USED IN THE CONSTRUCTION OF LIFE TABLES
FOR THE DOMINICAN REPUBLIC

	Growth Rates			Slopes of the Straight Lines of Adjustment of the $\log_e \dfrac{C'(x,\ x+5)}{_nL_5}$		
Year	Total	Male	Female	Male	Female	Average
1935	.0160	.01500	.01700	.014636	.017536	.016086
1950	.0255	.02303	.02797	.023380	.027715	.025548
1960	.0320	.02914	.03486	.029348	.035108	.032228

TABLE VII-3

ABRIDGED LIFE TABLE, DOMINICAN REPUBLIC, 1935
MALE

Age x n	l_x	$_n d_x$	$_n p_x$	$_n q_x$	$_n L_x$	T_x	e_x
0 1	100,000	24,996	.75004	.24996	76,716	2,987,974	29.88
1 4	75,004	10,844	.85542	.14458	276,496	2,911,258	38.81
0 5	100,000	35,840	.64160	.35840	353,212	2,987,974	29.88
5 5	64,160	4,854	.92434	.07566	303,507	2,634,761	41.07
10 5	59,306	2,307	.96111	.03889	290,574	2,331,254	39.31
15 5	56,999	2,597	.95443	.04557	279,158	2,040,680	35.80
20 5	54,402	3,272	.93985	.06015	264,122	1,761,522	32.38
25 5	51,130	3,570	.93018	.06982	246,778	1,497,400	29.29
30 5	47,560	3,759	.92097	.07903	228,553	1,250,622	26.30
35 5	43,801	4,083	.90678	.09322	209,056	1,022,069	23.33
40 5	39,718	4,518	.88624	.11376	187,600	813,013	20.47
45 5	35,200	4,915	.86035	.13965	163,915	625,413	17.77
50 5	30,284	5,182	.82890	.17110	138,598	461,498	15.24
55 5	25,103	5,306	.78861	.21139	112,281	322,900	12.86
60 5	19,796	5,234	.73561	.26439	85,781	210,619	10.64
65 5	14,562	4,920	.66216	.33784	60,254	124,838	8.57
70 5	9,643	4,215	.56283	.43717	37,060	64,583	6.70
75 5	5,427	3,059	.43641	.56359	18,649	27,523	5.07
80 5	2,368	1,691	.28588	.71412	6,958	8,874	3.75
85 +	677	677	0.00000	1.00000	1,917	1,917	2.83

TABLE VII-3 (continued)

ABRIDGED LIFE TABLE, DOMINICAN REPUBLIC, 1935
FEMALE

Age x n	l_x	$_n d_x$	$_n p_x$	$_n q_x$	$_n L_x$	T_x	e_x
0 1	100,000	23,138	.76862	.23138	78,631	2,994,935	29.95
1 4	76,862	11,313	.85281	.14719	282,998	2,916,305	37.94
0 5	100,000	34,451	.65549	.34451	361,628	2,994,935	29.95
5 5	65,549	5,373	.91803	.08197	309,075	2,633,307	40.17
10 5	60,176	2,862	.95244	.04756	293,574	2,324,232	38.62
15 5	57,314	3,159	.94488	.05512	279,288	2,030,657	35.43
20 5	54,155	3,812	.92961	.07039	261,545	1,751,370	32.34
25 5	50,343	4,106	.91845	.08155	241,509	1,489,825	29.59
30 5	46,237	4,178	.90963	.09037	220,756	1,248,316	27.00
35 5	42,059	4,163	.90102	.09898	199,843	1,027,560	24.43
40 5	37,896	4,116	.89139	.10861	179,160	827,718	21.84
45 5	33,780	4,165	.87671	.12329	158,579	648,558	19.20
50 5	29,616	4,330	.85379	.14621	137,377	489,979	16.54
55 5	25,285	4,570	.81928	.18072	115,190	352,602	13.94
60 5	20,716	4,818	.76741	.23259	91,688	237,412	11.46
65 5	15,898	4,871	.69361	.30639	67,257	145,724	9.17
70 5	11,027	4,483	.59340	.40660	43,516	78,467	7.12
75 5	6,543	3,514	.46300	.53700	23,134	34,951	5.34
80 5	3,030	2,123	.29937	.70063	9,135	11,817	3.90
85 +	907	907	0.00000	1.00000	2,682	2,682	2.96

TABLE VII-4

ABRIDGED LIFE TABLE, DOMINICAN REPUBLIC, 1950
MALE

Age x n	l_x	$_nd_x$	$_np_x$	$_nq_x$	$_nL_x$	T_x	e_x
0 1	100,000	16,433	.83567	.16433	84,573	4,356,456	43.56
1 4	83,567	6,385	.92360	.07640	320,435	4,271,883	51.12
0 5	100,000	22,818	.77182	.22818	405,007	4,356,456	43.56
5 5	77,182	3,004	.96108	.03892	375,483	3,951,449	51.20
10 5	74,178	1,641	.97787	.02213	366,772	3,575,966	48.21
15 5	72,537	2,036	.97193	.02807	358,181	3,209,194	44.24
20 5	70,500	2,634	.96264	.03736	346,158	2,851,012	40.44
25 5	67,867	2,817	.95849	.04151	332,249	2,504,854	36.91
30 5	65,050	2,875	.95580	.04420	318,133	2,172,605	33.40
35 5	62,174	3,105	.95006	.04994	303,313	1,854,473	29.83
40 5	59,069	3,557	.93978	.06022	286,814	1,551,160	26.26
45 5	55,512	4,229	.92382	.07618	267,471	1,264,346	22.78
50 5	51,283	5,081	.90092	.09908	244,301	996,875	19.44
55 5	46,202	6,080	.86841	.13159	216,481	752,574	16.29
60 5	40,122	7,158	.82160	.17840	183,425	536,092	13.36
65 5	32,964	8,117	.75375	.24625	145,096	352,667	10.70
70 5	24,847	8,428	.66080	.33920	103,066	207,571	8.35
75 5	16,419	7,519	.54202	.45798	62,287	104,505	6.36
80 5	8,899	5,340	.39999	.60001	29,576	42,217	4.74
85 +	3,560	3,560	0.00000	1.00000	12,642	12,642	3.55

CHAPTER VII. DOMINICAN REPUBLIC

TABLE VII-4 (continued)

ABRIDGED LIFE TABLE, DOMINICAN REPUBLIC, 1950
FEMALE

Age x n	l_x	$_nd_x$	$_np_x$	$_nq_x$	$_nL_x$	T_x	e_x
0 1	100,000	15,840	.84160	.15840	85,238	4,381,455	43.81
1 4	84,160	6,867	.91841	.08159	321,774	4,296,217	51.05
0 5	100,000	22,707	.77293	.22707	407,012	4,381,455	43.81
5 5	77,293	3,198	.95863	.04137	375,277	3,974,443	51.42
10 5	74,095	1,764	.97619	.02381	366,077	3,599,166	48.57
15 5	72,331	2,177	.96991	.03009	356,794	3,233,089	44.70
20 5	70,155	2,801	.96008	.03992	344,050	2,876,295	41.00
25 5	67,354	3,054	.95465	.04535	329,155	2,532,245	37.60
30 5	64,300	3,104	.95172	.04828	313,749	2,203,090	34.26
35 5	61,195	3,158	.94840	.05160	298,119	1,889,340	30.87
40 5	58,038	3,326	.94269	.05731	282,032	1,591,221	27.42
45 5	54,712	3,724	.93194	.06806	264,585	1,309,189	23.93
50 5	50,988	4,362	.91445	.08555	244,491	1,044,604	20.49
55 5	46,626	5,295	.88643	.11357	220,606	800,112	17.16
60 5	41,331	6,545	.84165	.15835	191,183	579,506	14.02
65 5	34,786	7,848	.77440	.22560	155,135	388,323	11.16
70 5	26,938	8,637	.67937	.32063	113,375	233,188	8.66
75 5	18,301	8,115	.55660	.44340	70,349	119,813	6.55
80 5	10,186	5,995	.41143	.58857	34,284	49,465	4.86
85 +	4,191	4,191	0.00000	1.00000	15,181	15,181	3.62

TABLE VII-5

ABRIDGED LIFE TABLE, DOMINICAN REPUBLIC, 1960
MALE

Age x n	l_x	$_nd_x$	$_np_x$	$_nq_x$	$_nL_x$	T_x	e_x
0 1	100,000	12,650	.87350	.12650	88,069	5,082,952	50.83
1 4	87,350	4,553	.94787	.05213	339,534	4,994,883	57.18
0 5	100,000	17,203	.82797	.17203	427,603	5,082,952	50.83
5 5	82,797	2,138	.97418	.02582	406,563	4,655,349	56.23
10 5	80,659	1,207	.98504	.01496	400,306	4,248,786	52.68
15 5	79,452	1,571	.98022	.01978	393,822	3,848,480	48.44
20 5	77,881	2,070	.97342	.02658	384,427	3,454,658	44.36
25 5	75,811	2,220	.97072	.02928	373,466	3,070,232	40.50
30 5	73,591	2,268	.96919	.03081	362,344	2,696,766	36.65
35 5	71,323	2,481	.96521	.03479	350,605	2,334,422	32.73
40 5	68,842	2,946	.95721	.04279	337,226	1,983,817	28.82
45 5	65,896	3,698	.94388	.05612	320,797	1,646,592	24.99
50 5	62,198	4,719	.92413	.07587	299,907	1,325,795	21.32
55 5	57,479	6,029	.89511	.10489	273,252	1,025,888	17.85
60 5	51,450	7,617	.85196	.14804	239,304	752,635	14.63
65 5	43,834	9,265	.78863	.21137	197,066	513,332	11.71
70 5	34,569	10,354	.70047	.29953	147,383	316,266	9.15
75 5	24,214	10,016	.58634	.41366	95,242	168,883	6.97
80 5	14,198	7,828	.44864	.55136	49,410	73,641	5.19
85 +	6,370	6,370	0.00000	1.00000	24,231	24,231	3.80

TABLE VII-5 (continued)

ABRIDGED LIFE TABLE, DOMINICAN REPUBLIC, 1960
FEMALE

Age x n	l_x	$_nd_x$	$_np_x$	$_nq_x$	$_nL_x$	T_x	e_x
0 1	100,000	10,883	.89117	.10883	89,810	5,349,399	53.49
1 4	89,117	4,440	.95018	.04982	346,876	5,259,589	59.02
0 5	100,000	15,323	.84677	.15323	436,686	5,349,399	53.49
5 5	84,677	2,173	.97434	.02566	415,954	4,912,713	58.02
10 5	82,504	1,303	.98421	.01579	409,297	4,496,760	54.50
15 5	81,202	1,617	.98009	.01991	402,375	4,087,462	50.34
20 5	79,585	2,057	.97415	.02585	392,973	3,685,088	46.30
25 5	77,527	2,230	.97123	.02877	382,070	3,292,114	42.46
30 5	75,297	2,279	.96974	.03026	370,817	2,910,044	38.65
35 5	73,018	2,371	.96753	.03247	359,236	2,539,227	34.78
40 5	70,648	2,607	.96309	.03691	346,929	2,179,991	30.86
45 5	68,040	3,097	.95449	.04551	332,856	1,833,062	26.94
50 5	64,943	3,866	.94048	.05952	315,604	1,500,207	23.10
55 5	61,078	5,006	.91805	.08195	293,729	1,184,603	19.39
60 5	56,072	6,676	.88093	.11907	264,922	890,873	15.89
65 5	49,396	8,803	.82179	.17821	226,475	625,952	12.67
70 5	40,593	10,779	.73445	.26555	177,164	399,477	9.84
75 5	29,814	11,332	.61989	.38011	120,389	222,313	7.46
80 5	18,481	9,496	.48616	.51384	66,402	101,924	5.52
85 +	8,985	8,985	0.00000	1.00000	35,522	35,522	3.95

TABLE VII-6

LIFE EXPECTANCY, DOMINICAN REPUBLIC
CENSUS YEARS

Year	Total*	Male	Female
1935	30.0	29.9	30.0
1950	43.7	43.6	43.8
1960	52.2	50.8	53.5

*Simple arithmetic average of male and
female.

NOTES

[1]Migration has not been significant in the Dominican Republic:
the foreign-born population in 1950 was 1.5% of the total population; most of these immigrants were from Haiti (Dirección General
de Estadística, Oficina Nacional del Censo, Tercer Censo Nacional
de Población, 1950, Ciudad Trujillo, 1958, pp. vii and 135).   In
1960, we found the same percentage of foreign-born (Secretariado
Técnico de la Presidencia, Oficina Nacional de Estadística, Divi-
sión de Censo de Población y Habitación, Cuarto Censo Nacional de
Población 1960: Resumen General, Santo Domingo, 1966, p. 33).

[2]This omission does not affect the proportional age distribution.

[3]A practical example of life table construction using Method B
is given in Appendix II.

VIII. ECUADOR

Only two censuses have been taken in Ecuador, the first in 1950 and the second in 1962. Thus we cannot construct life tables for years before 1950. Death registration is not complete; therefore, application of Method A is not recommended. Fortunately, conditions for the application of Method B are favorable. Fertility in the past seems to have been constant and very high (to judge from the age structure in both censuses). In addition, international migration, according to the total foreign-born enumerated in the censuses, could be considered negligible.

PROPORTIONAL AGE GROUP DISTRIBUTION OF THE POPULATION

A graphical cohort analysis of both censuses (Fig. VIII-1) shows that in general they are comparable, except for age groups under 20, which indicate higher underenumeration than other age groups. After a slight correction of age groups under 20, the age group distribution was smoothed according to the procedure explained in Appendix III. The proportional five-year age groups used in the life tables are presented in Table VIII-1.

ESTIMATION OF NATURAL GROWTH RATES

The natural growth rates for census years were estimated by considering the annual average intercensal geometric growth rate (27.9 per thousand) and the existing estimates.[1] Growth rates of 25.0 and 29.5 were estimated for 1950 and 1962 respectively.

CONSTRUCTION OF LIFE TABLES

Life tables were constructed using Method B, the proportional age group distribution (Table VIII-1), and the estimated growth rates given above. The United Nations set of $_5L_x$ values used in the quotient $\dfrac{C'(x, x+5)}{_5L_x}$ were levels 55 and 70 in 1950 and 1962 respectively. The slopes of the straight lines of adjustment and the growth rates used for each sex in the exponent of e (Eq. 5, Chap. I) are shown in Table VIII-2. The life tables obtained are presented in Tables VIII-3 and VIII-4 and a summary of life expectancy is given in Table VIII-5.[2]

FIGURE VIII-1

TEN-YEAR AGE GROUPS BY YEAR OF BIRTH, CENSUS POPULATION,

ECUADOR, 1950-1962, FEMALE

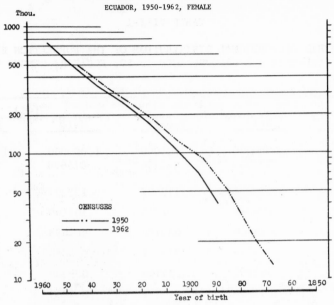

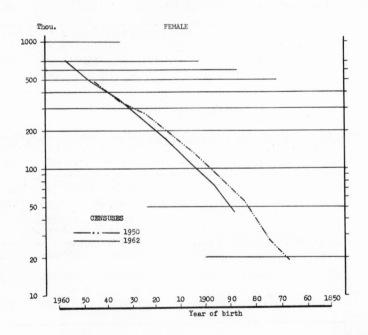

CHAPTER VIII. ECUADOR

TABLE VIII-1

SMOOTHED PROPORTIONAL DISTRIBUTION OF THE POPULATION BY SEX AND FIVE-YEAR AGE GROUPS, AGES 10-59, ECUADOR, CENSUS YEARS

Age Groups	1950 Male	1950 Female	1962 Male	1962 Female
Total	1.000000	1.000000	1.000000	1.000000
10-59	.632949	.635394	.616939	.622700
10-14	.120814	.113507	.123237	.119055
15-19	.104029	.101234	.103260	.102734
20-24	.088000	.089150	.084493	.087083
25-29	.074739	.077301	.070880	.074063
30-34	.062261	.065104	.059385	.061847
35-39	.052199	.054727	.049963	.051684
40-44	.042868	.044496	.041540	.042028
45-49	.035530	.036609	.034384	.034469
50-54	.029140	.029502	.027581	.027534
55-59	.023369	.023764	.022216	.022203

TABLE VIII-2

GROWTH RATES USED IN THE CONSTRUCTION OF LIFE TABLES FOR ECUADOR

Year	Growth Rates Total	Growth Rates Male	Growth Rates Female	Slopes of the Straight Lines of Adjustment of the $\log_e \frac{C'(x, x+5)}{{}_nL_5}$ Male	Female	Average
1950	.0267	.02690	.02650	.026734	.026324	.026529
1962	.0308	.03039	.03121	.030577	.031386	.030982

TABLE VIII-3

ABRIDGED LIFE TABLE, ECUADOR, 1950
MALE

Age x n	l_x	$_nd_x$	$_np_x$	$_nq_x$	$_nL_x$	T_x	e_x
0 1	100,000	15,143	.84857	.15143	85,748	4,664,597	46.65
1 4	84,857	5,620	.93377	.06623	327,226	4,578,850	53.96
0 5	100,000	20,763	.79237	.20763	412,974	4,664,597	46.65
5 5	79,237	2,534	.96802	.03198	387,222	4,251,623	53.66
10 5	76,703	1,326	.98271	.01729	380,206	3,864,401	50.38
15 5	75,377	1,730	.97705	.02295	373,130	3,484,195	46.22
20 5	73,647	2,316	.96856	.03144	362,680	3,111,065	42.24
25 5	71,331	2,499	.96497	.03503	350,368	2,748,385	38.53
30 5	68,832	2,561	.96280	.03720	337,833	2,398,017	34.84
35 5	66,271	2,800	.95775	.04225	324,569	2,060,184	31.09
40 5	63,471	3,281	.94830	.05170	309,541	1,735,615	27.34
45 5	60,190	4,016	.93327	.06673	291,444	1,426,074	23.69
50 5	56,174	4,975	.91143	.08857	269,097	1,134,630	20.20
55 5	51,198	6,142	.88003	.11997	241,439	865,533	16.91
60 5	45,056	7,466	.83429	.16571	207,504	624,094	13.85
65 5	37,590	8,728	.76781	.23219	166,905	416,591	11.08
70 5	28,862	9,343	.67629	.32371	121,046	249,686	8.65
75 5	19,519	8,612	.55877	.44123	75,098	128,640	6.59
80 5	10,907	6,351	.41766	.58234	36,877	53,542	4.91
85 +	4,555	4,555	0.00000	1.00000	16,665	16,665	3.66

TABLE VIII-3 (continued)

ABRIDGED LIFE TABLE, ECUADOR, 1950
FEMALE

Age x n	l_x	$_nd_x$	$_np_x$	$_nq_x$	$_nL_x$	T_x	e_x
0 1	100,000	13,302	.86698	.13302	87,569	4,897,395	48.97
1 4	86,698	5,548	.93601	.06399	334,781	4,809,825	55.48
0 5	100,000	18,850	.81150	.18850	422,351	4,897,395	48.97
5 5	81,150	2,595	.96802	.03198	396,693	4,475,044	55.15
10 5	78,555	1,459	.98143	.01857	389,155	4,078,351	51.92
15 5	77,096	1,834	.97621	.02379	381,401	3,689,195	47.85
20 5	75,262	2,372	.96849	.03151	370,615	3,307,795	43.95
25 5	72,890	2,582	.96458	.03542	358,009	2,937,180	40.30
30 5	70,308	2,636	.96251	.03749	344,983	2,579,171	36.68
35 5	67,673	2,718	.95983	.04017	331,627	2,234,189	33.01
40 5	64,955	2,929	.95490	.04510	317,639	1,902,562	29.29
45 5	62,025	3,395	.94526	.05474	302,026	1,584,923	25.55
50 5	58,630	4,133	.92951	.07049	283,341	1,282,897	21.88
55 5	54,497	5,206	.90447	.09553	260,276	999,556	18.34
60 5	49,291	6,719	.86368	.13632	230,770	739,280	15.00
65 5	42,571	8,503	.80025	.19975	192,812	508,510	11.94
70 5	34,068	9,925	.70867	.29133	146,244	315,698	9.27
75 5	24,143	9,900	.58993	.41007	95,301	169,454	7.02
80 5	14,243	7,811	.45155	.54845	49,661	74,153	5.21
85 +	6,431	6,431	0.00000	1.00000	24,492	24,492	3.81

TABLE VIII-4

ABRIDGED LIFE TABLE, ECUADOR, 1962
MALE

Age x n	l_x	$_nd_x$	$_np_x$	$_nq_x$	$_nL_x$	T_x	e_x
0 1	100,000	11,403	.88597	.11403	89,228	5,324,295	53.24
1 4	88,597	3,999	.95486	.04514	345,722	5,235,067	59.09
0 5	100,000	15,402	.84598	.15402	434,950	5,324,295	53.24
5 5	84,598	1,886	.97771	.02229	416,458	4,889,345	57.80
10 5	82,712	1,082	.98692	.01308	410,890	4,472,888	54.08
15 5	81,630	1,424	.98255	.01745	405,040	4,061,997	49.76
20 5	80,206	1,882	.97653	.02347	396,503	3,656,957	45.59
25 5	78,324	2,016	.97426	.02574	386,539	3,260,454	41.63
30 5	76,308	2,062	.97298	.02702	376,447	2,873,915	37.66
35 5	74,246	2,277	.96933	.03067	365,734	2,497,467	33.64
40 5	71,969	2,732	.96204	.03796	353,380	2,131,733	29.62
45 5	69,237	3,487	.94963	.05037	338,044	1,778,353	25.68
50 5	65,750	4,561	.93062	.06938	318,112	1,440,309	21.91
55 5	61,188	5,963	.90255	.09745	292,025	1,122,197	18.34
60 5	55,226	7,691	.86074	.13926	258,108	830,172	15.03
65 5	47,535	9,557	.79895	.20105	215,007	572,065	12.03
70 5	37,978	10,926	.71231	.28769	163,200	357,058	9.40
75 5	27,052	10,831	.59963	.40037	107,511	193,857	7.17
80 5	16,221	8,704	.46340	.53660	57,211	86,347	5.32
85 +	7,517	7,517	0.00000	1.00000	29,136	29,136	3.88

TABLE VIII-4 (continued)

ABRIDGED LIFE TABLE, ECUADOR, 1962
FEMALE

Age x n	l_x	$_nd_x$	$_np_x$	$_nq_x$	$_nL_x$	T_x	e_x
0 1	100,000	9,689	.90311	.09689	90,907	5,619,986	56.20
1 4	90,311	3,819	.95772	.04228	352,993	5,529,079	61.22
0 5	100,000	13,508	.86492	.13508	443,901	5,619,986	56.20
5 5	86,492	1,870	.97838	.02162	426,069	5,176,086	59.84
10 5	84,622	1,130	.98665	.01335	420,324	4,750,016	56.13
15 5	83,492	1,418	.98301	.01699	414,284	4,329,692	51.86
20 5	82,074	1,815	.97789	.02211	406,009	3,915,408	47.71
25 5	80,260	1,978	.97536	.02464	396,369	3,509,399	43.73
30 5	78,282	2,036	.97399	.02601	386,354	3,113,030	39.77
35 5	76,246	2,142	.97190	.02810	375,955	2,726,676	35.76
40 5	74,104	2,398	.96764	.03236	364,746	2,350,721	31.72
45 5	71,706	2,909	.95943	.04057	351,668	1,985,974	27.70
50 5	68,797	3,803	.94618	.05382	335,296	1,634,307	23.76
55 5	65,094	4,885	.92496	.07504	314,147	1,299,011	19.96
60 5	60,210	6,650	.88956	.11044	285,754	984,864	16.36
65 5	53,560	8,973	.83247	.16753	247,036	699,110	13.05
70 5	44,587	11,269	.74725	.25275	196,159	452,074	10.14
75 5	33,318	12,171	.63471	.36529	136,012	255,915	7.68
80 5	21,147	10,511	.50297	.49703	77,073	119,903	5.67
85 +	10,636	10,636	0.00000	1.00000	42,831	42,831	4.03

NEW LIFE TABLES FOR LATIN AMERICAN POPULATIONS

TABLE VIII-5

LIFE EXPECTANCY, ECUADOR
CENSUS YEARS

Year	Total*	Male	Female
1950	47.9	46.7	49.0
1962	54.7	53.2	56.2

*Simple arithmetic average of male and female.

NOTES

[1]O. Andrew Collver, Birth Rates in Latin America: New Estimates of Historical Trends and Fluctuations (Berkeley: Institute of International Studies, University of California, 1965) [Research Series, No. 7], p. 117.

[2]A practical example of life table construction using Method B is given in Appendix II.

IX. EL SALVADOR

Demographic information is available for El Salvador only for recent dates. Three national censuses have been taken, in 1930, 1950, and 1961. Death information by age groups is available for years since 1938,[1] but due to considerable under-registration, its use is not recommended. Fortunately for the purposes of this study, fertility has been virtually constant in El Salvador during past years, and international migration has been negligible prior to 1950. Therefore, life tables were constructed using Method B.

PROPORTIONAL AGE GROUP DISTRIBUTION OF THE POPULATION

The three censuses give the age group distribution of the population by sex. Therefore, we made a graphical cohort analysis of age group distribution by sex (Fig. IX-1) which reveals irregularities in some age groups: in 1935 the age group 20-29 appears to be overenumerated in relation to other age groups; in 1950, ages under 10 appear to be underenumerated; and, in 1961 we observed a dip in ages 10-34,[2] due to emigration (principally to Honduras).[3] After correcting for these irregularities by increasing or decreasing slightly the affected age groups, age group distributions were smoothed according to the procedure explained in Appendix III. Proportional age group distributions are given in Table IX-1.

ESTIMATION OF NATURAL GROWTH RATES

In spite of the irregularities in the particular age groups described above, the total completeness of all three censuses seems to be comparable. Therefore, we estimated natural growth rates by considering the intercensal geometric growth rates and the available estimates.[4] The rates calculated are 11.8, 27.1, and 32.0 per thousand for 1930, 1950, and 1961 respectively.

CONSTRUCTION OF LIFE TABLES

Life tables for each sex and year were constructed using Method B, the proportional age group distribution of the population (Table IX-1) and the estimates of the natural growth rates given above. The set of $_5L_x$ values from United Nations Model Life Tables used to obtain the quotient $\dfrac{C'(x, x+5)}{_5L_x}$ were levels 55 and 70 for both sexes in 1950 and 1960. For 1930 the levels were 15 for males and 20 for females. The slopes of the straight lines of

FIGURE IX-1

TEN-YEAR AGE GROUPS BY YEAR OF BIRTH, CENSUS POPULATION,

EL SALVADOR, 1930-1960, MALE

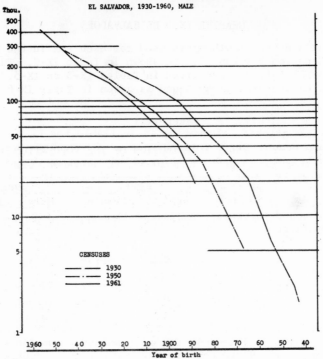

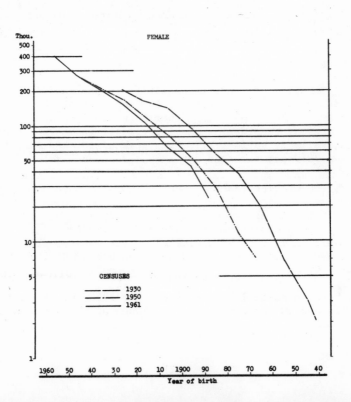

adjustment and the growth rates used for each sex in the application of Equation 5 (Chap. I) are shown in Table IX-2. The life tables for El Salvador are given in Tables IX-3 to IX-5.[5] A summary of the life expectancy found is given in Table IX-6.

TABLE IX-1

SMOOTHED PROPORTIONAL DISTRIBUTION OF THE POPULATION BY SEX AND FIVE-YEAR AGE GROUPS, AGES 10-59, EL SALVADOR, CENSUS YEARS

Age Groups	1930		1950		1961	
	Male	Female	Male	Female	Male	Female
Total	1.000000	1.000000	1.000000	1.000000	1.000000	1.000000
10-59	.674405	.681047	.654090	.664422	.606925	.619747
10-14	.115000	.113476	.124560	.121127	.122341	.122010
15-19	.104250	.104731	.107214	.107139	.100838	.102780
20-24	.093242	.095438	.090660	.093462	.084338	.086684
25-29	.079748	.084738	.077152	.080630	.070648	.073111
30-34	.071698	.072526	.064548	.067699	.058248	.060466
35-39	.061285	.061503	.054401	.056774	.048692	.050379
40-44	.050102	.049586	.045326	.046185	.040316	.041009
45-49	.041141	.040677	.037319	.037742	.033303	.033792
50-54	.032804	.032689	.029889	.030180	.026625	.027257
55-59	.025135	.025683	.023021	.023484	.021576	.022259

TABLE IX-2

GROWTH RATES USED IN THE CONSTRUCTION OF LIFE TABLES FOR EL SALVADOR

	Growth Rates			Slopes of the Straight Lines of Adjustment of the $\log_e \dfrac{C'(x,\ x+5)}{{}_nL_5}$		
Year	Total	Male	Female	Male	Female	Average
1930	.0118	.01157	.01203	.012565	.011046	.011806
1950	.0271	.02690	.02730	.027060	.027573	.027317
1961	.0320	.03167	.03233	.031200	.031854	.031527

TABLE IX-3

ABRIDGED LIFE TABLE, EL SALVADOR, 1930
MALE

Age x n	l_x	$_nd_x$	$_np_x$	$_nq_x$	$_nL_x$	T_x	e_x
0 1	100,000	25,123	.74877	.25123	76,626	2,877,627	28.78
1 4	74,877	11,145	.85116	.14884	275,388	2,801,001	37.41
0 5	100,000	36,268	.63732	.36268	352,014	2,877,627	28.78
5 5	63,732	5,226	.91801	.08199	300,430	2,525,612	39.63
10 5	58,507	2,658	.95457	.04543	285,680	2,225,183	38.03
15 5	55,849	2,905	.94798	.05202	272,597	1,939,503	34.73
20 5	52,944	3,521	.93349	.06651	256,168	1,666,906	31.48
25 5	49,422	3,762	.92388	.07612	237,725	1,410,738	28.54
30 5	45,660	3,893	.91473	.08527	218,678	1,173,012	25.69
35 5	41,767	4,150	.90064	.09936	198,669	954,334	22.85
40 5	37,616	4,505	.88024	.11976	177,072	755,665	20.09
45 5	33,112	4,817	.85453	.14547	153,668	578,594	17.47
50 5	28,295	5,000	.82329	.17671	129,054	424,926	15.02
55 5	23,295	5,049	.78328	.21672	103,841	295,872	12.70
60 5	18,246	4,915	.73063	.26937	78,796	192,031	10.52
65 5	13,331	4,563	.65769	.34231	54,973	113,234	8.49
70 5	8,768	3,866	.55903	.44097	33,583	58,261	6.64
75 5	4,901	2,777	.43336	.56664	16,784	24,678	5.03
80 5	2,124	1,522	.28353	.71647	6,220	7,894	3.72
85 +	602	602	0.00000	1.00000	1,674	1,674	2.78

TABLE IX-3 (continued)

ABRIDGED LIFE TABLE, EL SALVADOR, 1930
FEMALE

Age x n	l_x	$_nd_x$	$_np_x$	$_nq_x$	$_nL_x$	T_x	e_x
0 1	100,000	24,745	.75255	.24745	77,149	2,853,737	28.54
1 4	75,255	12,044	.83996	.16004	274,927	2,776,588	36.90
0 5	100,000	36,789	.63211	.36789	352,076	2,853,737	28.54
5 5	63,211	5,418	.91429	.08571	296,750	2,501,661	39.58
10 5	57,793	2,645	.95423	.04577	282,174	2,204,911	38.15
15 5	55,148	2,943	.94664	.05336	269,031	1,922,737	34.86
20 5	52,205	3,649	.93010	.06990	252,243	1,653,706	31.68
25 5	48,556	4,013	.91735	.08265	232,857	1,401,462	28.86
30 5	44,543	4,163	.90655	.09345	212,372	1,168,606	26.24
35 5	40,380	4,205	.89587	.10413	191,371	956,234	23.68
40 5	36,176	4,174	.88461	.11539	170,404	764,863	21.14
45 5	32,001	4,205	.86860	.13140	149,565	594,458	18.58
50 5	27,796	4,331	.84419	.15581	128,247	444,893	16.01
55 5	23,465	4,499	.80828	.19172	106,207	316,646	13.49
60 5	18,967	4,644	.75514	.24486	83,304	210,439	11.10
65 5	14,322	4,580	.68021	.31979	60,030	127,135	8.88
70 5	9,742	4,100	.57916	.42084	38,007	67,106	6.89
75 5	5,642	3,119	.44726	.55274	19,644	29,099	5.16
80 5	2,524	1,818	.27945	.72055	7,446	9,454	3.75
85 +	705	705	0.00000	1.00000	2,009	2,009	2.85

TABLE IX-4

ABRIDGED LIFE TABLE, EL SALVADOR, 1950
MALE

Age x n	l_x	$_nd_x$	$_np_x$	$_nq_x$	$_nL_x$	T_x	e_x
0 1	100,000	15,174	.84826	.15174	85,729	4,614,564	46.15
1 4	84,826	5,717	.93260	.06740	326,909	4,528,835	53.39
0 5	100,000	20,891	.79109	.20891	412,638	4,614,564	46.15
5 5	79,109	2,655	.96644	.03356	386,276	4,201,926	53.12
10 5	76,453	1,445	.98110	.01890	378,660	3,815,650	49.91
15 5	75,009	1,841	.97546	.02454	371,008	3,436,990	45.82
20 5	73,168	2,416	.96698	.03302	360,030	3,065,982	41.90
25 5	70,752	2,590	.96339	.03661	347,241	2,705,953	38.25
30 5	68,162	2,643	.96123	.03877	334,272	2,358,712	34.60
35 5	65,519	2,870	.95619	.04381	320,625	2,024,440	30.90
40 5	62,649	3,336	.94676	.05324	305,282	1,703,814	27.20
45 5	59,313	4,048	.93175	.06825	286,966	1,398,532	23.58
50 5	55,265	4,977	.90995	.09005	264,531	1,111,567	20.11
55 5	50,289	6,105	.87859	.12141	236,955	847,036	16.84
60 5	44,183	7,381	.83294	.16706	203,319	610,081	13.81
65 5	36,802	8,591	.76656	.23344	163,272	406,762	11.05
70 5	28,211	9,163	.67519	.32481	118,219	243,490	8.63
75 5	19,048	8,422	.55783	.44217	73,224	125,272	6.58
80 5	10,625	6,196	.41683	.58317	35,898	52,047	4.90
85 +	4,429	4,429	0.00000	1.00000	16,149	16,149	3.65

TABLE IX-4 (continued)

ABRIDGED LIFE TABLE, EL SALVADOR, 1950
FEMALE

Age x n	l_x	$_n d_x$	$_n p_x$	$_n q_x$	$_n L_x$	T_x	e_x
0 1	100,000	13,345	.86655	.13345	87,543	4,823,233	48.23
1 4	86,655	5,686	.93439	.06561	334,334	4,735,690	54.65
0 5	100,000	19,031	.80969	.19031	421,877	4,823,233	48.23
5 5	80,969	2,766	.96584	.03416	395,360	4,401,357	54.36
10 5	78,203	1,625	.97922	.02078	386,977	4,005,997	51.23
15 5	76,579	1,989	.97402	.02598	378,416	3,619,020	47.26
20 5	74,589	2,513	.96631	.03369	366,889	3,240,604	43.45
25 5	72,077	2,709	.96242	.03758	353,615	2,873,714	39.87
30 5	69,368	2,750	.96036	.03964	339,985	2,520,099	36.33
35 5	66,618	2,819	.95768	.04232	326,090	2,180,114	32.73
40 5	63,799	3,014	.95276	.04724	311,635	1,854,025	29.06
45 5	60,785	3,456	.94314	.05686	295,653	1,542,389	25.37
50 5	57,328	4,161	.92742	.07258	276,740	1,246,736	21.75
55 5	53,168	5,187	.90244	.09756	253,642	969,996	18.24
60 5	47,980	6,633	.86175	.13825	224,384	716,354	14.93
65 5	41,347	8,333	.79846	.20154	187,056	491,971	11.90
70 5	33,014	9,670	.70709	.29291	141,560	304,914	9.24
75 5	23,344	9,604	.58857	.41143	92,042	163,354	7.00
80 5	13,739	7,553	.45030	.54970	47,855	71,312	5.19
85 +	6,187	6,187	0.00000	1.00000	23,457	23,457	3.79

TABLE IX-5

ABRIDGED LIFE TABLE, EL SALVADOR, 1961
MALE

Age x n	l_x	$_nd_x$	$_np_x$	$_nq_x$	$_nL_x$	T_x	e_x
0 1	100,000	11,340	.88660	.11340	89,264	5,447,690	54.48
1 4	88,660	3,785	.95731	.04269	346,401	5,358,426	60.44
0 5	100,000	15,125	.84875	.15125	435,665	5,447,690	54.48
5 5	84,875	1,618	.98093	.01907	418,515	5,012,025	59.05
10 5	83,257	818	.99018	.00982	414,279	4,593,511	55.17
15 5	82,439	1,172	.98578	.01422	409,724	4,179,232	50.69
20 5	81,267	1,646	.97975	.02025	402,408	3,769,508	46.38
25 5	79,621	1,794	.97747	.02253	393,586	3,367,100	42.29
30 5	77,827	1,853	.97619	.02381	384,572	2,973,513	38.21
35 5	75,974	2,088	.97252	.02748	374,857	2,588,942	34.08
40 5	73,886	2,571	.96520	.03480	363,387	2,214,085	29.97
45 5	71,315	3,369	.95276	.04724	348,760	1,850,698	25.95
50 5	67,946	4,506	.93369	.06631	329,275	1,501,938	22.10
55 5	63,440	5,994	.90552	.09448	303,268	1,172,663	18.48
60 5	57,447	7,838	.86357	.13643	268,927	869,395	15.13
65 5	49,609	9,844	.80157	.19843	224,756	600,468	12.10
70 5	39,765	11,347	.71465	.28535	171,162	375,711	9.45
75 5	28,418	11,320	.60165	.39835	113,126	204,549	7.20
80 5	17,098	9,144	.46521	.53479	60,397	91,423	5.35
85 +	7,954	7,954	0.00000	1.00000	31,026	31,026	3.90

TABLE IX-5 (continued)

ABRIDGED LIFE TABLE, EL SALVADOR, 1961
FEMALE

Age x n	l_x	$_nd_x$	$_np_x$	$_nq_x$	$_nL_x$	T_x	e_x
0 1	100,000	9,626	.90374	.09626	90,943	5,753,276	57.53
1 4	90,374	3,601	.96016	.03984	353,681	5,662,333	62.65
0 5	100,000	13,227	.86773	.13227	444,625	5,753,276	57.53
5 5	86,773	1,597	.98159	.01841	428,158	5,308,652	61.18
10 5	85,176	863	.98987	.01013	423,764	4,880,494	57.30
15 5	84,313	1,162	.98622	.01378	419,038	4,456,730	52.86
20 5	83,152	1,573	.98108	.01892	412,009	4,037,692	48.56
25 5	81,578	1,750	.97854	.02146	403,540	3,625,683	44.44
30 5	79,828	1,822	.97717	.02283	394,628	3,222,143	40.36
35 5	78,006	1,944	.97508	.02492	385,261	2,827,515	36.25
40 5	76,062	2,221	.97080	.02920	374,995	2,442,254	32.11
45 5	73,841	2,764	.96257	.03743	362,729	2,067,259	28.00
50 5	71,077	3,606	.94927	.05073	346,971	1,704,530	23.98
55 5	67,471	4,859	.92798	.07202	326,148	1,357,558	20.12
60 5	62,612	6,733	.89246	.10754	297,639	1,031,411	16.47
65 5	55,879	9,210	.83519	.16481	258,151	733,771	13.13
70 5	46,669	11,682	.74968	.25032	205,654	475,621	10.19
75 5	34,987	12,706	.63683	.36317	143,061	269,967	7.72
80 5	22,281	11,031	.50490	.49510	81,332	126,906	5.70
85 +	11,250	11,250	0.00000	1.00000	45,573	45,573	4.05

TABLE IX-6

LIFE EXPECTANCY, EL SALVADOR
CENSUS YEARS

Year	Total*	Male	Female
1930	28.7	28.8	28.5
1950	47.2	46.2	48.2
1961	56.0	54.5	57.5

*Simple arithmetic average of male and
female.

NOTES

[1] El Salvador, Ministerio de Economía, Dirección General de
Estadística y Censo, Anuario Estadístico, San Salvador.

[2] Of the total foreign-born female population in El Salvador,
78% were in this age group. Most of these were enumerated in
the Department of San Salvador, where the capital is located (see
El Salvador, Ministerio de Economía, Dirección Nacional de Estadística y Censo, Tercer Censo Nacional de Población 1961, pp. 191-
195). The occurrence of such a high proportion of foreign-born
in the young age groups could be due to female migration for a
specific economic/employment reason, or perhaps because seasonal
male migration to Honduras and Guatemala from El Salvador has re-
sulted in marriages in those countries after which the wives then
returned to El Salvador with their husbands. Unfortunately, the
census publications do not list the foreign-born by country of
origin, so that it is not possible to substantiate our guesses.

[3] Honduras, Dirección General de Estadística y Censo, Secretaría
de Economía y Hacienda, Censo General de Honduras, Características
Generales y Educativas de la Población, Abril, 1961, p. 39.

[4] O. Andrew Collver, Birth Rates in Latin America: New Estimates of Historical Trends and Fluctuations (Berkeley: Institute
of International Studies, University of California, 1965) [Research
Series No. 7], p. 122.

[5] A practical example of life table construction using Method B
is given in Appendix II.

X. GUATEMALA

Seven censuses have been taken in Guatemala. The first census in 1778 (during the colonial period) was not taken for demographic purposes; thus, the information it contains is not useful for this study. The 1880 census is not available for study, and we were only able to obtain information by age and sex from the remaining five censuses (except for the 1893 census, where information is not available by sex). Unfortunately, the census enumerations in 1893, 1921, and 1940 have been modified and distorted.[1] In addition, a graphical cohort analysis shows that censuses for 1921, 1940, and 1950 are of questionable completeness when compared with the 1964 census (see Fig. X-1).[2] What is more, death registration is not reliable, particularly for those under one year old, and the age group distribution of deaths for 1963-1965 is not yet available at the time of this study.[3]

As a consequence of all these factors, it is impossible to construct life tables using Method A. But, since fertility has been virtually constant in the past, and international migration has been insignificant, life tables can be constructed using Method B. To do so, the proportional age group distribution of the population and the natural growth rates for census years must be established.

PROPORTIONAL AGE GROUP DISTRIBUTION OF THE POPULATION

The proportional age group distribution of the population was evidently not affected by the official changes made in the results of the enumerated censuses of 1893, 1921, and 1940, because every age group was modified by the same percentage. However, age distributions were affected here (as in other countries) by the misreporting of age or by specific underenumeration in some age groups.

A graphical cohort analysis (Fig. X-1) shows that age declaration was far from accurate. Yet before any corrections could be made, a regrouping of ages for the years 1893 and 1921 was required in order to obtain the usual ten-year age groups beginning and ending with ages ending in zero and nine respectively. The age groups of these two censuses were not grouped in the usual way. Age groups in the 1921 census were, for instance, 7-13, 18-20, 21-29. The regrouping was made using 1950 census information, under the assumption that the proportion of the age group 7-13 pertaining to ages 7-9 in the 1921 census was the same as that observed for the same ages in the 1950 census.[4] (The same assumptions were made for age 20 in relation to age group 18-20.) The same procedure

FIGURE X-1

TEN-YEAR AGE GROUPS BY YEAR OF BIRTH, CENSUS POPULATION,

GUATEMALA, 1921-1964, MALE

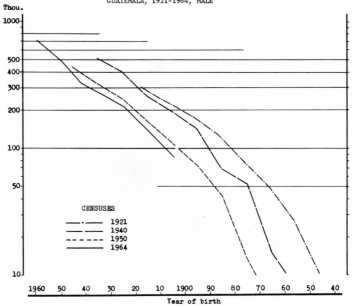

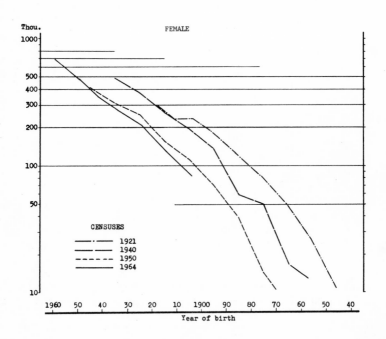

TABLE X-1

SMOOTHED PROPORTIONAL DISTRIBUTION OF THE POPULATION BY SEX AND FIVE-YEAR AGE GROUPS,
AGES 10-59, GUATEMALA, CENSUS YEARS

Age Groups	1893 Total	1921 Male	1921 Female	1940 Male	1940 Female	1950 Male	1950 Female	1964 Male	1964 Female
Total 10-59	1.000000 .652557	1.000000 .663535	1.000000 .678577	1.000000 .643986	1.000000 .646898	1.000000 .647658	1.000000 .654618	1.000000 .616045	1.000000 .626733
10-14	.117095	.116324	.113757	.119302	.117431	.122844	.122121	.127118	.129323
15-19	.106149	.105201	.105927	.103157	.103241	.106869	.107511	.105276	.107103
20-24	.094953	.093856	.097457	.087343	.089183	.091298	.093086	.082751	.084187
25-29	.082503	.082269	.086367	.075300	.077651	.077749	.079582	.070012	.071227
30-34	.068974	.070058	.073327	.064574	.067053	.064413	.065581	.059353	.060383
35-39	.056672	.058784	.061304	.055369	.057054	.053673	.054547	.052061	.052964
40-44	.043306	.046723	.048062	.046941	.046959	.043474	.044111	.042773	.043515
45-49	.034436	.037737	.038606	.038753	.037997	.035654	.036083	.031826	.032378
50-54	.027117	.029761	.030372	.030639	.029336	.028793	.029034	.025100	.025535
55-59	.021352	.022822	.023398	.022608	.020993	.022891	.022962	.019775	.020118

was used to modify 1893 census information. However, in this particular case, 1921 census information on age was used as a standard to separate the age groups 40-59 and 60-79 into decennial age groups. After regrouping, the age group distributions for all census years were smoothed according to the procedure explained in Appendix III, and the proportional distribution for ages 10-59 was calculated (Table X-1).

ESTIMATION OF NATURAL GROWTH RATES

The only intercensal growth rate which could be used to estimate natural growth rates is that of the period 1950-1964; growth rates for the previous intercensal periods are affected by the official "corrections" which were made in the earlier censuses.[5] Nevertheless, the intercensal growth rate for 1950-1954 should be considered with care, because the 1950 census seems to indicate some underenumeration when compared to the 1964 census.[6] Natural growth rates for the census years were estimated by considering previous estimates[7] and, once censuses were roughly corrected, intercensal geometric growth rates. The estimates of the natural growth rates are 11.2, 11.9, 16.1, 25.0, and 32.4 for 1893, 1921, 1940, 1950, and 1964 respectively.

CONSTRUCTION OF LIFE TABLES

Life tables were constructed by using Method B, the proportional age group distributions (Table X-1), and the estimates of the growth rates stated above. The set of United Nations $_5L_x$ values used in the quotient $\dfrac{C'(x,\ x+5)}{_5L_x}$ were those of level 10 for 1893 and 1921, and levels 20, 40, and 60 for 1940, 1950, and 1964 respectively. The slopes of the straight lines of adjustment and the growth rates used in the construction of life tables are shown in Table X-2. The life tables are given in Tables X-3 to X-7. A summary of the expectations of life at birth is presented in Table X-8.

TABLE X-2

GROWTH RATES USED IN THE CONSTRUCTION OF LIFE TABLES FOR GUATEMALA

				Slopes of the Straight Lines of Adjustment of the $\log_e \dfrac{C'(x,\ x+5)}{_nL_5}$		
		Growth Rates				
Year	Total	Male	Female	Male	Female	Average
1893	.0112					.013514
1921	.0119	.01180	.01200	.010534	.010813	.010674
1940	.0161	.01541	.01679	.014602	.016724	.015663
1950	.0250	.02463	.02537	.024070	.024789	.024430
1964	.0324	.03179	.03301	.031476	.033378	.032427

TABLE X-3

ABRIDGED LIFE TABLE, GUATEMALA, 1893
TOTAL

Age x n	l_x	$_nd_x$	$_np_x$	$_nq_x$	$_nL_x$	T_x	e_x
0 1	100,000	27,799	.72201	.27799	74,332	2,355,732	23.56
1 4	72,201	13,656	.81086	.18914	259,304	2,281,400	31.60
0 5	100,000	41,455	.58545	.41455	333,635	2,355,732	23.56
5 5	58,545	6,535	.88837	.11163	270,076	2,022,097	34.54
10 5	52,010	3,366	.93527	.06473	251,310	1,752,021	33.69
15 5	48,643	3,444	.92920	.07080	235,120	1,500,711	30.85
20 5	45,199	3,947	.91269	.08731	216,344	1,265,591	28.00
25 5	41,253	4,152	.89934	.10066	195,916	1,049,247	25.43
30 5	37,100	4,223	.88618	.11382	174,985	853,331	23.00
35 5	32,878	4,275	.86999	.13001	153,728	678,347	20.63
40 5	28,603	4,286	.85016	.14984	132,292	524,618	18.34
45 5	24,317	4,227	.82619	.17381	110,957	392,326	16.13
50 5	20,091	4,081	.79687	.20313	90,131	281,369	14.00
55 5	16,010	3,860	.75892	.24108	70,243	191,238	11.95
60 5	12,150	3,556	.70736	.29264	51,642	120,995	9.96
65 5	8,594	3,132	.63557	.36443	34,840	69,353	8.07
70 5	5,462	2,525	.53774	.46226	20,543	34,513	6.32
75 5	2,937	1,733	.41016	.58984	9,816	13,970	4.76
80 5	1,205	902	.25123	.74877	3,403	4,154	3.45
85 +	303	303	0.00000	1.00000	751	751	2.48

TABLE X-4

ABRIDGED LIFE TABLE, GUATEMALA, 1921
MALE

Age x n	l_x	$_n d_x$	$_n p_x$	$_n q_x$	$_n L_x$	T_x	e_x
0 1	100,000	28,442	.71558	.28442	73,575	2,558,854	25.59
1 4	71,558	12,749	.82184	.17816	258,551	2,485,279	34.73
0 5	100,000	41,191	.58809	.41191	332,126	2,558,854	25.59
5 5	58,809	5,508	.90635	.09365	274,062	2,226,728	37.86
10 5	53,301	2,391	.95514	.04486	260,236	1,952,666	36.63
15 5	50,910	2,568	.94955	.05045	248,745	1,692,430	33.24
20 5	48,342	3,220	.93338	.06662	233,960	1,443,685	29.86
25 5	45,121	3,578	.92070	.07930	216,786	1,209,725	26.81
30 5	41,543	3,860	.90709	.09291	198,270	992,939	23.90
35 5	37,683	4,246	.88732	.11268	178,089	794,669	21.09
40 5	33,437	4,667	.86042	.13958	155,786	616,580	18.44
45 5	28,770	4,918	.82905	.17095	131,616	460,794	16.02
50 5	23,852	4,905	.79434	.20566	106,913	329,178	13.80
55 5	18,946	4,686	.75266	.24734	82,823	222,265	11.73
60 5	14,260	4,278	.70000	.30000	60,286	139,442	9.78
65 5	9,982	3,716	.62777	.37223	40,244	79,156	7.93
70 5	6,267	2,953	.52873	.47127	23,375	38,911	6.21
75 5	3,313	1,983	.40163	.59837	10,963	15,536	4.69
80 5	1,331	996	.25126	.74874	3,730	4,574	3.44
85 +	334	334	0.00000	1.00000	844	844	2.52

TABLE X-4 (continued)

ABRIDGED LIFE TABLE, GUATEMALA, 1921
FEMALE

Age x n	l_x	$_nd_x$	$_np_x$	$_nq_x$	$_nL_x$	T_x	e_x
0 1	100,000	26,486	.73514	.26486	75,587	2,605,776	26.06
1 4	73,514	13,183	.82068	.17932	265,489	2,530,188	34.42
0 5	100,000	39,669	.60331	.39669	341,077	2,605,776	26.06
5 5	60,331	5,871	.90269	.09731	280,622	2,264,699	37.54
10 5	54,460	2,775	.94905	.05095	265,125	1,984,077	36.43
15 5	51,686	2,996	.94203	.05797	251,549	1,718,952	33.26
20 5	48,689	3,670	.92463	.07537	234,605	1,467,403	30.14
25 5	45,020	4,046	.91012	.08988	215,117	1,232,798	27.38
30 5	40,973	4,226	.89687	.10313	194,381	1,017,681	24.84
35 5	36,747	4,274	.88368	.11632	173,028	823,300	22.40
40 5	32,473	4,208	.87040	.12960	151,768	650,272	20.02
45 5	28,265	4,155	.85300	.14700	130,938	498,504	17.64
50 5	24,110	4,156	.82762	.17238	110,164	367,565	15.25
55 5	19,954	4,167	.79117	.20883	89,368	257,402	12.90
60 5	15,787	4,137	.73793	.26207	68,557	168,034	10.64
65 5	11,649	3,924	.66318	.33682	48,225	99,477	8.54
70 5	7,726	3,381	.56230	.43770	29,715	51,252	6.63
75 5	4,344	2,477	.42984	.57016	14,856	21,536	4.96
80 5	1,867	1,383	.25944	.74056	5,380	6,681	3.58
85 +	484	484	0.00000	1.00000	1,301	1,301	2.69

TABLE X-5

ABRIDGED LIFE TABLE, GUATEMALA, 1940
MALE

Age x n	l_x	$_nd_x$	$_np_x$	$_nq_x$	$_nL_x$	T_x	e_x
0 1	100,000	24,955	.75045	.24955	76,746	3,025,386	30.25
1 4	75,045	10,745	.85682	.14318	276,859	2,948,640	39.29
0 5	100,000	35,700	.64300	.35700	353,605	3,025,386	30.25
5 5	64,300	4,731	.92643	.07357	304,520	2,671,781	41.55
10 5	59,570	2,189	.96325	.03675	292,191	2,367,262	39.74
15 5	57,381	2,493	.95655	.04345	281,335	2,075,070	36.16
20 5	54,887	3,187	.94194	.05806	266,774	1,793,735	32.68
25 5	51,701	3,503	.93225	.06775	249,810	1,526,961	29.53
30 5	48,198	3,710	.92302	.07698	231,875	1,277,152	26.50
35 5	44,487	4,058	.90879	.09121	212,566	1,045,277	23.50
40 5	40,430	4,520	.88821	.11179	191,173	832,711	20.60
45 5	35,910	4,946	.86227	.13773	167,408	641,537	17.87
50 5	30,964	5,241	.83074	.16926	141,867	474,129	15.31
55 5	25,723	5,392	.79037	.20963	115,184	332,262	12.92
60 5	20,331	5,342	.73724	.26276	88,195	217,078	10.68
65 5	14,989	5,042	.66362	.33638	62,088	128,882	8.60
70 5	9,947	4,336	.56408	.43592	38,273	66,795	6.72
75 5	5,611	3,157	.43741	.56259	19,302	28,522	5.08
80 5	2,454	1,751	.28666	.71334	7,217	9,221	3.76
85 +	704	704	0.00000	1.00000	2,003	2,003	2.85

TABLE X-5 (continued)

ABRIDGED LIFE TABLE, GUATEMALA, 1940
FEMALE

Age x n	l_x	$_nd_x$	$_np_x$	$_nq_x$	$_nL_x$	T_x	e_x
0 1	100,000	23,080	.76920	.23080	78,671	3,046,269	30.46
1 4	76,920	11,176	.85471	.14529	283,502	2,967,598	38.58
0 5	100,000	34,256	.65744	.34256	362,173	3,046,269	30.46
5 5	65,744	5,205	.92083	.07917	310,474	2,684,097	40.83
10 5	60,539	2,705	.95532	.04468	295,792	2,373,623	39.21
15 5	57,834	3,023	.94772	.05228	282,246	2,077,831	35.93
20 5	54,811	3,705	.93241	.06759	265,111	1,795,585	32.76
25 5	51,106	4,026	.92122	.07878	245,540	1,530,474	29.95
30 5	47,080	4,126	.91237	.08763	225,117	1,284,934	27.29
35 5	42,955	4,135	.90374	.09626	204,405	1,059,816	24.67
40 5	38,820	4,112	.89408	.10592	183,803	855,411	22.04
45 5	34,708	4,187	.87936	.12064	163,179	671,608	19.35
50 5	30,521	4,384	.85636	.14364	141,788	508,429	16.66
55 5	26,137	4,659	.82175	.17825	119,247	366,641	14.03
60 5	21,478	4,946	.76972	.23028	95,204	247,394	11.52
65 5	16,532	5,031	.69569	.30431	70,046	152,190	9.21
70 5	11,501	4,656	.59518	.40482	45,457	82,144	7.14
75 5	6,845	3,666	.46445	.53555	24,239	36,687	5.36
80 5	3,179	2,224	.30058	.69942	9,600	12,448	3.92
85 +	956	956	0.00000	1.00000	2,848	2,848	2.98

TABLE X-6

ABRIDGED LIFE TABLE, GUATEMALA, 1950
MALE

Age x n	l_x	$_nd_x$	$_np_x$	$_nq_x$	$_nL_x$	T_x	e_x
0 1	100,000	18,989	.81011	.18989	82,199	3,994,386	39.94
1 4	81,011	7,487	.90759	.09241	307,783	3,912,187	48.29
0 5	100,000	26,475	.73525	.26475	389,983	3,994,386	39.94
5 5	73,525	3,310	.95498	.04502	355,796	3,604,403	49.02
10 5	70,215	1,623	.97689	.02311	346,968	3,248,607	46.27
15 5	68,592	2,035	.97034	.02966	338,526	2,901,639	42.30
20 5	66,557	2,710	.95928	.04072	326,296	2,563,112	38.51
25 5	63,847	2,956	.95371	.04629	311,838	2,236,817	35.03
30 5	60,891	3,069	.94959	.05041	296,893	1,924,979	31.61
35 5	57,822	3,359	.94191	.05809	280,959	1,628,087	28.16
40 5	54,463	3,860	.92912	.07088	263,052	1,347,128	24.73
45 5	50,603	4,525	.91057	.08943	242,154	1,084,077	21.42
50 5	46,077	5,296	.88505	.11495	217,664	841,922	18.27
55 5	40,781	6,127	.84975	.15025	189,123	624,258	15.31
60 5	34,654	6,924	.80019	.19981	156,449	435,135	12.56
65 5	27,730	7,509	.72921	.27079	120,183	278,686	10.05
70 5	20,221	7,424	.63285	.36715	82,190	158,503	7.84
75 5	12,797	6,261	.51071	.48929	47,245	76,313	5.96
80 5	6,535	4,144	.36596	.63404	20,988	29,068	4.45
85 +	2,392	2,392	0.00000	1.00000	8,081	8,081	3.38

TABLE X-6 (continued)

ABRIDGED LIFE TABLE, GUATEMALA, 1950
FEMALE

Age x n	l_x	$_n d_x$	$_n p_x$	$_n q_x$	$_n L_x$	T_x	e_x
0 1	100,000	17,165	.82835	.17165	84,021	4,151,668	41.52
1 4	82,835	7,533	.90906	.09094	315,018	4,067,647	49.11
0 5	100,000	24,698	.75302	.24698	399,038	4,151,668	41.52
5 5	75,302	3,441	.95431	.04569	364,364	3,752,630	49.83
10 5	71,861	1,833	.97449	.02551	354,719	3,388,266	47.15
15 5	70,028	2,262	.96770	.03230	345,101	3,033,547	43.32
20 5	67,766	2,936	.95667	.04333	331,797	2,688,446	39.67
25 5	64,830	3,226	.95024	.04976	316,121	2,356,649	36.35
30 5	61,603	3,296	.94650	.05350	299,798	2,040,528	33.12
35 5	58,307	3,350	.94255	.05745	283,191	1,740,730	29.85
40 5	54,958	3,494	.93643	.06357	266,187	1,457,539	26.52
45 5	51,464	3,856	.92508	.07492	247,995	1,191,351	23.15
50 5	47,608	4,452	.90648	.09352	227,338	943,356	19.81
55 5	43,156	5,311	.87693	.12307	203,153	716,018	16.59
60 5	37,845	6,423	.83028	.16972	173,948	512,865	13.55
65 5	31,422	7,507	.76108	.23892	138,993	338,917	10.79
70 5	23,914	8,026	.66438	.33562	99,598	199,924	8.36
75 5	15,888	7,315	.53957	.46043	60,219	100,326	6.31
80 5	8,573	5,225	.39049	.60951	28,307	40,106	4.68
85 +	3,348	3,348	0.00000	1.00000	11,799	11,799	3.52

TABLE X-7

ABRIDGED LIFE TABLE, GUATEMALA, 1964
MALE

Age x n	l_x	$_n d_x$	$_n p_x$	$_n q_x$	$_n L_x$	T_x	e_x
0 1	100,000	13,873	.86127	.13873	86,918	4,925,994	49.26
1 4	86,127	4,979	.94219	.05781	333,688	4,839,076	56.19
0 5	100,000	18,852	.81148	.18852	420,606	4,925,994	49.26
5 5	81,148	2,203	.97285	.02715	397,884	4,505,388	55.52
10 5	78,945	1,139	.98557	.01443	391,897	4,107,504	52.03
15 5	77,805	1,536	.98026	.01974	385,729	3,715,607	47.76
20 5	76,269	2,093	.97256	.02744	376,337	3,329,878	43.66
25 5	74,176	2,266	.96945	.03055	365,178	2,953,541	39.82
30 5	71,910	2,325	.96767	.03233	353,807	2,588,363	35.99
35 5	69,585	2,561	.96320	.03680	341,732	2,234,556	32.11
40 5	67,024	3,050	.95450	.04550	327,895	1,892,823	28.24
45 5	63,975	3,818	.94033	.05967	310,895	1,564,929	24.46
50 5	60,157	4,842	.91952	.08048	289,397	1,254,034	20.85
55 5	55,316	6,128	.88922	.11078	262,159	964,638	17.44
60 5	49,188	7,643	.84462	.15538	227,863	702,479	14.28
65 5	41,545	9,158	.77957	.22043	185,784	474,616	11.42
70 5	32,387	10,054	.68956	.31044	137,080	288,831	8.92
75 5	22,333	9,524	.57354	.42646	86,963	151,751	6.79
80 5	12,809	7,251	.43387	.56613	43,977	64,788	5.06
85 +	5,557	5,557	0.00000	1.00000	20,812	20,812	3.74

TABLE X-7 (continued)

ABRIDGED LIFE TABLE, GUATEMALA, 1964
FEMALE

Age x n	l_x	$_nd_x$	$_np_x$	$_nq_x$	$_nL_x$	T_x	e_x
0 1	100,000	10,895	.89105	.10895	89,803	5,326,889	53.27
1 4	89,105	4,479	.94974	.05026	346,752	5,237,086	58.77
0 5	100,000	15,374	.84626	.15374	436,555	5,326,889	53.27
5 5	84,626	2,221	.97375	.02625	415,579	4,890,334	57.79
10 5	82,405	1,350	.98362	.01638	408,684	4,474,754	54.30
15 5	81,055	1,662	.97950	.02050	401,531	4,066,071	50.16
20 5	79,394	2,099	.97357	.02643	391,913	3,664,540	46.16
25 5	77,295	2,269	.97065	.02935	380,812	3,272,626	42.34
30 5	75,027	2,314	.96915	.03085	369,374	2,891,815	38.54
35 5	72,712	2,403	.96695	.03305	357,623	2,522,441	34.69
40 5	70,309	2,635	.96252	.03748	345,164	2,164,818	30.79
45 5	67,674	3,119	.95391	.04609	330,964	1,819,654	26.89
50 5	64,555	3,879	.93991	.06009	313,622	1,488,690	23.06
55 5	60,676	5,006	.91750	.08250	291,710	1,175,068	19.37
60 5	55,670	6,658	.88041	.11959	262,942	883,359	15.87
65 5	49,012	8,759	.82130	.17870	224,648	620,416	12.66
70 5	40,253	10,707	.73402	.26598	175,629	395,769	9.83
75 5	29,547	11,242	.61951	.38049	119,274	220,139	7.45
80 5	18,304	9,412	.48581	.51419	65,748	100,865	5.51
85 +	8,893	8,893	0.00000	1.00000	35,117	35,117	3.95

NEW LIFE TABLES FOR LATIN AMERICAN POPULATIONS

TABLE X-8

LIFE EXPECTANCY, GUATEMALA
CENSUS YEARS

Year	Total*	Male	Female
1893	23.6		
1921	25.8	25.6	26.1
1940	30.4	30.3	30.5
1950	40.7	39.9	41.5
1964	51.3	49.3	53.3

*Simple arithmetic average of male and female.

NOTES

[1] República de Guatemala, Dirección General de Estadística, Sexto Censo de Población 1950, Guatemala, 1957, pp. i and ii.

[2] Data for 1964 are preliminary and were obtained directly from the Dirección General de Estadística of Guatemala.

[3] Our study was completed in the early months of 1967.

[4] Age distribution by individual age is given in the 1950 census, but not before.

[5] The effect of these corrections can easily be noted in Figure X-1, principally in the 1940 census.

[6] The diminution of the enumerated population in the cohorts in 1964 with respect to 1950 seems to be too small for a 14-year period, considering the high mortality rate of this country.

[7] O. Andrew Collver, Birth Rates in Latin America: New Estimates of Historical Trends and Fluctuations (Berkeley: Institute of International Studies, University of California, 1965) [Research Series No. 7], p. 128.

[8] An example of life table construction using Method B is given in Appendix II.

XI. HAITI

Haiti has taken only two censuses, in 1918-1919 and in 1950. Only the latter gives information by age and sex. Vital statistics have been poorly registered, and cannot be used in this study. Therefore, we constructed life tables for 1950 using Method B. The 1950 age group distributions of the population by sex[1] were smoothed according to the procedure explained in Appendix III. The results are given in Table XI-1. The growth rate for the total population was estimated at 20 per thousand for 1950.[2]

The United Nations set of $_5L_x$ values used in the quotient $\dfrac{C'(x, x+5)}{_5L_x}$ were those of level 40. The slopes of the straight lines of adjustment and the growth rates used for each sex are shown in Table XI-2. The life tables for each sex are given in Table XI-3,[3] and a summary of life expectancy is presented in Table XI-4.

TABLE XI-1

SMOOTHED PROPORTIONAL DISTRIBUTION OF THE POPULATION
BY SEX AND FIVE-YEAR AGE GROUPS, AGES 10-59, HAITI, 1950

Age Groups	Male	Female
Total	1.000000	1.000000
10-59	.683696	.687823
10-14	.118883	.112255
15-19	.105673	.104684
20-24	.092748	.096696
25-29	.081250	.086631
30-34	.069908	.075657
35-39	.060378	.064083
40-44	.051876	.051058
45-49	.043087	.041028
50-54	.034320	.031939
55-59	.025573	.023792

TABLE XI-2

GROWTH RATES USED IN THE CONSTRUCTION OF
THE LIFE TABLE FOR HAITI

Year	Growth Rates			Slopes of the Straight Lines of Adjustment of the $\log_e \dfrac{C'(x,x+5)}{{}_nL_5}$		
	Total	Male	Female	Male	Female	Average
1950	.0200	.01887	.02113	.019340	.021655	.020498

CHAPTER XI. HAITI

TABLE XI-3

ABRIDGED LIFE TABLE, HAITI, 1950
MALE

Age x n	l_x	$_nd_x$	$_np_x$	$_nq_x$	$_nL_x$	T_x	e_x
0 1	100,000	19,086	.80914	.19086	82,136	3,868,547	38.69
1 4	80,914	7,764	.90405	.09595	306,843	3,786,411	46.80
0 5	100,000	26,849	.73151	.26849	388,980	3,868,547	38.69
5 5	73,151	3,655	.95004	.04996	353,058	3,479,567	47.57
10 5	69,496	1,956	.97186	.02814	342,530	3,126,509	44.99
15 5	67,540	2,340	.96536	.03464	332,479	2,783,979	41.22
20 5	65,200	2,976	.95435	.04565	318,821	2,451,500	37.60
25 5	62,224	3,186	.94880	.05120	303,129	2,132,680	34.27
30 5	59,039	3,264	.94472	.05528	287,119	1,829,551	30.99
35 5	55,775	3,510	.93707	.06293	270,313	1,542,432	27.65
40 5	52,265	3,954	.92435	.07565	251,785	1,272,119	24.34
45 5	48,311	4,546	.90589	.09411	230,592	1,020,334	21.12
50 5	43,764	5,229	.88051	.11949	206,207	789,742	18.05
55 5	38,535	5,958	.84539	.15461	178,247	583,535	15.14
60 5	32,577	6,643	.79609	.20391	146,695	405,288	12.44
65 5	25,934	7,120	.72548	.27452	112,111	258,593	9.97
70 5	18,815	6,969	.62961	.37039	76,276	146,482	7.79
75 5	11,846	5,828	.50800	.49200	43,620	70,206	5.93
80 5	6,018	3,830	.36360	.63640	19,278	26,586	4.42
85 +	2,188	2,188	0.00000	1.00000	7,308	7,308	3.34

TABLE XI-3 (continued)

ABRIDGED LIFE TABLE, HAITI, 1950
FEMALE

Age x n	l_x	$_nd_x$	$_nP_x$	$_nq_x$	$_nL_x$	T_x	e_x
0 1	100,000	17,271	.82729	.17271	83,952	4,008,189	40.08
1 4	82,729	7,838	.90526	.09474	313,984	3,924,236	47.44
0 5	100,000	25,109	.74891	.25109	397,936	4,008189	40.08
5 5	74,891	3,819	.94900	.05100	361,354	3,610,252	48.21
10 5	71,071	2,196	.96910	.03090	349,849	3,248,898	45.71
15 5	68,875	2,592	.96237	.03763	338,486	2,899,049	42.09
20 5	66,283	3,221	.95140	.04860	323,642	2,560,564	38.63
25 5	63,062	3,469	.94500	.05500	306,651	2,236,921	35.47
30 5	59,593	3,500	.94128	.05872	289,213	1,930,271	32.39
35 5	56,093	3,514	.93735	.06265	271,686	1,641,058	29.26
40 5	52,579	3,614	.93126	.06874	253,965	1,369,371	26.04
45 5	48,965	3,918	.91998	.08002	235,303	1,115,407	22.78
50 5	45,047	4,438	.90148	.09852	214,513	880,103	19.54
55 5	40,609	5,194	.87210	.12790	190,635	665,590	16.39
60 5	35,415	6,173	.82570	.17430	162,330	474,955	13.41
65 5	29,242	7,109	.75690	.24310	128,995	312,624	10.69
70 5	22,133	7,509	.66073	.33927	91,924	183,630	8.30
75 5	14,624	6,778	.53649	.46351	55,273	91,706	6.27
80 5	7,846	4,804	.38770	.61230	25,838	36,433	4.64
85 +	3,042	3,042	0.00000	1.00000	10,595	10,595	3.48

TABLE XI-4

LIFE EXPECTANCY, HAITI
1950

Year	Total*	Male	Female
1950	39.4	38.7	40.1

*Simple arithmetic average of male and female.

NOTES

[1]United Nations, Demographic Yearbook, 1955, Table 10.

[2]Jacques St. Surin has estimated the growth rate for the period 1960-1965 at 22.91 per thousand (Haiti, Départment des Finances et des Affaires Économiques, Institute Haitien de Statistique, Guide Économique de la République d'Haiti, Port au Prince, July, 1964, p. 26). Another piece of research we considered was United Nations, Methods of Appraisal of Quality of Basic Data for Population Estimates, Manual II (ST/SOA/Series A, Population Studies No. 23) (New York, 1955), pp. 59-62.

[3]An example of life table construction using Method B is given in Appendix II.

XII. HONDURAS

In this century Honduras has taken nine censuses. Information for the total population is available in thirteen censuses,
the first dating back as early as 1791;[1] however, we find age
group distribution of the population by sex only since the 1930
census. The life tables which have been constructed for this
study use information from the 1930, 1940, 1950, and 1961 censuses.
We did not consider the 1935 and 1945 censuses because the variation of mortality before 1950 was very small.

Vital statistics, as they are registered, are not reliable, and their use for the construction of life tables is not
recommended. However, net international migration has been insignificant, and fertility can be considered virtually constant
throughout the period under consideration (1930-1961).[2] Thus,
life tables for Honduras could be constructed using Method B.

To supply the information needed for Method B, we had to
obtain the proportional age group distribution of the population
10-59 years old, as well as estimates of the natural growth rates
for the years for which life tables were to be constructed.

PROPORTIONAL AGE GROUP DISTRIBUTION OF THE POPULATION

A graphical cohort analysis (Fig. XII-1) shows that the
various censuses being considered are not comparable in completeness. In addition, the analysis shows that age group distribution
for 1950 presents a strange pattern when compared with that of the
previous and following censuses; there appears to have been some
underenumeration in the younger ages and some overenumeration in
the older ages. These errors in enumeration are confirmed by
comparing the mean age of the populations for each sex in all censuses (Table XII-1).

TABLE XII-1

MEAN AGE OF THE CENSUS POPULATION, HONDURAS, 1930-1961

	1930	1935	1940	1945	1950	1961
Male	21.7	22.5	22.6	22.7	24.0	21.0
Female	22.5	23.0	23.0	23.0	24.8	21.0

The increase of the mean age in the 1950 census is not acceptable. There is no indication that fertility during 1946-1950

150

FIGURE XII-1

TEN-YEAR AGE GROUPS BY YEAR OF BIRTH, CENSUS POPULATION,
HONDURAS, 1930-1961, MALE

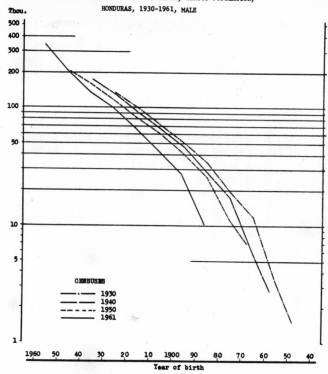

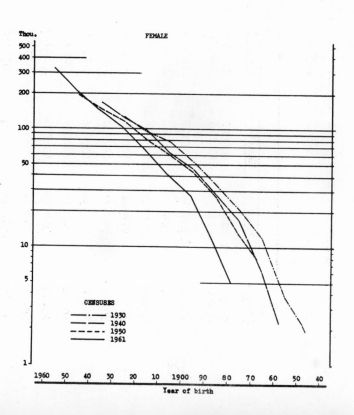

FEMALE

TABLE XII-2

SMOOTHED PROPORTIONAL DISTRIBUTION OF THE POPULATION BY SEX AND FIVE-YEAR AGE GROUPS,
AGES 10-59, HONDURAS, CENSUS YEARS

Age Groups	1930 Male	1930 Female	1940 Male	1940 Female	1950 Male	1950 Female	1961 Male	1961 Female
Total 10-59	1.000000 .645762	1.000000 .656341	1.000000 .646545	1.000000 .649457	1.000000 .619915	1.000000 .628238	1.000000 .597922	1.000000 .608916
10-14	.124194	.120527	.123144	.120585	.124019	.122413	.124986	.123331
15-19	.106947	.106784	.105836	.105487	.103959	.104668	.102678	.103441
20-24	.090331	.093214	.089211	.090774	.084967	.087646	.081734	.084569
25-29	.076866	.080507	.075996	.077987	.071314	.074244	.067606	.070779
30-34	.064431	.067817	.063860	.065599	.059851	.062160	.056484	.059137
35-39	.053948	.056459	.053940	.055092	.050362	.051912	.047250	.049188
40-44	.044110	.044789	.044935	.044923	.041835	.042129	.039015	.039734
45-49	.035780	.036059	.037049	.036765	.034479	.034365	.032118	.032415
50-54	.028096	.028394	.029696	.029405	.027683	.027417	.025847	.025958
55-59	.021059	.021791	.022878	.022840	.021446	.021284	.020204	.020364

was significantly low enough to increase the mean age of the population in 1950. Neither was migration significant during the 1945-1950 period--the foreign-born population consisted of 23,589 males and 15,436 females in 1945, and 19,168 males and 13,696 females in 1950.[3] Therefore, if fertility was unchanged and international migration was not significant, we must conclude that the age distribution for each sex, as given in the 1950 census, was not accurate. Thus we modified the proportional age group distribution 10-59 for 1950 somewhat by taking into account the age group distributions of the previous and subsequent censuses. Then we smoothed the age group distributions according to the procedure explained in Appendix III. The distributions for each sex can be seen in Table XII-2.[4]

ESTIMATION OF NATURAL GROWTH RATES

By taking different intercensal intervals, different annual growth rates were obtained for the same partial periods.[5] Then, after an analysis of these growth rates and existing estimates,[6] the following natural growth rates were calculated: 21.0, 22.0, 26.7, and 33.0 per thousand for 1930. 1940, 1950, and 1961 respectively.

CONSTRUCTION OF LIFE TABLES

The life tables for 1930, 1940, 1950, and 1961 were constructed using Method B, the proportional age group distribution from Table XII-2, and the estimates of the natural growth rates given above. The United Nations set of $_5L_x$ values used in the quotient $\frac{C'(x, x+5)}{_5L_x}$ were levels 30, 35, 45, and 65 for the years 1930-1940, 1950, and 1961 respectively. The slopes of the straight lines of adjustment and the growth rates used for each sex are in Table XII-3. The life tables obtained are given in Tables XII-4 to XII-7.[7] A summary of the life expectancy for each sex and year is presented in Table XII-8.

TABLE XII-3

GROWTH RATES USED IN THE CONSTRUCTION OF LIFE TABLES FOR HONDURAS

| Year | Growth Rates | | | Slopes of the Straight Lines of Adjustment of the $\log_e \frac{C'(x, x+5)}{_nL_5}$ | | |
	Total	Male	Female	Male	Female	Average
1930	.0210	.02090	.02110	.021929	.022136	.022033
1940	.0220	.02161	.02239	.021662	.022436	.022049
1950	.0267	.02607	.02733	.025945	.027201	.026573
1961	.0330	.03249	.03351	.031684	.032685	.032185

TABLE XII-4

ABRIDGED LIFE TABLE, HONDURAS, 1930
MALE

Age x n	l_x	$_nd_x$	$_np_x$	$_nq_x$	$_nL_x$	T_x	e_x
0 1	100,000	22,018	.77982	.22018	79,458	3,339,830	33.40
1 4	77,982	9,410	.87933	.12067	291,572	3,260,373	41.81
0 5	100,000	31,428	.68572	.31428	371,029	3,339,830	33.40
5 5	68,572	4,493	.93447	.06553	327,332	2,968,801	43.29
10 5	64,079	2,399	.96256	.03744	314,272	2,641,469	41.22
15 5	61,680	2,730	.95574	.04426	302,207	2,327,197	37.73
20 5	58,950	3,360	.94300	.05700	286,599	2,024,991	34.35
25 5	55,590	3,570	.93578	.06422	269,004	1,738,392	31.27
30 5	52,020	3,656	.92973	.07027	251,047	1,469,388	28.25
35 5	48,364	3,895	.91947	.08053	232,291	1,218,340	25.19
40 5	44,469	4,289	.90354	.09646	211,922	986,049	22.17
45 5	40,180	4,744	.88194	.11806	189,322	774,127	19.27
50 5	35,436	5,182	.85377	.14623	164,501	584,806	16.50
55 5	30,254	5,568	.81597	.18403	137,574	420,305	13.89
60 5	24,687	5,814	.76449	.23551	109,004	282,731	11.45
65 5	18,873	5,811	.69209	.30791	79,765	173,726	9.21
70 5	13,062	5,298	.59441	.40559	51,518	93,961	7.19
75 5	7,764	4,110	.47059	.52941	27,604	42,444	5.47
80 5	3,654	2,473	.32326	.67674	11,212	14,840	4.06
85 +	1,181	1,181	0.00000	1.00000	3,629	3,629	3.07

TABLE XII-4 (continued)

ABRIDGED LIFE TABLE, HONDURAS, 1930
FEMALE

Age x n	l_x	$_n d_x$	$_n p_x$	$_n q_x$	$_n L_x$	T_x	e_x
0 1	100,000	20,099	.79901	.20099	81,390	3,451,871	34.52
1 4	79,901	9,562	.88032	.11968	298,964	3,370,480	42.18
0 5	100,000	29,661	.70339	.29661	380,355	3,451,871	34.52
5 5	70,339	4,701	.93316	.06684	335,620	3,071,516	43.67
10 5	65,638	2,674	.95927	.04073	321,425	2,735,896	41.68
15 5	62,964	3,028	.95192	.04808	307,856	2,414,471	38.35
20 5	59,936	3,666	.93883	.06117	290,800	2,106,615	35.15
25 5	56,270	3,922	.93031	.06969	271,567	1,815,815	32.27
30 5	52,348	3,950	.92455	.07545	251,856	1,544,248	29.50
35 5	48,398	3,924	.91892	.08108	232,146	1,292,393	26.70
40 5	44,474	3,932	.91159	.08841	212,569	1,060,247	23.84
45 5	40,542	4,099	.89890	.10110	192,643	847,677	20.91
50 5	36,444	4,435	.87830	.12170	171,376	655,035	17.97
55 5	32,009	4,920	.84629	.15371	148,114	483,659	15.11
60 5	27,089	5,502	.79688	.20312	122,082	335,545	12.39
65 5	21,586	5,933	.72515	.27485	93,297	213,463	9.89
70 5	15,653	5,844	.62664	.37336	63,395	120,166	7.68
75 5	9,809	4,911	.49932	.50068	35,880	56,771	5.79
80 5	4,898	3,215	.34366	.65634	15,460	20,891	4.27
85 +	1,683	1,683	0.00000	1.00000	5,430	5,430	3.23

TABLE XII-5

ABRIDGED LIFE TABLE, HONDURAS, 1940
MALE

Age x n	l_x	$_nd_x$	$_np_x$	$_nq_x$	$_nL_x$	T_x	e_x
0 1	100,000	20,392	.79608	.20392	80,927	3,684,938	36.85
1 4	79,608	8,357	.89503	.10497	300,316	3,604,011	45.27
0 5	100,000	28,748	.71252	.28748	381,243	3,684,938	36.85
5 5	71,252	3,834	.94619	.05381	342,781	3,303,695	46.37
10 5	67,418	1,962	.97090	.02910	332,106	2,960,913	43.92
15 5	65,456	2,347	.96415	.03585	322,069	2,628,807	40.16
20 5	63,109	3,017	.95220	.04780	308,284	2,306,738	36.55
25 5	60,093	3,256	.94583	.05417	292,314	1,998,454	33.26
30 5	56,837	3,361	.94086	.05914	275,885	1,706,141	30.02
35 5	53,476	3,637	.93198	.06802	258,523	1,430,255	26.75
40 5	49,839	4,105	.91763	.08237	239,289	1,171,732	23.51
45 5	45,734	4,685	.89755	.10245	217,333	932,443	20.39
50 5	41,048	5,305	.87075	.12925	192,382	715,111	17.42
55 5	35,743	5,926	.83422	.16578	164,286	522,729	14.62
60 5	29,817	6,452	.78363	.21637	133,254	358,443	12.02
65 5	23,366	6,735	.71174	.28826	100,100	225,188	9.64
70 5	16,630	6,412	.61441	.38559	66,648	125,088	7.52
75 5	10,218	5,199	.49119	.50881	37,052	58,440	5.72
80 5	5,019	3,286	.34533	.65467	15,774	21,388	4.26
85 +	1,733	1,733	0.00000	1.00000	5,614	5,614	3.24

TABLE XII-5 (continued)

ABRIDGED LIFE TABLE, HONDURAS, 1940
FEMALE

Age x n	l_x	$_nd_x$	$_np_x$	$_nq_x$	$_nL_x$	T_x	e_x
0 1	100,000	18,591	.81409	.18591	82,736	3,809,074	38.09
1 4	81,409	8,465	.89602	.10398	307,327	3,726,338	45.77
0 5	100,000	27,055	.72945	.27055	390,063	3,809,074	38.09
5 5	72,945	4,005	.94510	.05490	350,807	3,419,011	46.87
10 5	68,940	2,204	.96802	.03198	339,155	3,068,204	44.51
15 5	66,735	2,618	.96076	.03924	327,764	2,729,049	40.89
20 5	64,117	3,304	.94847	.05153	312,638	2,401,285	37.45
25 5	60,813	3,592	.94093	.05907	295,114	2,088,647	34.35
30 5	57,221	3,646	.93628	.06372	276,996	1,793,532	31.34
35 5	53,574	3,665	.93160	.06840	258,708	1,516,537	28.31
40 5	49,910	3,743	.92500	.07500	240,272	1,257,829	25.20
45 5	46,166	4,016	.91301	.08699	221,046	1,017,557	22.04
50 5	42,150	4,497	.89331	.10669	199,855	796,510	18.90
55 5	37,653	5,182	.86237	.13763	175,829	596,655	15.85
60 5	32,471	6,037	.81408	.18592	147,854	420,826	12.96
65 5	26,434	6,785	.74333	.25667	115,618	272,972	10.33
70 5	19,649	6,966	.64549	.35451	80,715	157,353	8.01
75 5	12,683	6,099	.51916	.48084	47,231	76,638	6.04
80 5	6,585	4,173	.36620	.63380	21,251	29,407	4.47
85 +	2,411	2,411	0.00000	1.00000	8,156	8,156	3.38

TABLE XII-6

ABRIDGED LIFE TABLE, HONDURAS, 1950
MALE

Age x n	l_x	$_nd_x$	$_np_x$	$_nq_x$	$_nL_x$	T_x	e_x
0 1	100,000	17,703	.82297	.17703	83,388	4,182,934	41.83
1 4	82,297	6,899	.91617	.08383	314,218	4,099,546	49.81
0 5	100,000	24,602	.75398	.24602	397,606	4,182,934	41.83
5 5	75,398	3,133	.95845	.04155	365,938	3,785,328	50.20
10 5	72,265	1,615	.97765	.02235	357,260	3,419,390	47.32
15 5	70,651	2,022	.97139	.02861	348,822	3,062,130	43.34
20 5	68,629	2,663	.96120	.03880	336,754	2,713,308	39.54
25 5	65,966	2,880	.95635	.04365	322,607	2,376,554	36.03
30 5	63,087	2,965	.95300	.04700	308,111	2,053,947	32.56
35 5	60,121	3,223	.94639	.05361	292,771	1,745,836	29.04
40 5	56,898	3,695	.93505	.06495	275,622	1,453,065	25.54
45 5	53,203	4,369	.91788	.08212	255,571	1,177,442	22.13
50 5	48,834	5,196	.89360	.10640	231,741	921,871	18.88
55 5	43,638	6,119	.85977	.14023	203,495	690,131	15.82
60 5	37,519	7,067	.81165	.18835	170,537	486,635	12.97
65 5	30,452	7,854	.74207	.25793	133,070	316,098	10.38
70 5	22,597	7,971	.64726	.35274	92,829	183,028	8.10
75 5	14,626	6,922	.52673	.47327	54,766	90,199	6.17
80 5	7,704	4,751	.38335	.61665	25,183	35,433	4.60
85 +	2,953	2,953	0.00000	1.00000	10,249	10,249	3.47

TABLE XII-6 (continued)

ABRIDGED LIFE TABLE, HONDURAS, 1950
FEMALE

Age x n	l_x	$_nd_x$	$_np_x$	$_nq_x$	$_nL_x$	T_x	e_x
0 1	100,000	15,852	.84148	.15852	85,231	4,363,454	43.63
1 4	84,148	6,903	.91797	.08203	321,653	4,278,223	50.84
0 5	100,000	22,755	.77245	.22755	406,884	4,363,454	43.63
5 5	77,245	3,243	.95802	.04198	374,923	3,956,570	51.22
10 5	74,002	1,807	.97558	.02442	365,501	3,581,647	48.40
15 5	72,195	2,217	.96929	.03071	356,008	3,216,147	44.55
20 5	69,978	2,836	.95947	.04053	343,076	2,860,139	40.87
25 5	67,142	3,085	.95405	.04595	328,017	2,517,062	37.49
30 5	64,057	3,131	.95112	.04888	312,467	2,189,046	34.17
35 5	60,926	3,180	.94780	.05220	296,714	1,876,579	30.80
40 5	57,746	3,344	.94210	.05790	280,526	1,579,865	27.36
45 5	54,402	3,735	.93135	.06865	263,007	1,299,339	23.88
50 5	50,668	4,364	.91388	.08612	242,879	1,036,332	20.45
55 5	46,304	5,285	.88587	.11413	219,014	793,453	17.14
60 5	41,020	6,517	.84112	.15888	189,683	574,439	14.00
65 5	34,502	7,801	.77391	.22609	153,822	384,756	11.15
70 5	26,702	8,573	.67895	.32105	112,344	230,935	8.65
75 5	18,129	8,045	.55624	.44376	69,665	118,591	6.54
80 5	10,084	5,939	.41109	.58891	33,929	48,926	4.85
85 +	4,145	4,145	0.00000	1.00000	14,997	14,997	3.62

TABLE XII-7

ABRIDGED LIFE TABLE, HONDURAS, 1961
MALE

Age x n	l_x	$_nd_x$	$_np_x$	$_nq_x$	$_nL_x$	T_x	e_x
0 1	100,000	12,553	.87447	.12553	88,126	5,263,374	52.63
1 4	87,447	4,231	.95161	.04839	340,562	5,175,248	59.18
0 5	100,000	16,784	.83216	.16784	428,688	5,263,374	52.63
5 5	83,216	1,735	.97915	.02085	409,667	4,834,686	58.10
10 5	81,481	811	.99005	.00995	405,412	4,425,019	54.31
15 5	80,670	1,194	.98520	.01480	400,873	4,019,607	49.83
20 5	79,476	1,719	.97837	.02163	393,298	3,618,735	45.53
25 5	77,757	1,893	.97565	.02435	384,026	3,225,436	41.48
30 5	75,864	1,964	.97411	.02589	374,484	2,841,410	37.45
35 5	73,900	2,209	.97011	.02989	364,193	2,466,926	33.38
40 5	71,691	2,719	.96208	.03792	352,076	2,102,733	29.33
45 5	68,973	3,540	.94868	.05132	336,626	1,750,657	25.38
50 5	65,433	4,657	.92883	.07117	316,305	1,414,031	21.61
55 5	60,776	6,098	.89966	.10034	289,658	1,097,725	18.06
60 5	54,678	7,858	.85629	.14371	254,961	808,067	14.78
65 5	46,820	9,709	.79263	.20737	211,026	553,107	11.81
70 5	37,111	10,984	.70402	.29598	158,626	342,081	9.22
75 5	26,127	10,728	.58940	.41060	103,029	183,455	7.02
80 5	15,399	8,448	.45138	.54862	53,721	80,426	5.22
85 +	6,951	6,951	0.00000	1.00000	26,705	26,705	3.84

CHAPTER XII. HONDURAS

TABLE XII-7 (continued)

ABRIDGED LIFE TABLE, HONDURAS, 1961
FEMALE

Age x n	l_x	$_nd_x$	$_np_x$	$_nq_x$	$_nL_x$	T_x	e_x
0 1	100,000	10,780	.89220	.10780	89,871	5,556,751	55.57
1 4	89,220	4,090	.95416	.04584	347,989	5,466,880	61.27
0 5	100,000	14,870	.85130	.14870	437,859	5,556,751	55.57
5 5	85,130	1,736	.97960	.02040	419,314	5,118,892	60.13
10 5	83,394	874	.98951	.01049	414,824	4,699,577	56.35
15 5	82,519	1,208	.98536	.01464	410,002	4,284,753	51.92
20 5	81,311	1,676	.97939	.02061	402,576	3,874,752	47.65
25 5	79,635	1,875	.97646	.02354	393,512	3,472,176	43.60
30 5	77,760	1,948	.97495	.02505	383,977	3,078,663	39.59
35 5	75,813	2,067	.97274	.02726	373,985	2,694,687	35.54
40 5	73,746	2,340	.96828	.03172	363,116	2,320,702	31.47
45 5	71,406	2,883	.95962	.04038	350,260	1,957,586	27.41
50 5	68,523	3,732	.94554	.05446	333,893	1,607,325	23.46
55 5	64,791	4,990	.92299	.07701	312,423	1,273,432	19.65
60 5	59,801	6,837	.88567	.11433	283,297	961,010	16.07
65 5	52,964	9,205	.82620	.17380	243,487	677,712	12.80
70 5	43,759	11,448	.73839	.26161	191,496	434,226	9.92
75 5	32,311	12,171	.62330	.37670	130,828	242,730	7.51
80 5	20,140	10,286	.48929	.51071	72,549	111,902	5.56
85 +	9,854	9,854	0.00000	1.00000	39,353	39,353	3.99

161

TABLE XII-8

LIFE EXPECTANCY, HONDURAS
CENSUS YEARS

Year	Total*	Male	Female
1930	34.0	33.4	34.5
1940	37.5	36.8	38.1
1950	42.7	41.8	43.6
1960	54.1	52.6	55.6

*Simple arithmetic average of male and female.

NOTES

[1] Honduras, Dirección General de Estadística y Censos, Resumen General del Censo de Población 1950, Tegucigalpa, 1952, p. 13.

[2] Honduras, Dirección General de Estadística y Censos, Secretaria de Economía y Hacienda, Anuario Estadístico 1962, Tegucigalpa, Julio, 1963.

[3] Honduras, Dirección General de Estadística y Censos, Resumen General del Censo de Población 1945, Tegucigalpa, 1947, p. 10, and Resumen General del Censo de Población 1950, Tegucigalpa, 1952, p. 16.

[4] The population age distribution data were taken from: Honduras, Dirección General de Estadística y Censos, Secretaria de Economía y Hacienda, Censo Nacional de Honduras, Características Generales Educativas de la Población, Abril, 1961, Tegucigalpa, 1964, p. 5, and Resumen General del Censo de Población 1945, Tegucigalpa, 1947, p. 8 (where the 1940 age group distribution is published); for the 1930 age group distribution see U. S. Department of Commerce, Bureau of the Census, U.S. Census Summary, 1945, Table 7, p. 58.

[5] We considered, for example, the periods 1930-1935, 1930-1940, 1935-1940, etc.

[6] O. Andrew Collver, Birth Rates in Latin America: New Estimates of Historical Trends and Fluctuations (Berkeley: Institute of International Studies, University of California, 1965) [Research Series No. 7], p. 136.

[7] In Appendix II, we use the case of Honduras, 1940, for an example of life table construction by Method B.

XIII. MEXICO

Mexico is one of the few Latin American countries with a regular censal history. The country has had eight national censuses from 1895 through 1960, all of them taken in years ending in zero, except for the first, in 1895, and the 1921 census. A census was not taken in 1920 because civil war during the decade 1910-1920 prevented it. Some vital statistics are available for the period 1877-1910,[1] but there is a complete lack of information for the period 1910-1921. In 1922, after the Civil War, the statistical series again began to be published.

Life tables for the period preceding the Civil War were constructed using Method B, because vital statistics before 1922 are unreliable, and because the completeness of the censuses-- principally that of 1895--is questionable (see Fig. XIII-1).[2] For the period following the Civil War, however, Method A was applied, because the available information was sufficient to permit a complete evaluation of the statistics.

LIFE TABLES FOR 1895, 1900, AND 1910; CONSTRUCTION BY METHOD B

To construct life tables using Method B, we needed the proportional age group distribution of the population aged 10-59 by sex, and estimates of the natural growth rates for 1895, 1900, and 1910.

Proportional Age Group Distribution of the Population

Age groups in the three censuses taken before the Civil War differ in form from those of subsequent censuses. In the first three censuses age groups do not begin with ages ending in 0 or 5, as is the practice at the present time; they end in ages ending in 0 and 5.[3] Because the tendency of the population to report ages ending in 0 and 5 has the effect of reducing rather than increasing ages, age groups ending in 0 and 5 can cause more distortion from the actual age group distribution than grouping beginning with ages 0 and 5.[4]

Therefore, before smoothing the age group distribution, we attempted regrouping ages into the standard groups. To do this, it was necessary to estimate the total number of persons enumerated in each age ending in zero--including, of course, those who are not actually at those ages as well as those who are.

In order to estimate the number of such persons, we used the 1950 census, which was the first Mexican census publishing an age distribution of the population by individual ages. From 1950 census information we calculated the percentages of persons declar-

163

FIGURE XIII-1

TEN-YEAR AGE GROUPS BY YEAR OF BIRTH, CENSUS POPULATION, MEXICO, 1895-1960, MALE

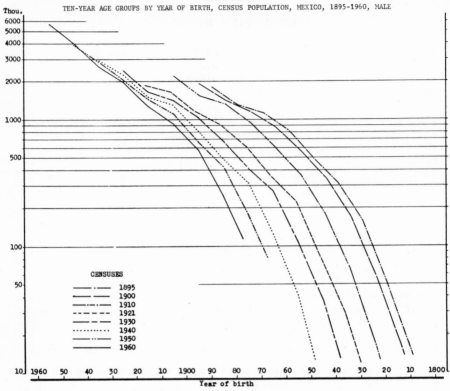

FEMALE

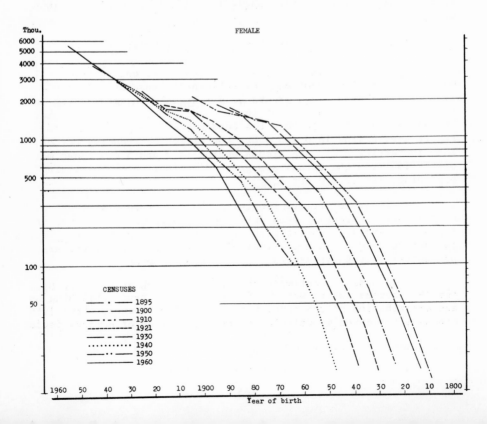

ing an age ending in zero within each ten-year age group ending in
a zero.[5] Assuming the same percentages for the 1895, 1900, and
1910 censuses, we estimated the number of persons declaring ages
ending in zero.[6] After regrouping, the ten-year age groups were
smoothed and separated into five-year age groups according to the
procedure explained in Appendix III. Because the absolute numbers
of these age group distributions were needed to make a cohort
analysis, the population catalogued as "unknown" was spread proportionately among all age groups. The six proportional age group
distributions for ages 10-59 for these three years are presented
in Table XIII-1.

TABLE XIII-1

SMOOTHED PROPORTIONAL DISTRIBUTION OF THE POPULATION BY
SEX AND FIVE-YEAR AGE GROUPS, AGES 10-59, MEXICO, CENSUS YEARS

| Age | 1895 | | 1900 | | 1910 | |
Groups	Male	Female	Male	Female	Male	Female
Total	1.000000	1.000000	1.000000	1.000000	1.000000	1.000000
10-59	.663023	.681081	.664163	.681574	.656162	.672734
10-14	.114731	.115256	.115982	.115929	.116355	.115747
15-19	.102455	.105890	.102942	.106122	.102788	.105545
20-24	.090384	.096196	.090243	.096023	.089621	.095135
25-29	.079636	.084957	.079250	.084682	.078388	.083678
30-34	.069536	.072459	.069028	.072259	.068103	.071331
35-39	.059549	.061102	.059222	.060975	.058124	.059953
40-44	.049063	.049131	.049298	.049195	.047932	.047894
45-49	.040411	.039938	.040708	.040032	.039394	.038831
50-54	.031979	.031518	.032207	.031613	.031057	.030630
55-59	.025279	.024634	.025383	.024744	.024400	.023990

Estimation of Natural Growth Rate

The natural growth rate for the period 1895-1910 could
have been calculated easily, if vital statistics had been reliable.
Unfortunately, this is not the case. There is obvious under-
registration in the birth statistics for these years, and their
use is not recommended;[7] also, an examination of information for
the first three censuses and intercensal vital statistics reveals
inconsistencies which make their use as recorded inadvisable.[8]
Thus to estimate the natural growth rate it was necessary to evaluate the completeness of the censuses, using a cohort analysis.
For such an analysis the number of births during the 1895-1910
period was not needed; it was necessary, however, to examine the

deaths and net international migration for the cohorts during the two intercensal periods.

Deaths. For a cohort analysis we needed to know the number of deaths during each intercensal period pertaining to the cohorts aged 0 and over and 5 and over at the beginning of each intercensal period. To establish these cohort deaths, it was necessary to obtain the age distribution by individual ages for the ages 0-9 for the period 1895-1910 and for ages 10-14 for 1905-1910. The following death statistics were available: total deaths and deaths under one year for the period 1896-1900; deaths in the age groups 0-5 and 6-15 for the period 1896-1900; and deaths in the ages 0-6 and 7-14 for 1901 and 1902.[9]

First, we estimated deaths in the age groups 1-4, 5-9, and 10-14, by comparing the trend of the proportion of deaths occurring in these age groups to the trend of total deaths during the period 1896-1902. We broke down these age groups into individual ages using a semilogarithmic graph of the accumulated number of deaths.[10] The separation factors used to obtain the deaths belonging to the cohorts 0 and over and 5 and over, enumerated at the beginning of each intercensal period, were 1/3 for deaths under one year, and 1/2 for the other ages. The results obtained are given in Table XIII-2.

TABLE XIII-2

REGISTERED DEATHS BY COHORTS, MEXICO, 1895-1911
(thousands)

| Period | Cohort Ages at the Beginning of the Period | |
	Age 0 and Over	Age 5 and Over
1895-1901	1,391.5	1,142.1
1901-1911	2,666.5	2,328.3

International Migration. To estimate the amount of international migration during the period 1895-1910, it was necessary to use census information, because data from registers were first published in 1909. The foreign-born population enumerated in Mexican censuses was used to estimate immigration, and U.S. migratory statistics of Mexicans entering the U.S. were used to estimate emigration.[11] To estimate immigration, the total number of foreign-born and the number of foreign-born aged 5 and over enumerated in the censuses of 1895 and 1900 were multiplied by the corresponding intercensal survival ratio for the total population.[12] Since ages of the foreign-born were not available, it was necessary for us to estimate the foreign-born population aged 5 and over in 1895 and 1900, aged 10 and over in 1900 and 1910, and aged 15 and over in 1910. We did so using the age distribution of foreign populations enumerated in other countries.[13] We assumed the proportion of foreign-born in the specific ages to be the same for all three

years. The estimates we obtained are: 98.0 percent for ages 5 and
over, 93.5 percent for ages 10 and over, and 84.0 percent for ages
15 and over. We calculated the net immigrant movement by comparing the estimates of the foreign-born enumerated in the censuses
with the survivors from the previous census (Table XIII-3, col. 3).

The number of Mexicans entering the United States was 746
for the period 1896-1900, and 49,642 for the period 1901-1910.[14]
The same age distribution used for immigrants was used for these
emigrants (Table XIII-3, col. 4). Thus to establish the net international migration, we obtained the difference between net immigration and emigration estimates (Table XIII-3, col. 5).

TABLE XIII-3

NET MIGRATION WITHIN COHORTS, MEXICO, 1895-1911
(thousands)

Period	Cohort Age at the Beginning of the Period	Net Immigration	Net Emigration	Net Migration (3)-(4)
(1)	(2)	(3)	(4)	(5)
1896-1900	0 and over	10.5	.7	9.8
	5 and over	9.8	.7	9.1
1901-1910	0 and over	63.2	47.4	15.8
	5 and over	54.5	44.0	10.2

Evaluation of Censuses by Cohort Analysis. Once we
obtained information on deaths and migration, we made a retrospec-
tive cohort analysis of census figures. Census populations were
shifted to the end of each census year[15]; then, the expected populations for 1900 and 1895 were obtained (Table XIII-4) by adding
the population cohorts enumerated in 1910 and 1900, and the per-
tinent death and net migration. Our analysis of Table XIII-4
begins with column 3. By taking the population aged 10 and over
in 1911, adding to this figure the deaths during the period 1901-
1911, and subtracting from that sum the net migration pertaining
to the cohorts over the period, we can establish an expected
population for January 1, 1901. This expected population turns
out to be 161.4 thousand less than the census figures for that
date. If we apply the same process to the population aged 15 and
over on January 1, 1911, during the same period, the difference
between the expected and estimated population increases to 316.4
thousand (col. 4). These differences are not equal because in
column 3 we have included the age group 0-4 in 1900; as might be
expected, this age group shows a higher degree of omission than
the others. To account for the negative values in the differences

(cols. 3 and 4) we considered three possibilities: (a) that the 1910 census contained a higher degree of omission than that of 1900; (b) that emigration was of a much larger magnitude than estimated; or (c) that not all the deaths which occurred over the period were registered. Of these possibilities, the one we accepted as most likely to be correct is the under-registration of deaths.[16] We therefore assumed the difference of 316.4 thousand to be due to omission in the death registers; deaths were thus under-registered (col. 4) by 13.6 percent. Increasing the deaths in column 3 (those 2,666.5 thousand belonging to all the cohorts enumerated in 1900) by the 13.6 percent of omission, we obtained the figure 3,029.1 thousand. Using this figure, the total expected population for 1901 (col. 3) becomes 13,828.9 thousand, which is larger by 201.2 thousand than the estimate based on official census data. This positive difference between the expected and estimated population figures should probably be attributed to underenumeration in the 0-4 age group of the 1900 census.[17]

TABLE XIII-4

COHORT ANALYSIS FOR 1896-1911, MEXICO

(thousands)

	1896-1901		1901-1911	
	Cohort Age at the End of the Period			
	5 and Over	10 and Over	10 and Over	15 and Over
	(1)*	(2)	(3)	(4)
Survivors at the end of the period	11,687.4	9,834.3	10,815.6	9,052.8
Cohort deaths during the period	1,391.5	1,142.1	2,666.5	2,328.3
Estimated net migration	+9.8	+9.1	+15.8	+10.2
Expected population at the beginning of the period (1)+(2)-(3)	13,069.1	10,967.3	13,466.3	11,370.9
Estimated population at the beginning of the period	12,647.1	10,866.0	13,627.7	11,687.4
Difference (4)-(5)	422.0	101.3	-161.4	-316.4

*Column numbers are given for purposes of identification in text discussion.

We can follow practically the same procedure for the period 1895-1900 (Table XIII-4, cols. 1 and 2). The number of registered deaths was corrected by assuming the same omission for this period as for the period 1900-1910 (13.6 percent). Thus, the total deaths belonging in the cohorts aged 5 and over and aged 0 and over in 1895 (cols. 1 and 2) become 1,297.4 and 1,580.9 thousand respectively. Using the corrected deaths, the expected populations aged 0 and over and aged 5 and over in 1896 are 13,258.5 and 11,127.6 thousand respectively (instead of 13,069.1 and 10,967.3 according to official census data). Therefore, our results differ from census population by 256.6 thousand for ages 5 and over, and 611.4 thousand for ages 0 and over.[18] The figure 256.6 thousand was accepted for the number of persons in ages 5 and over who were not enumerated in the 1895 census. In other words the 1895 census has an underenumeration of 4.8 percent in relation to the two subsequent censuses.[19]

Since we established that the 1900 and 1910 censuses are of comparable completeness, we calculated the average annual geometric growth rate, considering migration, at 10.4 per thousand. For the period 1895-1900, taking into account the estimated expected population (13,258.5 and 13,828.9 thousand for January 1, 1896 and January 1, 1901 respectively), we calculated an intercensal annual geometric growth rate of 8.4 per thousand.[20] Using the average annual geometric growth rates of 8.4 and 10.4 for the 1895-1900 and 1900-1910 periods, we estimated the natural growth rates of the population for census years at 7.6, 9.0, and 12.2 per thousand for 1895, 1900, and 1910 respectively.

Construction of Life Tables for 1895, 1900, and 1910

Life tables for these three years were constructed using Method B, the proportional age group distribution (Table XIII-1), and the estimates of the natural growth rates given above. The set of $_5L_x$ values used in obtaining the quotient $\frac{C'(x, x+5)}{_5L_x}$ from the United Nations Model Life Tables were those from level 10 for 1895 and 1900, and from level 15 for 1910. The slopes of the straight lines of adjustment and the growth rates used in the application of Equation 5 (Chap. I) for each sex are given in Table XIII-5. The life tables constructed by this method are presented in Tables XIII-6, XIII-7, and XIII-8.[21]

TABLE XIII-5

GROWTH RATES USED IN THE CONSTRUCTION OF LIFE TABLES FOR MEXICO

	Growth Rates			Slopes of the Straight Lines of Adjustment of the $\log_e \frac{C'(x, x+5)}{_nL_5}$		
Year	Total	Male	Female	Male	Female	Average
1895	.0076	.00670	.00850	.007470	.009642	.008556
1900	.0090	.00785	.01015	.007432	.009607	.008520
1910	.0122	.01129	.01311	.011172	.012977	.012075

TABLE XIII-6

ABRIDGED LIFE TABLE, MEXICO, 1895
MALE

Age x n	l_x	$_nd_x$	$_np_x$	$_nq_x$	$_nL_x$	T_x	e_x
0 1	100,000	28,632	.71368	.28632	73,433	2,426,756	24.27
1 4	71,368	13,143	.81584	.18416	257,006	2,353,323	32.97
0 5	100,000	41,775	.58225	.41775	330,439	2,426,756	24.27
5 5	58,225	5,996	.89702	.10298	269,909	2,096,317	36.00
10 5	52,229	2,851	.94542	.05458	253,696	1,826,408	34.97
15 5	49,378	2,965	.93995	.06005	240,039	1,572,712	31.85
20 5	46,413	3,531	.92393	.07607	223,484	1,332,673	28.71
25 5	42,882	3,801	.91137	.08863	204,981	1,109,189	25.87
30 5	39,082	3,990	.89790	.10210	185,575	904,207	23.14
35 5	35,091	4,269	.87834	.12166	164,998	718,632	20.48
40 5	30,822	4,571	.85171	.14829	142,872	553,634	17.96
45 5	26,252	4,708	.82065	.17935	119,484	410,762	15.65
50 5	21,544	4,604	.78629	.21371	96,075	291,278	13.52
55 5	16,940	4,319	.74504	.25496	73,673	195,203	11.52
60 5	12,621	3,876	.69291	.30709	53,083	121,530	9.63
65 5	8,745	3,311	.62143	.37857	35,077	68,447	7.83
70 5	5,434	2,590	.52337	.47663	20,167	33,370	6.14
75 5	2,844	1,714	.39748	.60252	9,362	13,203	4.64
80 5	1,131	850	.24849	.75151	3,153	3,841	3.40
85 +	281	281	0.00000	1.00000	688	688	2.45

TABLE XIII-6 (continued)

ABRIDGED LIFE TABLE, MEXICO, 1895
FEMALE

Age x n	l_x	$_nd_x$	$_np_x$	$_nq_x$	$_nL_x$	T_x	e_x
0 1	100,000	26,709	.73291	.26709	75,422	2,450,964	24.51
1 4	73,291	13,644	.81383	.18617	263,677	2,375,542	32.41
0 5	100,000	40,353	.59647	.40353	339,098	2,450,964	24.51
5 5	59,647	6,437	.89208	.10792	275,767	2,111,866	33.41
10 5	53,210	3,298	.93801	.06199	257,524	1,836,099	34.51
15 5	49,911	3,436	.93116	.06884	241,511	1,578,575	31.63
20 5	46,475	4,000	.91393	.08607	222,637	1,337,063	28.77
25 5	42,476	4,265	.89959	.10041	201,782	1,114,426	26.24
30 5	38,210	4,337	.88649	.11351	180,223	912,644	23.88
35 5	33,873	4,286	.87346	.12654	158,569	732,421	21.62
40 5	29,587	4,132	.86033	.13967	137,477	573,852	19.40
45 5	25,455	3,993	.84314	.15686	117,237	436,375	17.14
50 5	21,462	3,905	.81804	.18196	97,495	319,138	14.87
55 5	17,557	3,827	.78202	.21798	78,176	221,643	12.62
60 5	13,730	3,715	.72940	.27060	59,277	143,468	10.45
65 5	10,014	3,450	.65552	.34448	41,215	84,190	8.41
70 5	6,565	2,916	.55582	.44418	25,102	42,975	6.55
75 5	3,649	2,099	.42469	.57531	12,404	17,873	4.90
80 5	1,550	1,154	.25550	.74450	4,440	5,469	3.53
85 +	396	396	0.00000	1.00000	1,028	1,028	2.60

TABLE XIII-7

ABRIDGED LIFE TABLE, MEXICO, 1900
MALE

Age x n	l_x	$_nd_x$	$_np_x$	$_nq_x$	$_nL_x$	T_x	e_x
0 1	100,000	28,522	.71478	.28522	73,516	2,502,552	25.03
1 4	71,478	12,914	.81934	.18066	257,906	2,429,036	33.98
0 5	100,000	41,435	.58565	.41435	331,422	2,502,552	25.03
5 5	58,565	5,713	.90245	.09755	272,324	2,171,130	37.07
10 5	52,852	2,585	.95108	.04892	257,492	1,898,805	35.93
15 5	50,266	2,737	.94554	.05446	245,081	1,641,313	32.65
20 5	47,529	3,354	.92943	.07057	229,539	1,396,232	29.38
25 5	44,175	3,675	.91680	.08320	211,789	1,166,693	26.41
30 5	40,500	3,918	.90325	.09675	192,881	954,905	23.58
35 5	36,581	4,259	.88357	.11643	172,515	762,024	20.83
40 5	32,322	4,629	.85678	.14322	150,271	589,509	18.24
45 5	27,693	4,831	.82554	.17446	126,420	439,238	15.86
50 5	22,862	4,779	.79098	.20902	102,258	312,818	13.68
55 5	18,083	4,530	.74948	.25052	78,881	210,560	11.64
60 5	13,553	4,106	.69704	.30296	57,174	131,679	9.72
65 5	9,447	3,541	.62512	.37488	38,005	74,505	7.89
70 5	5,905	2,796	.52649	.47351	21,981	36,499	6.18
75 5	3,109	1,866	.39989	.60011	10,265	14,518	4.67
80 5	1,245	932	.25009	.74991	3,478	4,253	3.42
85 +	311	311	0.00000	1.00000	775	775	2.49

TABLE XIII-7 (continued)

ABRIDGED LIFE TABLE, MEXICO, 1900
FEMALE

Age x n	l_x	$_nd_x$	$_np_x$	$_nq_x$	$_nL_x$	T_x	e_x
0 1	100,000	26,548	.73452	.26548	75,542	2,561,476	25.61
1 4	73,452	13,311	.81878	.18122	264,986	2,485,934	33.84
0 5	100,000	39,859	.60141	.39859	340,528	2,561,476	25.61
5 5	60,141	6,030	.89974	.10026	279,270	2,220,948	36.93
10 5	54,111	2,923	.94598	.05402	262,999	1,941,678	35.88
15 5	51,188	3,122	.93901	.06099	248,730	1,678,679	32.79
20 5	48,066	3,766	.92166	.07834	231,230	1,429,948	29.75
25 5	44,301	4,111	.90719	.09281	211,340	1,198,718	27.06
30 5	40,189	4,261	.89399	.10601	190,355	987,378	24.57
35 5	35,928	4,281	.88084	.11916	168,899	797,023	22.18
40 5	31,647	4,190	.86760	.13240	147,671	628,124	19.85
45 5	27,457	4,111	.85026	.14974	126,994	480,453	17.50
50 5	23,346	4,087	.82496	.17504	106,501	353,459	15.14
55 5	19,259	4,071	.78863	.21137	86,119	246,958	12.82
60 5	15,188	4,016	.73556	.26444	65,852	160,839	10.59
65 5	11,172	3,787	.66105	.33895	46,174	94,986	8.50
70 5	7,385	3,246	.56050	.43950	28,360	48,813	6.61
75 5	4,139	2,366	.42841	.57159	14,132	20,453	4.94
80 5	1,773	1,315	.25833	.74167	5,101	6,321	3.56
85 +	458	458	0.00000	1.00000	1,219	1,219	2.66

TABLE XIII-8

ABRIDGED LIFE TABLE, MEXICO, 1910
MALE

Age x n	l_x	$_nd_x$	$_np_x$	$_nq_x$	$_nL_x$	T_x	e_x
0 1	100,000	26,672	.73328	.26672	75,200	2,731,490	27.31
1 4	73,328	11,874	.83807	.16193	267,569	2,656,290	36.22
0 5	100,000	38,546	.61454	.38546	342,769	2,731,490	27.31
5 5	61,454	5,340	.91310	.08690	288,273	2,388,721	38.87
10 5	56,113	2,513	.95522	.04478	274,034	2,100,448	37.43
15 5	53,600	2,729	.94909	.05091	261,802	1,826,414	34.07
20 5	50,871	3,370	.93376	.06624	246,215	1,564,612	30.76
25 5	47,502	3,673	.92268	.07732	228,402	1,318,397	27.75
30 5	43,829	3,879	.91150	.08850	209,602	1,089,995	24.87
35 5	39,950	4,198	.89492	.10508	189,505	880,393	22.04
40 5	35,752	4,591	.87158	.12842	167,548	690,889	19.32
45 5	31,161	4,885	.84324	.15676	143,708	523,340	16.79
50 5	26,276	4,983	.81036	.18964	118,929	379,632	14.45
55 5	21,293	4,909	.76944	.23056	94,096	260,703	12.24
60 5	16,384	4,644	.71656	.28344	70,075	166,606	10.17
65 5	11,740	4,183	.64371	.35629	47,912	96,531	8.22
70 5	7,557	3,442	.54456	.45544	28,589	48,619	6.43
75 5	4,115	2,395	.41802	.58198	13,864	20,031	4.87
80 5	1,720	1,259	.26813	.73187	4,938	6,167	3.58
85 +	461	461	0.00000	1.00000	1,229	1,229	2.66

TABLE XIII-8 (continued)

ABRIDGED LIFE TABLE, MEXICO, 1910
FEMALE

Age x n	l_x	$_nd_x$	$_np_x$	$_nq_x$	$_nL_x$	T_x	e_x
0 1	100,000	24,826	.75174	.24826	77,090	2,787,648	27.88
1 4	75,174	12,226	.83736	.16264	274,237	2,710,557	36.06
0 5	100,000	37,053	.62947	.37053	351,328	2,787,648	27.88
5 5	62,947	5,643	.91035	.08965	294,862	2,436,320	38.70
10 5	57,304	2,856	.95016	.04984	279,189	2,141,458	37.37
15 5	54,448	3,124	.94263	.05737	265,054	1,862,269	34.20
20 5	51,325	3,790	.92615	.07385	247,459	1,597,215	31.12
25 5	47,534	4,114	.91345	.08655	227,470	1,349,756	28.40
30 5	43,420	4,225	.90270	.09730	206,579	1,122,285	25.85
35 5	39,195	4,231	.89206	.10794	185,360	915,706	23.36
40 5	34,965	4,166	.88086	.11914	164,351	730,346	20.89
45 5	30,799	4,161	.86491	.13509	143,640	565,995	18.38
50 5	26,638	4,246	.84061	.15939	122,643	422,355	15.86
55 5	22,392	4,370	.80485	.19515	101,135	299,712	13.38
60 5	18,022	4,471	.75194	.24806	78,989	198,576	11.02
65 5	13,552	4,373	.67733	.32267	56,679	119,587	8.82
70 5	9,179	3,885	.57671	.42329	35,733	62,909	6.85
75 5	5,294	2,936	.44529	.55471	18,391	27,176	5.13
80 5	2,357	1,702	.27786	.72214	6,941	8,785	3.73
85 +	655	655	0.00000	1.00000	1,845	1,845	2.82

NEW LIFE TABLES FOR LATIN AMERICAN POPULATIONS

LIFE TABLES FOR 1921, 1929-1931, 1939-1941, 1949-1951, AND 1959-1961; CONSTRUCTION BY METHOD A

The life tables for these years were constructed using Method A, after available vital statistics and population data were evaluated.

Analysis of Death Statistics

In this section we will analyze death statistics for the purposes of evaluating the enumerated census population and obtaining death information for the construction of life tables.

To evaluate the enumerated census population, an estimate of the cohort deaths during each intercensal period was required, as well as a breakdown of deaths by individual ages. To obtain the desired death information we needed to know deaths classified by five-year age groups and by individual ages between 0 and 4 for every census year and for adjacent years. Before we could proceed, however, we had to deal with two types of irregularity in death registration, total omission in death registration in rural areas, and differential omission in death registration of children under one year old (caused mainly by the frequent omission in death registration of children a few days old).

Total Omission in Death Registration. Urban-rural death rates differ widely between Mexican states. In addition, greater differences have been observed between states in rural death rates than in urban death rates. For example, it has been observed that Tamaulipas in 1939-1941 had a rural mortality rate 3.2 times smaller than its urban rate, 5.3 times smaller than Queretaro's urban rate, 3.2 times smaller than the rural rate for the entire country, and 3.3 times smaller than the total mortality rate for the country. Similar comparisons can be made with the rates of Baja California Territorio Norte and Quintana Roo for other years.

An analysis of these differences in urban-rural death rates was made in a previous study.[22] Mexican states were grouped into two categories according to whether or not a developed index indicated probable omission in the rural area. The conclusions of the study were first, that under-registration of rural deaths at least exists in Mexico, and second, that the rural death rate is higher than the urban in spite of what death statistics show.

In the present study, in order to obtain an idea of the amount of under-registration, we established limits between which the probable omission could vary after considering the following assumptions: (a) rural deaths in those states with poor rural registration must be increased in order to obtain the same rural death rate as those states with better registration[23]; (b) the minimum level of a rural death rate is the level of the registered rural death rate for the whole country; and (c) the minimum level of each state's rural death rate is the urban death rate for that state.

For 1959-1961 calculation of omission using these three assumptions gives very close results. Therefore, we considered their mean point (5 percent) to be the estimated omission for registered deaths. The omission in death registration for 1910 (12 percent) was available because life table construction by Method B allows for such estimation.[24] We estimated the omission for the years 1939-1941 and 1949-1951 in the same way we had estimated omission for 1959-1961; for 1930 and 1921 we interpolated levels of omission between 1910 and 1939-1941, 1949-1951, and 1959-1961. The results are given in Table XIII-9.

TABLE XIII-9

UNDER-REGISTRATION OF DEATHS UNDER AGE ONE,
AND AGE ONE YEAR AND OVER, MEXICO, 1921-1960
(percent)

Year	Total	Under Age One	Age One Year and Over
1921	11.9	11.9	11.9
1930	11.2	11.2	11.2
1940	9.9	10.4	9.8
1950	8.5	10.4	7.8
1960	5.0	8.0	3.6

Differential Omission in Deaths of Children Under One Year Old. Once we had estimated the total under-registration of deaths, we made an analysis of the omission in death registration for age under one year in order to establish more realistic infant mortality figures (see Appendix V). We found that registration of deaths under one day was incomplete, a circumstance which could have been due not only to omission, but to a misdeclaration of age, which would affect the completeness of registration for the under-one-year-old death figure.

We found that the relative difference in omission between ages under one year and other ages decreased for dates further in the past. When total omission is high, the relative difference between the omission in ages under one and ages over one is lower than when total omission is low, because the improvement in completeness is more probable for deaths over one year old than for deaths under one year old. These differences are presented in Table XIII-9, taking into account that the differential omission in these ages does not affect the total omission already estimated.

Death Statistics by Age. Death statistics began to be published again in 1922, after the end of the Civil War. Information on mortality is given by sex and age, but there have been some differences in the breakdown by age as time has passed. The age groups published in the vital statistics are as follows:

1922-1927: Under 1, 1, 2-5, 6-9, and then twenty-year age groups;

1928-1935: Under 1, 1-9, and then twenty-year age groups;

1936-1961: Under 1, 1-4, and then five-year age groups.

There are some exceptions for the last period. For 1947 and 1948, only total deaths--both sexes combined--and deaths for the age group under one year are available. For 1949, information on deaths over 10 years of age is given by twenty-year age groups. From 1950-1961, deaths 0-4 are given by individual ages. However, the death information needed to analyze the censuses and to construct life tables differs somewhat from the information given in the official sources. The death information required is: (a) the individual age distribution for ages 0-4 for every year; (b) the individual age distribution for ages 5-9 for the five years before each census; and (c) the five-year age groups from 5-84 for census and adjacent years. As a consequence, when the information available differed from that required, estimates of the required breakdown by age were made.

The available death information shows many irregularities, due to misreporting of age. The existence of these irregularities to some extent justifies the method we used in the following estimation of individual ages. Before estimating the individual age distribution 1-4, we estimated the age group 1-5 for the years 1928-1939, using the age group 1-9 and considering the proportion of the 1-5 age group to the 1-9 age group in previous and subsequent years.

Our next steps were: (a) to break down ages 1-4 for 1922-1949, making semilogarithmic graphs of the accumulated deaths at ages 1, 5 (or 6, according to the information for that year), 10, 15, and 19 [25] (the details of these calculations are given in Appendix V); (b) to determine the individual age distribution for the age group 5-9 for the five years preceding each census[26]

and to establish the quinquennial age groups for age 20 and over
for the years where this information was not available by reading the values from a semilogarithmic graph of the accumulated
deaths; (c) to break down twenty-year average groups in 1949 into quinquennial age groups by considering the same distribution
for the years 1950 and 1951; (d) to estimate the age-sex distribution of deaths for 1947 and 1948 in accordance with the observed
age-sex distribution from the previous and subsequent years;
(e) for 1921, a year for which there is no death information
available, we assumed the total number of deaths and the age-sex
distribution to be the same as that observed in 1922.

Once the required age distribution had been estimated, we
corrected the number of deaths for the estimated omission as shown
in Table XIII-9. Then we found the total intercensal cohort
deaths of the population cohorts enumerated at the beginning of
each intercensal period. We used a separation factor of 1/2 for
ages 1-9 and the separation factors given in Table XIII-10 for
age under one year to calculate cohort deaths, which are given in
Table XIII-11.

TABLE XIII-10

SEPARATION FACTOR FOR DEATHS UNDER AGE ONE,
MEXICO, 1921-1960

Separation Factor	1921	1931	1941	1951
Male	.344	.339	.332	.317
Female	.346	.343	.339	.335

Source: Appendix IV

TABLE XIII-11

COHORT DEATHS FROM THE POPULATION ALIVE AT
THE BEGINNING OF EACH INDICATED PERIOD, MEXICO, 1921-1960

	1921-1930	1931-1940	1941-1950	1951-1960	1941-1960
Male	1,213,475	1,408,103	1,405,240	1,317,107	2,446,232
Female	1,175,908	1,365,229	1,327,398	1,207,767	2,271,803

TABLE XIII-12

DEATHS BY SEX AND AGE GROUPS USED IN THE CONSTRUCTION
OF LIFE TABLES, MEXICO, CENSUS YEARS
MALE

Age Groups	1921	1929-31	1939-41	1949-51	1959-61
Total	209,164	249,071	254,560	249,126	218,961
0	60,260	63,711	64,735	70,599	69,786
1	21,092	28,511	28,613	25,907	16,227
2	10,018	19,708	16,444	15,352	9,169
3	4,425	8,269	8,012	8,251	5,311
4	2,023	4,714	4,630	4,643	3,165
0-4	97,818	124,912	122,434	124,752	103,658
5-9	8,860	12,457	12,143	10,010	7,545
10-14	4,523	5,475	5,608	4,638	3,610
15-19	7,735	6,481	6,565	6,031	4,688
20-24	8,752	8,122	7,623	6,778	5,469
25-29	9,520	9,261	8,693	7,001	5,956
30-34	9,929	9,582	9,594	7,167	6,293
35-39	9,391	8,918	9,816	7,606	6,430
40-44	8,155	8,026	9,070	7,999	6,382
45-49	7,241	7,382	8,080	8,068	6,653
50-54	6,921	7,203	7,546	7,681	7,370
55-59	6,735	7,637	7,849	7,594	8,134
60-64	5,942	7,756	8,230	8,094	8,429
65-69	4,731	6,881	7,759	8,254	8,377
70-74	3,668	5,750	6,886	7,816	8,019
75-79	3,016	4,542	5,638	6,520	7,395
80-84	2,672	3,978	4,845	5,428	5,903
85 +	3,554	4,707	6,181	7,689	8,650

TABLE XIII-12 (continued)

DEATHS BY SEX AND AGE GROUPS USED IN THE CONSTRUCTION
OF LIFE TABLES, MEXICO, CENSUS YEARS
FEMALE

Age Groups	1921	1929-31	1939-41	1949-51	1959-61
Total	198,706	238,698	240,469	228,086	196,441
0	52,985	54,142	54,538	58,364	57,529
1	21,925	27,707	28,413	25,846	16,321
2	10,521	20,328	16,960	15,903	9,548
3	4,505	8,530	8,319	8,612	5,433
4	2,084	4,863	4,777	4,819	3,228
0-4	92,020	115,570	113,007	113,544	92,059
5-9	8,303	11,817	11,554	9,644	7,132
10-14	3,803	4,864	4,789	3,912	2,874
15-19	6,969	6,913	6,564	5,396	3,855
20-24	8,360	8,191	7,671	5,934	4,547
25-29	9,328	8,945	8,274	6,043	4,820
30-34	9,542	9,124	8,523	5,882	4,895
35-39	8,628	8,447	8,354	5,999	4,855
40-44	7,591	7,293	7,609	6,084	4,728
45-49	6,872	6,543	6,751	5,984	4,876
50-54	6,234	6,348	6,389	5,838	5,464
55-59	5,922	6,634	7,023	6,293	6,375
60-64	5,414	7,054	7,861	7,319	7,185
65-69	4,483	6,926	7,738	7,896	7,674
70-74	3,734	6,395	7,162	7,387	7,838
75-79	3,386	5,399	6,138	7,027	7,639
80-84	3,465	5,312	6,293	6,800	7,242
85 +	4,652	6,923	8,769	11,104	12,383

TABLE XIII-13

NUMBER OF DEATHS FOR SELECTED AGES AND YEARS
(CORRECTED BY ESTIMATED UNDER-REGISTRATION), MEXICO
MALE

Years	Age				
	0	1	2	3	4
1925	65,138				
1926	60,566	22,808			
1927	55,790	21,112	15,285		
1928	60,677	27,073	18,257	7,685	
1929	63,979	28,225	19,480	8,691	4,727
1930	65,263	29,472	20,148	8,888	4,895
1935	61,572				
1936	62,303	28,996			
1937	64,461	30,645	17,406		
1938	63,299	27,497	15,634	7,411	
1939	63,329	27,940	16,022	7,757	4,497
1940	66,198	30,552	17,556	8,562	4,928
1945	65,120				
1946	65,999	28,574			
1947	62,739	22,618	13,217		
1948	65,590	22,834	13,398	7,029	
1949	72,571	27,240	16,016	8,460	4,681
1950	68,502	23,072	13,058	7,011	4,010
1955	68,753				
1956	60,785	15,372			
1957	70,466	20,866	12,137		
1958	68,669	18,769	10,992	6,168	
1959	69,983	16,010	9,609	5,563	3,321
1960	71,117	17,007	9,123	5,340	3,141

TABLE XIII-13 (continued)

NUMBER OF DEATHS FOR SELECTED AGES AND YEARS
(CORRECTED BY ESTIMATED UNDER-REGISTRATION), MEXICO
FEMALE

Years	Age				
	0	1	2	3	4
1925	56,175				
1926	52,283	22,235			
1927	47,579	24,043	15,413		
1928	51,469	26,455	18,918	7,756	
1929	55,078	27,578	20,019	9,156	4,878
1930	55,105	28,624	20,818	9,312	5,080
1935	51,364				
1936	52,347	28,110			
1937	55,049	30,383	17,987		
1938	54,236	27,337	16,239	7,698	
1939	53,945	27,917	16,675	8,119	4,680
1940	55,412	29,926	17,856	8,774	5,022
1945	54,032				
1946	55,675	28,448			
1947	52,408	23,052	13,937		
1948	54,466	23,846	14,397	7,248	
1949	59,777	27,246	16,520	8,432	5,162
1950	56,566	22,803	13,438	7,723	4,217
1955	56,810				
1956	49,798	15,445			
1957	59,073	20,981	12,573		
1958	57,242	19,119	11,317	6,365	
1959	58,334	16,248	9,829	5,577	3,444
1960	58,022	16,937	9,520	5,576	3,109

NEW LIFE TABLES FOR LATIN AMERICAN POPULATIONS

In order to obtain death distributions for the life tables, we used annual averages for 1929-1931, 1939-1941, 1949-1951, and 1959-1961. The same distribution of deaths given for 1922 was assumed for 1921, a year for which information was not published. The five-year age group distributions of deaths were smoothed,[27] and the final age group distribution of deaths corrected for omission (Table XIII-12). Finally, because an estimate of the individual age distribution of the population aged 0-4 in 1930, 1940, 1950, and 1960 was needed, we found deaths for some single age groups in particular years (for periods five years before census years)(Table XIII-13). See Appendix V for an explanation of our procedure.

Analysis of Census Population

In order to evaluate the completeness of the censuses, it was necessary to make a cohort analysis for the total population enumerated at the beginning of each intercensal period, rather than by age groups, because census information by age was not sufficiently accurate for a detailed analysis, and because international migration was not available by age.[28] Information on deaths needed for this analysis is provided in the preceding section. The necessary information on international migration is provided below.

International Migration. Mexico has been experiencing international migration for a long time. The major migration streams have been crossing the frontier to the U.S., and Americans have been entering Mexico. Some Europeans, principally Spaniards, have come to Mexico in the past, and it is not possible to forget the effect of the "movimiento de braceros," although statistics and regulations pertaining to this movement have only existed since 1942.[29] It is very difficult to determine the extent to which international migration has affected the Mexican population. Statistics on migration are not reliable, and it was necessary for us to make estimates.

The available statistics on migration to and from Mexico are not broken down by age and sex, except in a few special cases.[30] Thus, we decided not to use them, and decided instead to estimate the international migration movement of the foreign-born in and out of Mexico by an indirect procedure, using Mexican census information on foreign-born residents of Mexico.[31] In order to estimate the international migratory movement of Mexicans, we considered information from U.S. censuses on the number of Mexicans enumerated in the U.S.[32]

Estimate of Net International Migratory Movement of Mexicans. An estimate of the net emigration of native Mexicans can be obtained by comparing the survivors of the Mexican-born population enumerated in the U.S. census at time t-10 with those

enumerated in the U.S. census at time t. U.S. censuses have
given figures of Mexican-born, by age and sex, since 1940. For
1920 and 1930, then, as information is not given by age and sex,
an estimate of the age structure is required. This estimate was
made considering: (a) the total number of Mexicans enumerated in
U.S. censuses, in order to obtain an idea of the trend and therefore of the age of that population; and (b) the observed age distribution for subsequent years.

We can conclude from the figures in Table XIII-14 that:
(a) during 1920-1930, the emigration of Mexicans from Mexico
to the U.S. was considerable; (b) in the next decade (1930-1940)
the net movement of migration was in the other direction, and
apparently some Mexicans returned to Mexico; (c) from 1940-
1960, Mexicans were migrating to the U.S., principally during the
first decade, 1940-1950. Therefore, it is possible for us to
assume that the age distribution of 1930 must have been closer to
that of 1950 than to that of 1940 or 1960, given the characteristics of the migration movement during 1920-1930 and 1940-1950
(large movements during both periods). On the other hand, the
age distribution for 1920 can be considered, for the same reasons,
similar to that of 1960. Thus, the total number of Mexicans
enumerated in the 1930 and 1920 censuses were distributed using
the same proportional age group distribution of Mexicans enumerated
in the 1950 and 1960 U.S. censuses respectively.

TABLE XIII-14

MEXICAN-BORN PERSONS ENUMERATED IN THE UNITED STATES CENSUSES,
1920-1960

	1920	1930	1940	1950	1960
Total	486,418	641,462	374,433	451,490	468,684
Male	276,526	361,787	197,965	246,905	254,034
Female	209,892	279,675	176,468	204,585	214,650

The survival ratios for each five-year age group needed
to estimate the survivors of those enumerated in each census were
calculated using U.S. life tables.[33] By multiplying each five-
year age group of Mexicans enumerated in the U.S. at time t-10 by
the corresponding survival ratio, the survivors in time t were

obtained. These were then compared with the Mexicans enumerated at the same time in order to estimate the net emigration of Mexicans for each intercensal period (Table XIII-15).

Estimation of Net International Migration of Foreign-Born into Mexico. We estimated the international migration into Mexico using census information for the enumerated foreign-born. In this particular case, it was impossible to make an estimation using five-year age groups as we had in the previous case of emigration, because Mexican censuses do not give an age breakdown of the foreign-born population. Therefore, we made our estimate using the total foreign-born population enumerated at the beginning of each intercensal period and an estimate of the survival ratio for that population during the period.

Thus it was necessary that we estimate the enumerated foreign-born population of age 10 and over for 1930, 1940, 1950, and 1960 (for 1960, of age 20 and over as well). We did so by considering the age distribution of the foreign-born observed in other countries. The variation of the foreign-born population under 10 years old in each census can be correlated to the total foreign-born female population, because children generally migrate with their mothers. In addition, we would expect that there would be almost the same number of each sex in the foreign-born population enumerated under 10 years old.

Between 1921 and 1930 Mexico received a large flow of migrants (in fact, the number of foreign-born females was doubled) (Table XIII-16). It is reasonable to assume that some of these females were carrying their children, and as a consequence we can expect, in 1930, a higher proportion of migrants under 10 years old than would be the case during times when migration was not so great.

The number of foreign-born enumerated in the 1940 census was considerably lower than the number of foreign-born enumerated in 1930. It seems, therefore, that immigration into Mexico during the 1930-1940 decade was negligible. As a consequence, we would expect to find a low proportion of foreign-born under 10 years old in the 1940 census. During 1940-1950, migration was again significant (again, the number of foreign-born females doubled during that period); thus an increase in the proportion of enumerated foreign-born aged under 10 years would be expected in 1950, and also in 1960, because the migration was significant during the decade 1950-1960. For 1960 we also estimated the proportion of foreign-born under 20 years old. We estimated the proportion of foreign-born under 10 years old for each census (and under 20 for 1960) by taking into account (a) the total changes of this particular female population in Mexico, and (b) the age distribution of the enumerated foreign-born in other countries.[34] The estimated proportions of foreign-born under age 10 were 8.5, 2.6,

TABLE XIII-15

MEXICAN MIGRATION TO THE UNITED STATES

	Male					Female				
	1921-1930	1931-1940	1941-1950	1951-1960	1941-1960	1921-1930	1931-1940	1941-1950	1951-1960	1941-1960
(1) Total Mexicans enumerated in the U.S. Censuses at the beginning of the period	276,526	361,787	197,965	246,905	197,965	209,892	279,675	176,468	204,585	176,468
(2) Estimated Survivors at the end of the period	211,510	266,322	164,415	197,498	122,934	152,191	205,542	149,552	166,522	116,546
(3) Enumerated Mexicans 10 years old and over in the U.S. Censuses at the end of the period	348,841	196,924	238,070	242,114	219,397*	267,549	175,419	195,715	202,795	180,021*
(4) Estimated migration (3)-(2)	137,331	-69,398	73,655	44,616	96,463	115,358	-30,123	46,163	36,273	63,473

*20 years old and over

TABLE XIII-16

FOREIGN-BORN POPULATION ENUMERATED IN MEXICO, 1921-1960

	1921	1930	1940	1950	1960
Total	100,854	159,876	105,350	182,343	223,468
Male	70,134	95,717	65,087	99,138	120,118
Female	30,720	64,159	40,263	83,205	103,350

6.5, and 8.5 percent for the years 1930, 1940, 1950, and 1960 respectively. For 1960 we estimated a proportion of 27.3 percent
for ages under 20. For ages under 10 we assumed the same absolute
number of persons in each sex; for ages of 10 to 20 years old in
1960 we used a sex ratio of 102.2 males for each 100 females.
Given the estimate of foreign-born by sex in these age groups, we
found the foreign-born population 10 and over and 20 and over by
subtracting these estimates from the total foreign-born in each
sex (Table XIII-17).

TABLE XIII-17

ESTIMATED FOREIGN-BORN POPULATION IN MEXICO

Year	10 Years Old and Over		20 Years Old and Over	
	Male	Female	Male	Female
1930	90,521	58,963		
1940	64,033	39,210		
1950	94,579	78,647		
1960	112,855	96,088	89,375	73,107

In order to establish the net movement of foreign-born
into Mexico for each census date, the number of survivors from
the foreign-born enumerated in the previous census was required.
And, in order to obtain the number of those survivors, we needed

to find the survival ratios for every intercensal period. We assumed the survival ratio for the foreign-born population to be the same as that for the total population.[35] Thus survival ratios were calculated by taking

$$_nP^t_{x+} = \frac{P^{t+n}_{x+n+}}{P^t_{x+}} ,$$

where P means population, x the age, n the period, and t time.[36] The surviving foreign-born from each ten-year interval were compared with those enumerated at the same time. The difference was attributed to immigration (Table XIII-18). Then, taking the difference between the estimated net international migration of Mexicans and the estimated net international migration of the foreign-born population in Mexico, we established the net amount of international migration experienced by Mexico during each intercensal period (Table XIII-19). The figures we obtained were later used to analyze the completeness of the five censuses since 1921.

Cohort Analysis. Once we had estimated intercensal migration and established the corrected death for the cohorts (Tables XIII-11 and XIII-19), we could evaluate the completeness of the census population data through a cohort analysis. In order to have population information in equidistant ten-year periods, the total population for each sex for 1930, 1940, 1950, and 1960 was shifted to the end of each year (e.g., to December 31). Information for the 1921 census was shifted to the beginning of that year (e.g., to January 1). The total growth rates used for shifting the population were: 15, 17, 22, 28, and 34 per thousand for the years 1921, 1930, 1940, 1950, and 1960 respectively. The same proportion of census population aged 10 and over to total population was maintained at the shifted dates (this is true also of age 20 and over in 1961).

For a better cohort analysis we needed an estimate of the age groups 0-4 for all censuses except 1961. Census information shows practically no variation in the proportion of total population enumerated in the age group 0-4 since 1930--for 1921 the proportion was lower due to the decline of fertility during the Civil War.[37] Thus, we can assume (because fertility has been constant) that the completeness in this particular age group seems to have been the same over time; therefore it will be sufficient to estimate the completeness of only one census year. We chose the year 1961 because, of all the censuses considered, the census of this year presents the highest proportion of total population in the ages 0-4. We concluded, therefore, that omission for this year could be considered minimal. Using deaths by single years

TABLE XIII-18

NET MIGRATION OF FOREIGN-BORN INTO MEXICO

	Male					Female				
	1921-1930	1931-1940	1941-1950	1951-1960	1941-1960	1921-1930	1931-1940	1941-1950	1951-1960	1941-1960
(1) Total foreign-born enumerated at the beginning of the period	70,134	95,717	65,087	99,138	65,087	30,720	64,159	40,263	83,205	40,263
(2) Estimated survivors at the end of the period	57,110	78,967	57,823	89,928	51,028	25,562	53,631	36,752	75,043	32,142
(3) Estimate of those enumerated 10 years old and over at the end of the period	90,521	64,033	94,579	112,855	89,375*	58,963	39,210	78,647	96,088	73,107*
(4) Estimated migration (3)-(2)	33,411	-14,934	36,756	22,927	38,347	33,401	-14,421	41,895	21,045	40,965

*20 years old and over

TABLE XIII-19

NET INTERNATIONAL MIGRATION, MEXICO 1921-1960

	Male					Female				
	1921-1930	1931-1940	1941-1950	1951-1960	1941-1960	1921-1930	1931-1940	1941-1950	1951-1960	1941-1960
(1) Net Immigration of foreign-born to Mexico	33,411	-14,934	36,756	22,927	38,347	33,401	-14,421	41,895	21,045	40,965
(2) Net emigration of Mexicans	137,331	-69,398	73,655	44,616	96,463	155,358	-30,123	46,163	36,273	63,475
(3) Net international migration to Mexico (1)-(2)	-103,920	54,464	-36,899	-21,689	-58,116	-121,957	15,702	-4,268	-15,228	-22,510

for ages 0-4 which had been corrected for the omission previously established in Table XIII-9, and registered births for the period 1955-1960, we constructed a Lexis' diagram for each sex in order to estimate the expected population in the age group 0-4.[38] As can be seen in Table XIII-20, the estimated omission for both sexes was approximately 15 percent of the enumerated population.[39] The population in the age group 0-4 for the previous census years was estimated assuming the same percentage of omission. Using these estimates of the population 0-4, cohort deaths from Table XIII-11, and migration data from Table XIII-19, it was possible to make the cohort analysis which is presented in Table XIII-21. The analysis was made retrospectively, beginning with the more recent censuses, because we assumed that later census information was the most accurate.

Assuming that the census taken at the end of each inter-censal period is accurate, the following conclusions would result (see Table XIII-21):

(a) If the enumeration of population of age 10 and over in 1960 is correct, the 1950 census presents an underenumeration of approximately 100,000 males and an overenumeration of 100,000 females.

(b) If the enumeration of the population aged 10 and over in the 1950 census is correct, the 1940 census presents an approximate underenumeration of 320,000 males and 430,000 females.

(c) If the enumeration of population of age 10 and over in 1940 is correct, the 1930 census presents an overnumeration of 100,000 in each sex.

(d) Enumerated populations in the 1930 and the 1921 censuses are comparable.

(e) If the population aged 20 and over in 1960 is correct, the 1940 census presents an underenumeration of 310,000 males and 190,000 females.

Masculinity ratios were calculated for the total popula-tion in each census; they are 95.5, 96.3, 97.4, 97.0, and 99.5 for the years 1921, 1930, 1940, 1950, and 1960 respectively. The strange decline of masculinity in 1950 and the sudden increase in 1960 aided us in our analysis of the censuses. From these ratios and statements (a), (b), (c), and (e), we obtained some rough conclusions about underenumeration. It seems that there was underenumeration of females in 1960, of males in 1950, and of both sexes in 1940. We estimated the magnitude of this underenumeration at about 100,000 females in 1960, 100,000 males in 1950, and 350,000 of each sex in 1940.[40]

TABLE XIII-20

ESTIMATED POPULATION, AGES 0-4
MEXICO, 1960

Year of Birth	Births	Cohort Deaths		Survivors		Age at Census Date	Survivors at Census Date
		Up to the Beginning of 1960	Up to the End of 1960	At the Beginning of 1960	At the End of 1960		
Male							
1960	824,166				774,313	0	771,408
1959	818,011	48,848	78,616	769,163	739,395	1	699,239
1958	744,924	76,726	89,792	668,198	655,132	2	665,024
1957	764,285	91,616	98,847	672,669	665,438	3	651,354
1956	737,980	97,514	101,755	640,466	636,225	4	620,472
1955	710,924	102,808		608,116			
Female							
1960	784,008		39,455		744,553	0	737,504
1959	771,595	39,550	66,596	732,045	705,009	1	666,906
1958	702,654	65,203	78,432	637,451	624,222	2	633,137
1957	720,917	80,888	88,411	640,029	632,506	3	615,744
1956	689,742	86,955	91,273	602,787	598,469	4	615,744
1955	666,993	91,615		575,378			

		Total	Male	Female
(1)	Total Estimated Population Aged 0-4	6,646,128	3,407,396	3,238,732
(2)	Enumerated Census Population Aged 0-4	5,776,747	2,936,387	2,840,360
(3)	[(1) + (2)] - 1	.1505	.1604	.1403

TABLE XIII-21

COHORT ANALYSIS, MEXICO, 1921-1960

Period and Sex	Census Population Age Ten Years and Over at the End of the Period (1)	Cohort Deaths During the Period (2)	Migration in the Cohort During the Period (3)	Expected Population at the Beginning of the Period (4)	Census Population at the Beginning of the Period (5)(a)	Difference (4)-(5) (6)
1951-1960						
Male	11,977,513	1,317,107	- 21,689	13,316,309	13,204,905	111,404
Female	12,272,121	1,207,767	- 15,328	13,495,216	13,599,943	-104,726
1941-1950						
Male	8,966,272	1,405,240	- 36,891	10,408,403	10,092,385	316,018
Female	9,454,557	1,327,398	- 4,268	10,786,223	10,354,188	432,035
1931-1940						
Male	6,928,487	1,408,103	+ 54,464	8,282,126	8,398,416	-116,290
Female	7,282,702	1,365,229	+ 15,699	8,632,232	8,712,273	- 80,041
1921-1930						
Male	5,741,215	1,213,475	-103,919	7,058,609	7,050,381	8,228
Female	6,132,615	1,175,908	-106,207	7,414,730	7,370,298	44,432
1941-1960						
Male	7,912,846(b)	2,446,232	- 42,439	10,401,517	10,092,385	309,132
Female	8,265,463(a)	2,271,803	- 4,499	10,541,765	10,354,188	187,577

(a) Corrected by omission in age group 0 to 4   (b) 20 years old and over

CHAPTER XIII. MEXICO

In relative numbers the magnitude of these omissions is: 0.8 percent for female population 10 years old and over in 1960, 1.1 percent for male population 10 years old and over in 1950, and 3.5 percent for the total population in 1940. Masculinity ratios by five-year age groups give us an idea how to spread these underenumerated persons. We decided to: (a) spread the 100,000 omitted females in 1960 among ages 30-59;[41] (b) spread the 100,000 omitted males in 1950 among ages 10-49;[42] (c) spread the omission of 3.5 percent in the 1940 census proportionate to the enumerated population in each age group.

Once these corrections were made, the only kind of smoothing done was to redistribute the ten-year age groups into five-year age groups[43] for ages 10 and over (for the formula used, see Appendix III). The age group 5-9 was considered accurate, and was not modified. Because life table construction by Method A requires a breakdown of ages under 5, it was necessary to estimate the individual ages 0-4 for each census. For 1960, this had already been done (Table XIII-20). For 1930, 1940, and 1950 a procedure similar to that used for 1960 was followed.[44] The smoothed age distribution of population by sex for all years is given in Table XIII-22.

Construction of Life Tables

The basic information needed to construct life tables by Method A--corrected age distributions of the population (Table XIII-22) and the age distribution of deaths (Table XIII-12)--is given in the preceding sections. Life tables for each sex were thus constructed using Method A for 1921, 1929-1931, 1939-1941, 1949-1951, and 1959-1961. These are presented in Tables XIII-23 to XIII-27. A summary of the life expectancy for each year is given in Table XIII-28.

TABLE XIII-22

POPULATION BY SEX AND AGE GROUPS USED IN THE CONSTRUCTION
OF LIFE TABLES, MEXICO, CENSUS YEARS
MALE

Age Groups	1921	1930	1940	1950	1960
0	298,800	356,055	403,577	542,562	771,408
1	222,507	299,027	350,962	487,235	699,239
2	194,914	255,082	324,536	461,848	665,023
3	177,566	238,597	298,626	427,550	651,354
4	165,321	243,744	278,162	405,766	620,472
5-9	949,258	1,169,178	1,491,930	1,868,258	2,715,994
10-14	891,722	890,391	1,238,814	1,549,127	2,178,664
15-19	787,768	784,671	1,055,703	1,334,036	1,809,471
20-24	626,067	753,330	819,558	1,127,123	1,415,587
25 29	542,473	669,192	724,788	959,642	1,194,963
30-34	497,000	566,916	725,935	794,589	1,071,413
35-30	425,446	477,043	624,870	685,481	904,167
40-44	341,935	384,569	469,664	617,436	702,836
45-49	274,232	309,428	371,523	511,327	586,741
50-54	203,117	232,493	282,497	372,847	512,602
55-59	159,964	185,631	224,651	294,915	423,403
60-64	133,258	157,478	187,705	246,381	330,745
65-69	97,443	117,407	139,385	184,282	246,843
70-74	51,572	65,809	79,025	120,771	154,495
75-79	30,422	40,269	48,169	55,846	98,887
80-84	17,287	23,061	26,871	71,651	55,998
85 +		22,690			

TABLE XIII-22 (continued)

POPULATION BY SEX AND AGE GROUPS USED IN THE CONSTRUCTION
OF LIFE TABLES, MEXICO, CENSUS YEARS
FEMALE

Age Groups	1921	1930	1940	1950	1960
0	288,200	341,582	384,989	516,097	737,504
1	220,552	288,873	339,529	465,712	666,906
2	193,319	245,811	311,897	437,520	633,137
3	175,638	226,751	284,578	399,653	615,744
4	163,525	231,631	264,532	373,855	585,446
5-9	907,877	1,124,532	1,436,297	1,813,074	2,618,444
10-14	881,128	882,790	1,202,776	1,541,460	2,118,938
15-19	814,837	813,516	1,056,808	1,358,004	1,812,291
20-24	730,300	853,271	898,325	1,225,317	1,540,833
25-29	642,089	762,281	806,943	1,049,826	1,318,256
30-34	546,091	606,296	771,715	828,931	1,073,054
35-39	458,818	503,785	662,410	705,417	936,627
40-44	369,555	413,918	508,495	636,664	732,398
45-49	295,471	334,384	405,368	526,993	608,413
50-54	219,708	252,278	310,348	384,491	525,126
55-59	170,657	199,659	244,874	306,480	431,208
60-64	135,708	163,827	197,099	261,414	334,302
65-69	97,672	120,570	144,593	197,827	250,762
70-74	52,306	67,196	82,485	131,412	161,956
75-79	31,352	41,431	50,937	62,169	107,499
80-84	18,637	24,754	29,648		65,263
85 +					35,248

TABLE XIII-23

ABRIDGED LIFE TABLE, MEXICO, 1921
MALE

Age x n	l_x	$_nd_x$	$_np_x$	$_nq_x$	$_nL_x$	T_x	e_x
0 1	100,000	17,708	.82292	.17708	88,384	3,366,341	33.66
1 1	82,292	7,704	.90638	.09362	77,747	3,277,957	39.83
2 1	74,588	3,696	.95045	.04955	72,629	3,200,210	42.91
3 1	70,892	1,739	.97547	.02453	69,988	3,127,581	44.12
4 1	69,153	878	.98730	.01270	68,696	3,057,593	44.21
0 5	100,000	31,725	.68275	.31725	377,444	3,366,341	33.66
5 5	68,275	2,349	.96560	.03440	335,503	2,988,897	43.78
10 5	65,926	1,901	.97116	.02884	324,878	2,653,394	40.25
15 5	64,025	2,741	.95719	.04281	313,273	2,328,516	36.37
20 5	61,284	3,811	.93781	.06219	296,893	2,015,243	32.88
25 5	57,473	4,552	.92080	.07920	275,985	1,718,350	29.90
30 5	52,921	4,887	.90765	.09235	252,388	1,442,365	27.26
35 5	48,034	5,134	.89312	.10688	227,335	1,189,977	24.77
40 5	42,900	5,019	.88301	.11699	201,953	962,642	22.44
45 5	37,881	4,932	.86980	.13020	177,075	760,689	20.08
50 5	32,949	4,924	.85056	.14944	152,435	583,614	17.71
55 5	28,025	4,895	.82533	.17467	127,888	431,179	15.39
60 5	23,130	4,828	.79127	.20873	103,580	303,291	13.11
65 5	18,302	4,657	.74555	.25445	79,868	199,711	10.91
70 5	13,645	4,419	.67615	.32385	57,178	119,843	8.78
75 5	9,226	3,971	.56959	.43041	36,203	62,665	6.79
80 5	5,255	2,968	.43520	.56480	18,780	26,462	5.04
85 +	2,287	2,287	0.00000	1.00000	7,682	7,682	3.36

TABLE XIII-23 (continued)

ABRIDGED LIFE TABLE, MEXICO, 1921
FEMALE

Age x n	l_x	$_nd_x$	$_np_x$	$_nq_x$	$_nL_x$	T_x	e_x
0 1	100,000	16,415	.83585	.16415	89,265	3,564,228	35.64
1 1	83,585	7,971	.90464	.09536	78,882	3,474,963	41.57
2 1	75,614	3,917	.94820	.05180	73,538	3,396,081	44.91
3 1	71,691	1,808	.97478	.02522	70,757	3,322,543	46.34
4 1	69,889	930	.98669	.01331	69,405	3,251,786	46.53
0 5	100,000	31,041	.68959	.31041	381,847	3,564,228	35.64
5 5	68,959	2,369	.96565	.03435	338,873	3,182,381	46.15
10 5	66,590	1,692	.97459	.02541	328,720	2,843,508	42.70
15 5	64,898	2,445	.96233	.03767	318,378	2,514,788	38.75
20 5	62,453	3,369	.94606	.05394	303,843	2,196,410	35.17
25 5	59,084	4,026	.93186	.06814	285,355	1,892,567	32.03
30 5	55,058	4,455	.91909	.08091	264,153	1,607,212	29.19
35 5	50,603	4,588	.90933	.09067	241,545	1,343,059	26.54
40 5	46,015	4,603	.89997	.10003	218,568	1,101,514	23.94
45 5	41,412	4,662	.88742	.11258	195,405	882,946	21.32
50 5	36,750	4,775	.87007	.12993	171,813	687,541	18.71
55 5	31,975	4,910	.84644	.15356	147,600	515,728	16.13
60 5	27,065	5,062	.81297	.18703	122,670	368,128	13.60
65 5	22,003	5,234	.76212	.23788	96,930	245,458	11.16
70 5	16,769	5,335	.68185	.31815	70,508	148,528	8.86
75 5	11,434	4,921	.56962	.43038	44,868	78,020	6.82
80 5	6,513	3,679	.43513	.56487	23,368	33,152	5.09
85 +	2,834	2,834	0.00000	1.00000	9,784	9,784	3.45

TABLE XIII-24

ABRIDGED LIFE TABLE, MEXICO, 1930
MALE

Age x n	l_x	$_nd_x$	$_np_x$	$_nq_x$	$_nL_x$	T_x	e_x
0 1	100,000	16,430	.83570	.16430	89,140	3,301,523	33.02
1 1	83,570	8,395	.89955	.10045	78,617	3,212,383	38.44
2 1	75,175	5,089	.93230	.06770	72,478	3,133,766	41.69
3 1	70,086	2,419	.96549	.03451	68,828	3,061,288	43.68
4 1	67,667	1,392	.97943	.02057	66,943	2,992,460	44.22
0 5	100,000	33,725	.66275	.33725	376,006	3,301,523	33.02
5 5	66,275	3,774	.94306	.05694	321,940	2,925,517	44.14
10 5	62,501	2,056	.96710	.03290	307,365	2,603,577	41.66
15 5	60,445	2,350	.96112	.03888	296,350	2,296,212	37.99
20 5	58,095	3,059	.94734	.05266	282,828	1,999,862	34.42
25 5	55,036	3,633	.93399	.06601	266,098	1,717,034	31.20
30 5	51,403	4,019	.92181	.07819	246,968	1,450,936	28.23
35 5	47,384	4,206	.91124	.08876	226,405	1,203,968	25.41
40 5	43,178	4,320	.89995	.10005	205,090	977,563	22.64
45 5	38,858	4,552	.88286	.11714	182,910	772,473	19.88
50 5	34,306	4,927	.85638	.14362	159,213	589,563	17.19
55 5	29,379	5,244	.82151	.17849	133,785	430,350	14.65
60 5	24,135	5,356	.77808	.22192	107,285	296,565	12.29
65 5	18,779	5,280	.71883	.28117	80,695	189,280	10.08
70 5	13,499	4,968	.63197	.36803	55,075	108,585	8.04
75 5	8,531	4,096	.51987	.48013	32,415	53,510	6.27
80 5	4,435	2,692	.39301	.60699	15,445	21,095	4.76
85 +	1,743	1,743	0.00000	1.00000	5,650	5,650	3.24

TABLE XIII-24 (continued)

ABRIDGED LIFE TABLE, MEXICO, 1930
FEMALE

Age x n	l_x	$_nd_x$	$_np_x$	$_nq_x$	$_nL_x$	T_x	e_x
0 1	100,000	14,829	.85171	.14829	90,257	3,470,085	34.70
1 1	85,171	8,518	.89999	.10001	80,145	3,379,828	39.68
2 1	76,653	5,510	.92812	.07188	73,733	3,299,683	43.05
3 1	71,143	2,670	.96247	.03753	69,755	3,225,950	45.34
4 1	68,473	1,525	.97773	.02227	67,680	3,156,195	46.09
0 5	100,000	33,052	.66948	.33052	381,570	3,470,085	34.70
5 5	66,948	3,742	.94411	.05589	325,385	3,088,515	46.13
10 5	63,206	1,920	.96962	.03038	311,230	2,763,130	43.72
15 5	61,286	2,274	.96290	.03710	300,745	2,451,900	40.01
20 5	59,012	2,865	.95145	.04855	287,898	2,151,155	36.45
25 5	56,147	3,352	.94030	.05970	272,355	1,863,257	33.19
30 5	52,795	3,698	.92996	.07004	254,730	1,590,902	30.13
35 5	49,097	3,862	.92134	.07866	235,830	1,336,172	27.21
40 5	45,235	3,942	.91286	.08714	215,320	1,100,342	24.33
45 5	41,293	4,072	.90139	.09861	196,285	884,022	21.41
50 5	37,221	4,403	.88171	.11829	175,098	687,737	18.48
55 5	32,818	4,916	.85020	.14980	151,800	512,639	15.62
60 5	27,902	5,432	.80532	.19468	125,430	360,839	12.93
65 5	22,470	5,870	.73876	.26124	97,675	235,409	10.48
70 5	16,600	5,852	.64747	.35253	63,370	137,734	8.30
75 5	10,748	4,996	.53517	.46483	41,250	69,364	6.45
80 5	5,752	3,412	.40682	.59318	20,230	28,114	4.89
85 +	2,340	2,340	0.00000	1.00000	7,884	7,884	3.37

TABLE XIII-25

ABRIDGED LIFE TABLE, MEXICO, 1940
MALE

Age x n	l_x	$_nd_x$	$_np_x$	$_nq_x$	$_nL_x$	T_x	e_x
0 1	100,000	14,664	.85336	.14664	90,204	3,766,931	37.67
1 1	85,336	6,982	.91818	.08182	81,216	3,676,727	43.09
2 1	78,354	3,757	.95205	.04795	76,363	3,595,511	45.89
3 1	74,597	1,991	.97331	.02669	73,562	3,519,148	47.18
4 1	72,606	1,242	.98291	.01709	71,960	3,445,586	47.46
0 5	100,000	28,636	.71364	.28636	393,305	3,766,931	37.67
5 5	71,364	3,198	.95517	.04483	348,826	3,373,626	47.27
10 5	68,166	1,671	.97549	.02451	336,652	3,024,800	44.37
15 5	66,495	2,013	.96973	.03027	327,444	2,688,148	40.43
20 5	64,482	2,820	.95626	.04374	315,360	2,360,704	36.61
25 5	61,662	3,409	.94311	.05689	299,789	2,045,344	33.17
30 5	58,253	3,828	.93428	.06572	281,697	1,745,555	29.96
35 5	54,425	4,182	.92316	.07684	261,671	1,463,858	26.90
40 5	50,243	4,522	.90999	.09001	239,911	1,202,187	23.93
45 5	45,721	4,835	.89426	.10574	216,519	962,276	21.05
50 5	40,886	5,223	.87224	.12776	191,374	745,757	18.24
55 5	35,663	5,656	.84140	.15860	164,174	554,383	15.55
60 5	30,007	5,931	.80236	.19764	135,207	390,209	13.00
65 5	24,076	6,204	.74233	.25767	104,871	255,002	10.59
70 5	17,872	6,200	.65306	.34694	73,861	150,131	8.40
75 5	11,672	5,350	.54163	.45837	44,984	76,270	6.53
80 5	6,322	3,706	.41387	.58613	22,346	31,286	4.95
85 +	2,616	2,616	0.00000	1.00000	8,940	8,940	3.42

TABLE XIII-25 (continued)

ABRIDGED LIFE TABLE, MEXICO, 1940
FEMALE

Age x n	l_x	$_nd_x$	$_np_x$	$_nq_x$	$_nL_x$	T_x	e_x
0 1	100,000	13,052	.86948	.13052	91,373	3,983,698	39.84
1 1	86,948	7,158	.91767	.08233	82,725	3,892,325	44.77
2 1	79,790	4,079	.94888	.05112	77,628	3,809,600	47.75
3 1	75,711	2,195	.97101	.02899	74,570	3,731,972	49.29
4 1	73,516	1,382	.98120	.01880	72,797	3,657,402	49.75
0 5	100,000	27,866	.72134	.27866	399,093	3,983,698	39.84
5 5	72,134	3,254	.95490	.04510	352,533	3,584,605	49.69
10 5	68,880	1,536	.97771	.02229	340,562	3,232,072	46.92
15 5	67,344	1,998	.97032	.02968	331,726	2,891,510	42.94
20 5	65,346	2,418	.96301	.03699	320,686	2,559,784	39.17
25 5	62,928	3,051	.95152	.04848	307,015	2,239,098	35.58
30 5	59,877	3,313	.94467	.05533	291,105	1,932,083	32.27
35 5	56,564	3,537	.93746	.06254	273,979	1,640,978	29.01
40 5	53,027	3,762	.92904	.07096	255,729	1,366,999	25.78
45 5	49,265	4,062	.91755	.08245	236,168	1,111,270	22.56
50 5	45,203	4,578	.89874	.10126	214,571	875,102	19.36
55 5	40,625	5,376	.86767	.13233	189,687	660,531	16.26
60 5	35,249	6,319	.82071	.17929	160,449	470,844	13.36
65 5	28,930	7,268	.74882	.25118	126,482	310,395	10.73
70 5	21,662	7,370	.65978	.34022	89,888	183,913	8.49
75 5	14,292	6,509	.54458	.45542	55,190	94,025	6.58
80 5	7,783	4,558	.41435	.58565	27,521	38,835	4.99
85 +	3,225	3,225	0.00000	1.00000	11,314	11,314	3.51

TABLE XIII-26

ABRIDGED LIFE TABLE, MEXICO, 1950
MALE

Age x n	l_x	$_nd_x$	$_np_x$	$_nq_x$	$_nL_x$	T_x	e_x
0 1	100,000	11,994	.88006	.11994	91,832	4,615,612	46.16
1 1	88,006	4,970	.94353	.05647	85,074	4,523,780	51.40
2 1	83,036	2,686	.96765	.03235	81,612	4,438,706	53.46
3 1	80,350	1,529	.98097	.01903	79,555	4,357,094	54.23
4 1	78,821	910	.98845	.01155	78,348	4,277,539	54.27
0 5	100,000	22,089	.77911	.22089	416,421	4,615,612	46.16
5 5	77,911	2,184	.97198	.02802	384,095	4,199,191	53.90
10 5	75,727	1,248	.98352	.01648	375,516	3,815,096	50.38
15 5	74,479	1,582	.97876	.02124	368,442	3,439,580	46.18
20 5	72,897	2,155	.97043	.02957	359,098	3,071,138	42.13
25 5	70,742	2,592	.96336	.03664	347,231	2,712,040	38.34
30 5	68,150	2,987	.95616	.04384	333,282	2,364,809	34.70
35 5	65,163	3,382	.94811	.05189	317,360	2,031,527	31.18
40 5	61,781	3,850	.93768	.06232	299,281	1,714,167	27.75
45 5	57,931	4,424	.92364	.07636	278,596	1,414,886	24.42
50 5	53,507	5,100	.90468	.09532	254,786	1,136,290	21.24
55 5	48,407	5,838	.87938	.12062	227,439	881,504	18.21
60 5	42,569	6,560	.84592	.15408	196,445	654,065	15.37
65 5	36,009	7,290	.79754	.20246	161,821	457,620	12.71
70 5	28,719	7,830	.72736	.27264	124,020	295,799	10.30
75 5	20,889	7,600	.63619	.36381	85,446	171,779	8.22
80 5	13,289	6,299	.52601	.47399	50,700	86,333	6.50
85 5	6,990	4,185	.40123	.59877	24,488	35,633	5.10
90 5	2,805	2,037	.27364	.72636	8,931	11,145	3.97
95 +	768	768	0.00000	1.00000	2,214	2,214	2.88

TABLE XIII-26 (continued)

ABRIDGED LIFE TABLE, MEXICO, 1950
FEMALE

Age x n	l_x	$_nd_x$	$_np_x$	$_nq_x$	$_nL_x$	T_x	e_x
0 1	100,000	10,610	.89390	.10610	92,966	4,899,698	49.00
1 1	89,390	5,105	.94289	.05711	86,378	4,806,732	53.77
2 1	84,285	2,957	.96492	.03508	82,718	4,720,354	56.00
3 1	81,328	1,727	.97877	.02123	80,430	4,637,636	57.02
4 1	79,601	1,030	.98706	.01294	79,065	4,557,206	57.25
0 5	100,000	21,429	.78571	.21429	421,557	4,899,698	49.00
5 5	78,571	2,240	.97150	.02850	387,256	4,478,141	56.99
10 5	76,331	1,095	.98564	.01436	378,918	4,090,885	53.59
15 5	75,236	1,338	.98222	.01778	372,834	3,711,967	49.34
20 5	73,898	1,769	.97607	.02393	365,069	3,339,133	45.19
25 5	72,129	2,107	.97078	.02922	355,379	2,974,064	41.23
30 5	70,022	2,453	.96497	.03503	343,978	2,618,685	37.40
35 5	67,569	2,777	.95890	.04110	330,904	2,274,707	33.66
40 5	64,792	3,094	.95224	.04776	316,226	1,943,803	30.00
45 5	61,698	3,527	.94283	.05717	299,672	1,627,577	26.38
50 5	58,171	4,209	.92764	.07236	280,330	1,327,905	22.83
55 5	53,962	5,209	.90347	.09653	256,786	1,047,575	19.41
60 5	48,753	6,446	.86779	.13221	227,650	790,789	16.22
65 5	42,307	7,758	.81661	.18339	192,140	563,139	13.31
70 5	34,547	8,757	.74655	.25345	150,853	370,999	10.74
75 5	25,792	8.877	.65582	.34418	106,769	220,146	8.54
80 5	16,915	7,712	.54405	.45595	65,295	113,377	6.70
85 5	9,203	5,375	.41551	.58449	32,566	48,082	5.22
90 5	3,824	2,747	.28160	.71840	12,252	15,516	4.06
95 +	1,077	1,077	0.00000	1.00000	3,264	3,264	3.03

TABLE XIII-27

ABRIDGED LIFE TABLE, MEXICO, 1960
MALE

Age x n	l_x	$_n d_x$	$_n p_x$	$_n q_x$	$_n L_x$	T_x	e_x
0 1	100,000	8,279	.91721	.08279	94,196	5,637,516	56.38
1 1	91,721	2,565	.97203	.02797	90,208	5,543,320	60.44
2 1	89,156	1,221	.98630	.01370	88,509	5,453,112	61.16
3 1	87,935	780	.99113	.00887	87,529	5,364,603	61.01
4 1	87,155	407	.99533	.00467	86,943	5,277,074	60.55
0 5	100,000	13,252	.86748	.13252	447,385	5,637,516	56.38
5 5	86,748	1,204	.98612	.01388	430,730	5,190,131	59.83
10 5	85,544	779	.99089	.00911	425,772	4,759,401	55.64
15 5	84,765	1,062	.98747	.01253	421,171	4,333,629	51.12
20 5	83,703	1,582	.98109	.01891	414,559	3,912,458	46.74
25 5	82,121	2,003	.97561	.02439	405,597	3,497,899	42.59
30 5	80,118	2,336	.97085	.02915	394,752	3,092,302	38.60
35 5	77,782	2,751	.96462	.03538	382,033	2,697,550	34.68
40 5	75,031	3,321	.95574	.04426	366,851	2,315,517	30.86
45 5	71,710	3,977	.94454	.05546	348,606	1,948,666	27.17
50 5	67,733	4,758	.92976	.07024	326,440	1,600,060	23.62
55 5	62,975	5,782	.90818	.09182	300,421	1,273,290	20.22
60 5	57,193	6,849	.88025	.11975	268,842	972,869	17.01
65 5	50,344	8,143	.83825	.16175	231,362	704,027	13.98
70 5	42,201	9,673	.77079	.22921	186,822	472,665	11.20
75 5	32,528	10,517	.67668	.32332	136,348	285,843	8.79
80 5	22,011	9,755	.55683	.44317	85,669	149,495	6.79
85 5	12,256	7,157	.41606	.58394	43,390	63,826	5.21
90 5	5,099	3,735	.26756	.73244	16,159	20,436	4.01
95 +	1,364	1,364	0.00000	1.00000	4,277	4,277	3.13

TABLE XIII-27 (continued)

ABRIDGED LIFE TABLE, MEXICO, 1960
FEMALE

Age x n	l_x	$_nd_x$	$_np_x$	$_nq_x$	$_nL_x$	T_x	e_x
0 1	100,000	7,274	.92726	.07274	95,054	5,957,633	59.58
1 1	92,726	2,606	.97190	.02810	91,188	5,862,579	63.22
2 1	90,120	1,337	.98516	.01484	89,411	5,771,391	64.04
3 1	88,783	784	.99117	.00883	88,375	5,681,980	64.00
4 1	87,999	491	.99442	.00558	87,744	5,593,605	63.56
0 5	100,000	12,492	.87508	.12492	451,772	5,957,633	59.58
5 5	87,508	1,206	.98621	.01379	434,525	5,505,861	62.92
10 5	86,302	660	.99236	.00764	429,862	5,071,336	58.76
15 5	85,642	857	.98999	.01001	426,070	4,641,474	54.20
20 5	84,785	1,227	.98552	.01448	420,859	4,215,404	49.72
25 5	83,558	1,531	.98167	.01833	413,962	3,794,545	45.41
30 5	82,027	1,819	.97783	.02217	405,586	3,380,583	41.21
35 5	80,208	2,096	.97387	.02613	395,801	2,974,997	37.09
40 5	78,112	2,474	.96832	.03168	384,375	2,579,196	33.02
45 5	75,638	2,987	.96051	.03949	370,721	2,194,821	29.02
50 5	72,651	3,746	.94844	.05156	353,889	1,824,100	25.11
55 5	68,905	4,957	.92807	.07193	332,132	1,470,211	21.34
60 5	63,948	6,510	.89820	.10180	303,466	1,138,079	17.80
65 5	57,438	8,424	.85333	.14667	266,130	834,613	14.53
70 5	49,014	10,504	.78569	.21431	218,808	568,483	11.60
75 5	38,510	11,816	.69328	.30672	163,019	349,675	9.08
80 5	26,698	11,391	.57332	.42668	105,011	186,656	6.99
85 5	15,307	8,731	.42962	.57038	54,706	81,645	5.33
90 5	6,576	4,753	.27715	.72285	20,996	26,939	4.10
95 +	1,823	1,823	0.00000	1.00000	5,943	5,943	3.26

TABLE XIII-28

LIFE EXPECTANCY, MEXICO,
CENSUS YEARS

Year	Total*	Male	Female
1895	24.4	24.3	24.5
1900	25.3	25.0	25.6
1910	27.6	27.3	27.9
1921	34.7	33.7	35.6
1930	33.9	33.0	34.7
1940	38.8	37.7	39.8
1950	47.6	46.2	49.0
1960	58.0	56.4	59.6

*Simple arithmetic average of male and
female.

NOTES

[1] México, Secretaría de Economía, Dirección General de Estadística, Estadísticas Sociales del Porfiriato 1877-1910, México D.F., 1956.

[2] It is possible that the statistics of the period immediately following the Civil War are not as accurate as might be desired, and therefore, the use of Method B for this period might seem preferable; however, the reduction of fertility during the wartime period and the considerable international migration which had occurred rendered the use of Method B inadvisable. For a graphical analysis of census data, see Figure XIII-1.

[3] The age groups are not, for example, 20-24, 25-29, etc., but rather 21-25, 26-30, etc.

[4] This distortion can be seen in the masculinity ratios for some age groups. Because age-heaping is not equal for both sexes, being greater, in general, for females than for males, the irregularities in the sex ratios are notable:

Age Group	1895	1900	1910
0-10	104.7	104.5	104.1
11-30	91.7	91.6	91.4
31-60	101.4	100.8	100.3
61 +	119.7	113.8	106.6

[5] We estimated, for example, the percentage of those aged 30 within the 21-30 age group.

[6] It is unlikely that the habits of age-reporting in 1950 were identical to those in the 1894-1910 period. However, for the purpose of our estimates, the 1950 data seem a reasonable indicator, especially since we know that even in 1950 age-declarations were still highly inaccurate. How inaccurate they were can be assessed by calculating the Myers' index to the 1950 data. The value of 27.5 was given for male declarations in Mexico, and 35.8 for female declarations (the average of the two being 31.7). For other countries the Myers' index average is: Peru, 1940--30.6; Russia, 1897--20.5; Brazil, 1940--16.3; Australia, 1933--4.0.; and Sweden, 1939--1.2.

[7]It is certain that births were underenumerated during these periods, because births and deaths as listed were practically the same, as the following figures show (in thousands):

	1896-1900	1901-1910
Deaths	2,277.3	4,725.4
Births	2,273.0	4,844.5

Nevertheless, the census data give the increment of population during the periods 1896-1900 and 1901-1910 as 974.8 and 1553.1 thousand respectively.

[8]The inconsistencies can be seen as follows: According to the census data, the average annual intercensal growth rate was 14.8 per thousand between 1895 and 1900, but only 10.8 per thousand between 1900 and 1910. To what could this decline be due? In the censuses of 1895, 1900, and 1910 the percentage of the total population aged 10 and under was reported as 30.8, 30.6, and 31.5 respectively. The slight variation among these percentages indicates that there was no notable change in fertility during the 15 years in question. Moreover, as we will show later on, the net migration during this period, although higher for the years 1900-1910 than for 1895-1900, was, on the whole, insignificant. Therefore, the decline in the growth rate, if it actually occurred, would have to have been largely due to rising mortality. However, according to the registered deaths, the average annual death rate during the first five years was 34.7 per thousand, while in the last ten years it fell to 32.9 per thousand. It is probable that there was extensive under-registration of deaths, but if we can assume that omission did not increase over the years, then mortality had declined from the earlier period, and not risen. This fact, coupled with a constant fertility and an insignificant migration factor, is inconsistent with a declining intercensal geometric growth rate, particularly one of the magnitude previously indicated.

[9]México, Ministerio de Fomento, Dirección General de Estadística, Boletín Demográfico de la República Mexicana, 1896-1904.

[10]We used the same method for some years of the period 1921-1950; for an example, see Appendix IV.

[11]There are no statistics on the number of Mexican residents in the United States who returned to Mexico during this period, but because of the political unrest in Mexico and the limited mobility of the people, we can assume that the number is insignificant. It is assumed that the United States absorbs virtually all Mexican emigration, as can be deduced from the small number of Mexicans listed in the censuses of other countries of the world.

[12] The censuses did not give the age structure of the foreign-born. Thus it was not possible to use survival ratios by age groups. We calculated the survival ratio for all ages as follows:

$$_nP_{x+} = \frac{P^n_{x+n+}}{P^0_{x+}}$$

where:

$_nP_{x+}$ is the survival ratio for the population aged x and over at the beginning of the period for the n year period;

P^0_{x+} is the population aged x and over in the census for year 0;

P^n_{n+n+} is the population aged x+n and over in the census for year n.

In this case, x=0, 5 and n=5, 10

The differences obtained using these total survival ratios instead of survival ratios by age groups could be considered insignificant for the purposes of making an evaluation of the censuses. The total foreign-born enumerated in Mexico represent .4, .4, and .8 percent of the total population in 1895, 1900, and 1910, respectively.

[13] Argentina, 1895; Venezuela, 1950; Guatemala, 1950; Chile, 1952; Colombia, 1951.

[14] U.S., Department of Commerce, Bureau of the Census, Historical Statistics of the U.S.: Colonial Times to 1957, Washington, D.C., 1961, p. 58.

[15] Since the three censuses were taken in the month of October, the estimate is made only for a two-month period. The annual growth rates applied to these two-month periods are 7, 9, and 11 per thousand for the years 1895, 1900, and 1910, respectively. (The intercensal growth rate between 1900 and 1910 is 10.8.)

[16] Upon examining the death statistics by states, we must conclude that, in some cases, there is a notable omission. In 1895 the official death rate per thousand persons for some states is: Colima, 40.30; Federal District, 43.17; Morelos, 47.30; and Yucatan, 41.62. For others it is much lower: Baja California, 14.53; Chiapas, 10.44: Chihuahua, 19.98; Durango, 19.59; and Sonora, 14.04. The death rate for the entire country for the same year is 30.97.

[17] This figure, 201.2 thousand, represents 10.4 percent of the total enumerated in the age group 0-4; that is, 9.4 percent of the actual population 0-4 as estimated. In other words, one out of every 10 children in this age group was not enumerated in 1900.

[18] The difference between the figures 611.4 and 256.6 is mainly due to the inclusion of ages 0-4 in the analysis. It was deduced from these figures that the age group 0-4 in the 1895 census had an underenumeration of 19.9 percent over the enumerated population in these ages. This underenumeration includes that which is normal for this age group and that common to all ages (4.8 percent).

[19] Supporting this conclusion about the omission in the 1895 census is the following paragraph from the "Introduction" of the General Population Census of 1930 (Ministry of Economics, Office of Statistics, p. xiii) concerning the 1895 census:

> Since census experience was lacking, and since the population was classified in three categories: present, absent and passing through, this census can be considered as the forerunner of that of 1900, and lent itself to frequent duplications, omissions and errors.

[20] The rate for the official censuses of population is 14.8 per thousand.

[21] An example of life table construction by Method B is given in Appendix II.

[22] E. Arriaga, "Rural-Urban Mortality in Developing Countries and an Index for Detecting Rural Underregistration" Demography, Vol. 4, No. 1 (July, 1967).

[23] Ibid. In 1959-1961, for example, those states with better registration have death rates of 13.3 rural and 11.0 urban per thousand; for those states with poor rural registration the rates are 9.1 rural and 11.2 urban per thousand. In 1949-1951 the same happened. For the states with better registration the rates were 19.3 rural and 16.8 urban; and for states with poor rural registration, 13.6 rural and 16.4 urban.

[24] The crude mortality rate was calculated, taking the addition $m = \Sigma \, _n m_x \, C(x, x+5)$ where $_n m_x$ are the central mortality rates for the age group x to x+n, and $C(x, x+5)$ is the smoothed proportion of population in the same age group to total population. By comparing the estimated with the registered crude death rate, we obtained an idea of the omission.

[25]Given information for the age under one, this method of estimating individual distribution is acceptable. We tested the method on the years 1950-1961, for which information on individual ages 0-4 is available, and it was proven to be satisfactorily accurate.

[26]In addition, we found the individual age distribution for ages 10-14 in 1951-1955, and for ages 15-19 in 1956-1961.

[27]The smoothing was done using five-year age groups from 10-84. The formula used to obtain the smoothed age groups 25-69 was:

$$Q^*_{x,x+5} = \frac{1}{48}(-Q_{x-15,x-10} +12Q_{x-5,x} +24Q_{x,x+5} +15Q_{x+5,x+10} -2Q_{x+5,x+20}).$$

For the two five-year age groups 15-19 and 20-24, the formula used was:

$$Q^*_{x,x+5} = \frac{1}{48}(8Q_{x-5,x} +24Q_{x,x+5} +21Q_{x+5,x+10} -6Q_{x+5,x+20} +Q_{x+25,x+30}).$$

We used the inverse order of the coefficients for the age groups 70-74 and 75-79. Each $Q_{x,x+5}$ stands for the five-year age group aged x to x+5, and the asterisk (*) means "smoothed." The age groups 5-9, 10-14, and 80-84 were not smoothed.

[28]Census information deficiencies were due to incorrect declaration of age. We could not correct these deficiencies by smoothing, however, because to some extent the irregularities were due to a real break in the age-pattern arising from fertility changes during the Civil War.

[29]"The movimento de braceros" is a temporary movement of Mexican agricultural and farm workers to the U.S., which in some years has surpassed 100,000.

[30]Statistics have been published about those who left and those who entered Mexico for the period 1921-1960, but neither age nor sex is given (see México, Secretaria de Economía, Dirección General de Estadística, Anuario Estadístico). Information by sex and age is given only for immigrants but, because the proportion of persons entering Mexico who are immigrants is too small, its utilization is not advisable (United Nations, Sex and Age of International Migrants: Statistics for 1918-1947 (New York, 1953), p. 89 ff). The principal problem in dealing with Mexican migration is the movement of "braceros." This seasonal migration is registered in both countries (Mexico and the U.S.), but it is still impossible to reconstruct a complete picture of the whole movement or to make both registers agree. Above all, it seems that information is lacking about Mexicans returning from the U.S. to Mexico. It is suspected that a lot of "braceros" do not return. Some of

those who do return are not in the same category as they were previously. They stay in the U.S. more than the legally permitted time, and, after becoming illegal residents, are deported. There are a large number of Mexicans deported during some years. Another factor impairs a good comparison between U.S. and Mexican statistics on "braceros"--Mexico publishes statistics for the calender year, while the U.S. publishes statistics for the year ending June 30.

[31] Also, the statistics of migrants and the number of foreigners enumerated in Mexican censuses are not in agreement. This can be due to the fact that in Mexico, according to census definition, a foreigner would be enumerated if he had a resident visa and six months of residence at the census date.

[32] It should be noted that the total number of native-born Mexicans enumerated in countries other than the U.S. is insignificant. In addition, the use of census information is made easier by the favorable fact that Mexico and the U.S. have had practically the same census dates since 1930, the difference between them being less than two months.

[33] The life tables used in the calculation of survival ratios were the following:
U.S., Department of Commerce, Bureau of the Census, U.S. Life Tables, 1930, Washington, D.C., 1936. For the period 1921-1930: Tables IV-C and IV-D, "Life Table for Negro Male (Female) in the Registration States of 1920: 1919-1921," pp. 32-35.
U.S., Department of Commerce, Bureau of the Census, U.S. Life Table and Actuarial Tables, by Thomas N.E. Greville. For the period 1941-1950: Tables 11 and 12, "Life Table for Other Races (All Except White and Negro) Male (Female) in the U.S., 1929 to 1931," pp. 8-11.
U.S., Department of Health, Education, and Welfare, Public Health Service, National Office of Vital Statistics, Life Tables for 1941-51, by Monroe-Carlson Gustav Sirken. For the period 1951-1960: Tables 8 and 9, "Life Table for Non-White Male (Female)," pp. 22-25.

[34] Argentina, 1895; Colombia, 1951; Guatemala, 1950; Venezuela, 1950.

[35] Of course, because of the difference in age structure between total and foreign-born populations, it is not correct to assume that the survival ratios are the same for both. But because we are dealing with estimates, and because the errors that can be made are very small with respect to the total population, we felt we could make such an assumption. The total foreign-born population in Mexico has always been under one percent of the total

population except in the 1921 and 1930 censuses, when it just exceeded that figure. Possible errors are therefore insignificant.

[36]Before making the calculation of the survival ratios, we corrected the age group 0-4 in each census for underenumeration. Considering births and deaths for the period 1955-1960, we estimated that there was (as will be explained in the census analysis) an omission of about 15% in the ages 0-4 in 1960. The small percentage of omission was assumed for the other censuses. We then calculated the survival ratios for the periods 1921-1930, 1931-1940, 1941-1950, 1951-1960 and 1941-1960 respectively; their values were: for males, .8143, .8250, .8884, .9070, and .7840; and for females .8321, .8359, .9128, .9019, and .7983. The levels of survival ratios for each sex in 1951-1961 and for females in 1941-1951 are not what we would expect. Nevertheless, they can be explained by incorrect declaration of age, or by different underenumeration in each sex (as will be evident in the census analysis). In any case, we used the calculated values because we had assumed previously that the foreign-born population had the same error of enumeration as the total population.

[37]Also the ratio for 1940 can be accepted as slightly lower than those for 1930, 1950, and 1960, because young mothers (with high fertility) were relatively fewer than in other years, due to the decline of fertility during 1910-1920.

[38]Roland Pressat, L'Analyse Démographique (Paris: Presses Universitaires de France, 1961).

[39]There are two possible explanations for our finding a higher degree of omission for males than for females. First, there might be a larger degree of late registration for males than for females. Also, there might have been enumeration of females over 5 years old as under 5 years old. Possibly, when the age of a female had to be estimated, there was a tendency to attribute a lower age to females than to males, because girls seem smaller than boys of the same age.

[40]We began with the 1930-1940 period, where the same underenumeration for both sexes is shown in the 1940 census. Therefore, the observed differences between sexes in 1940-1950, 1950-1960, and 1940-1960 indicate different omissions for each sex in 1950 and 1960. This indication is confirmed by the trend of total sex ratio in all the censuses. After the adjustment for males in 1950 and females in 1960, we determined the sex ratio for these two censuses at 97.7 and 98.9 respectively.

[41]We spread 50,000 into the age group 30-39, 27,000 into the age group 40-49 and 23,000 into the age group 50-59.

[42]We spread 30,000 into 10-19, 35,000 into 20-29, 30,000 into 30-39 and 5,000 into 40-49.

[43]We made the redistribution principally in order to maintain the effect of the change of fertility during 1910-1920 and because the ten-year age group distributions could be considered smooth.

[44]For 1921 we used a different method to obtain the individual age distribution from 0 to 4; see Appendix IV.

XIV. NICARAGUA

Population information for Nicaragua has been available since 1778,[1] but the only national censuses were those of 1906 and after--1920, 1940, 1950, and 1963.[2] Age group distribution is available for total population beginning in 1920, and for each sex beginning with the 1940 census. Our study of mortality in Nicaragua therefore begins with the year 1920.

Vital statistics, especially death statistics, are incomplete. This fact makes the use of registered deaths in the construction of the life tables inadvisable. As in previous cases, fertility seems to have been without significant change during the period considered, and international net migration was almost nil. Therefore, Method B was used to construct life tables. Proportional age group distributions were obtained from census information, and estimates of the natural growth rates for each census year were established.

PROPORTIONAL AGE GROUP DISTRIBUTION OF THE POPULATION

A graphical cohort analysis is presented in Figure XIV-1; from this analysis it appears that the last three censuses are comparable in completeness and that age group distributions do not present any notable irregularities. Therefore, in order to obtain the proportional five-year age group distribution by sex (and for both sexes combined for 1920), the census information was smoothed according to the procedure explained in Appendix III. The distributions for ages 10-59 are presented in Table XIV-1.

ESTIMATION OF NATURAL GROWTH RATE

The censuses seem to be comparable in completeness. Therefore, we estimated natural growth rates by considering the intercensal annual geometric growth rates, which were 28.9 for the period 1950-1963, 23.4 for the period 1940-1950, and 13.5 for the period 1920-1940. Using these intercensal growth rates, we obtained the following growth rates for each census year: 12.7, 20.5, 25.5, and 32.0 for 1920, 1940, 1950, and 1963 respectively.

CONSTRUCTION OF LIFE TABLES

Life tables were constructed using Method B, the proportional age group distributions shown in Table XIV-1, and the estimated growth rates for the total population given above. The

FIGURE XIV-1

TEN-YEAR AGE GROUPS BY YEAR OF BIRTH, CENSUS POPULATION,
NICARAGUA, 1940-1963, MALE

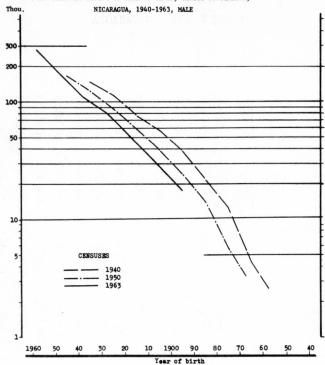

FEMALE

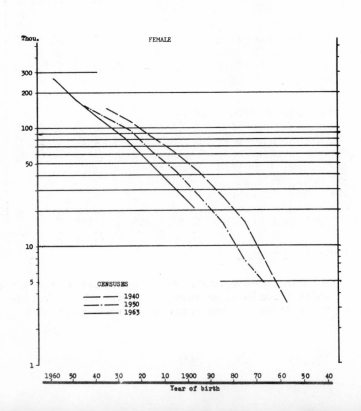

TABLE XIV-1

SMOOTHED PROPORTIONAL DISTRIBUTION OF THE POPULATION BY SEX AND FIVE-YEAR AGE GROUPS, AGES 10-59, NICARAGUA, CENSUS YEARS

Age Groups	1920 Total	1940 Male	1940 Female	1950 Male	1950 Female	1960 Male	1960 Female
Total	1.000000	1.000000	1.000000	1.000000	1.000000	1.000000	1.000000
10-59	.662973	.648168	.651006	.638803	.653523	.589382	.603818
10-14	.123294	.125044	.121102	.125506	.121080	.125617	.123218
15-19	.109862	.107532	.105046	.107678	.106893	.102548	.103161
20-24	.096363	.090677	.089561	.090446	.092882	.080919	.084120
25-29	.082536	.077105	.076929	.076196	.079745	.066496	.070165
30-34	.067642	.064627	.065225	.062573	.066302	.055281	.058287
35-39	.055423	.054121	.055301	.051839	.055175	.045968	.048316
40-44	.043012	.044332	.046010	.041964	.044291	.037625	.038866
45-49	.034650	.035891	.037950	.034159	.036002	.030832	.031753
50-54	.027782	.028045	.030430	.027239	.028717	.024742	.025581
55-59	.022409	.020794	.023451	.021203	.022434	.019354	.020351

United Nations set of $_5L_x$ values used in the quotient $\dfrac{C'(x,\ x+5)}{_5L_x}$
were: level 10 for 1920, level 30 for 1940, level 40 for 1950,
and level 60 for 1963. The slopes of the straight lines of adjustment, and the growth rates used for each sex are given in
Table XIV-2. The life tables are presented in Tables XIV-3 to
XIV-6.[3] A summary of life expectancy for Nicaragua is given in
Table XIV-7.

TABLE XIV-2

GROWTH RATES USED IN THE CONSTRUCTION OF
LIFE TABLES FOR NICARAGUA

	Growth Rates			Slopes of the Straight Lines of Adjustment of the $\log_e \dfrac{C'(x,\ x+5)}{_nL_5}$		
Year	Total	Male	Female	Male	Female	Average
1920	.0127					.013719
1940	.0205	.02166	.01934	.022201	.019824	.021013
1950	.0255	.02598	.02502	.025939	.024988	.025464
1963	.0330	.03294	.03306	.031880	.031987	.031934

CHAPTER XIV. NICARAGUA

TABLE XIV-3

ABRIDGED LIFE TABLE, NICARAGUA, 1920
TOTAL

Age x n	l_x	$_nd_x$	$_np_x$	$_nq_x$	$_nL_x$	T_x	e_x
0 1	100,000	27,677	.72323	.27677	74,423	2,434,990	24.35
1 4	72,323	13,405	.81465	.18535	260,294	2,360,567	32.64
0 5	100,000	41,082	.58918	.41082	334,717	2,434,990	24.35
5 5	58,918	6,232	.89423	.10577	272,712	2,100,273	35.65
10 5	52,686	3,089	.94138	.05862	255,411	1,827,561	34.69
15 5	49,598	3,213	.93523	.06477	240,510	1,572,150	31.70
20 5	46,385	3,775	.91861	.08139	222,740	1,331,640	28.71
25 5	42,610	4,040	.90519	.09481	203,018	1,108,900	26.02
30 5	38,570	4,168	.89194	.10806	182,507	905,882	23.49
35 5	34,402	4,278	.87564	.12436	161,378	723,375	21.03
40 5	30,124	4,347	.85569	.14431	139,778	561,997	18.66
45 5	25,776	4,342	.83155	.16845	117,996	422,219	16.38
50 5	21,434	4,243	.80205	.19795	96,471	304,223	14.19
55 5	17,191	4,060	.76385	.23615	75,674	207,752	12.08
60 5	13,132	3,783	.71195	.28805	55,996	132,078	10.06
65 5	9,349	3,369	.63969	.36031	38,023	76,082	8.14
70 5	5,980	2,744	.54123	.45877	22,565	38,060	6.36
75 5	3,237	1,900	.41289	.58711	10,852	15,495	4.79
80 5	1,336	998	.25316	.74684	3,787	4,643	3.47
85 +	338	338	0.00000	1.00000	856	856	2.53

TABLE XIV-4

ABRIDGED LIFE TABLE, NICARAGUA, 1940
MALE

Age x n	l_x	$_nd_x$	$_np_x$	$_nq_x$	$_nL_x$	T_x	e_x
0 1	100,000	21,972	.78028	.21972	79,489	3,387,771	33.88
1 4	78,028	9,290	.88094	.11906	291,993	3,308,282	42.40
0 5	100,000	31,262	.68738	.31262	371,482	3,387,771	33.88
5 5	68,738	4,346	.93678	.06322	328,532	3,016,289	43.88
10 5	64,392	2,259	.96492	.03508	316,194	2,687,756	41.74
15 5	62,133	2,605	.95807	.04193	304,799	2,371,562	38.17
20 5	59,528	3,256	.94531	.05469	289,763	2,066,763	34.72
25 5	56,272	3,485	.93807	.06193	272,638	1,777,000	31.58
30 5	52,787	3,590	.93200	.06800	255,061	1,504,362	28.50
35 5	49,197	3,851	.92172	.07828	236,581	1,249,301	25.39
40 5	45,346	4,274	.90575	.09425	216,363	1,012,719	22.33
45 5	41,072	4,760	.88409	.11591	193,761	796,357	19.39
50 5	36,312	5,234	.85585	.14415	168,770	602,596	16.60
55 5	31,077	5,657	.81797	.18203	141,489	433,826	13.96
60 5	25,420	5,939	.76636	.23364	112,380	292,336	11.50
65 5	19,481	5,966	.69377	.30623	82,436	179,956	9.24
70 5	13,515	5,462	.59585	.40415	53,373	97,520	7.22
75 5	8,053	4,254	.47178	.52822	28,667	44,147	5.48
80 5	3,799	2,567	.32425	.67565	11,672	15,480	4.07
85 +	1,232	1,232	0.00000	1.00000	3,807	3,807	3.09

TABLE XIV-4 (continued)

ABRIDGED LIFE TABLE, NICARAGUA, 1940
FEMALE

Age x n	l_x	n^d_x	n^p_x	n^q_x	n^L_x	T_x	e_x
0 1	100,000	20,046	.79954	.20046	81,426	3,509,192	35.09
1 4	79,954	9,423	.88215	.11785	299,454	3,427,766	42.87
0 5	100,000	29,469	.70531	.29469	380,880	3,509,192	35.09
5 5	70,531	4,530	.93577	.06423	337,012	3,128,312	44.35
10 5	66,001	2,513	.96193	.03807	323,651	2,791,299	42.29
15 5	63,488	2,886	.95454	.04546	310,844	2,467,648	38.87
20 5	60,602	3,550	.94142	.05858	294,434	2,156,804	35.59
25 5	57,052	3,829	.93288	.06712	275,721	1,862,370	32.64
30 5	53,222	3,880	.92710	.07290	256,415	1,586,650	29.81
35 5	49,343	3,875	.92146	.07854	237,001	1,330,235	26.96
40 5	45,467	3,905	.91411	.08589	217,615	1,093,234	24.04
45 5	41,562	4,099	.90138	.09862	197,761	875,619	21.07
50 5	37,463	4,468	.88073	.11927	176,415	677,858	18.09
55 5	32,995	4,994	.84863	.15137	152,890	501,443	15.20
60 5	28,001	5,626	.79908	.20092	126,367	348,553	12.45
65 5	22,375	6,105	.72715	.27285	96,839	222,186	9.93
70 5	16,270	6,046	.62836	.37164	65,984	125,347	7.70
75 5	10,223	5,104	.50076	.49924	37,449	59,363	5.81
80 5	5,119	3,354	.34493	.65507	16,181	21,914	4.28
85 +	1,766	1,766	0.00000	1.00000	5,734	5,734	3.25

TABLE XIV-5

ABRIDGED LIFE TABLE, NICARAGUA, 1950
MALE

Age x n	l_x	$_nd_x$	$_np_x$	$_nq_x$	$_nL_x$	T_x	e_x
0 1	100,000	19,038	.80962	.19038	82,167	3,930,251	39.30
1 4	80,962	7,626	.90580	.09420	307,310	3,848,084	47.53
0 5	100,000	26,664	.73336	.26664	389,477	3,930,251	39.30
5 5	73,336	3,484	.95249	.04751	354,414	3,540,774	48.28
10 5	69,851	1,792	.97435	.02565	344,725	3,186,360	45.62
15 5	68,060	2,190	.96783	.03217	335,466	2,841,636	41.75
20 5	65,870	2,846	.95679	.04321	322,507	2,506,170	38.05
25 5	63,024	3,074	.95123	.04877	307,418	2,183,663	34.65
30 5	59,951	3,169	.94713	.05287	291,927	1,876,244	31.30
35 5	56,781	3,437	.93947	.06053	275,543	1,584,318	27.90
40 5	53,344	3,909	.92672	.07328	257,313	1,308,774	24.53
45 5	49,435	4,538	.90821	.09179	236,258	1,051,461	21.27
50 5	44,897	5,264	.88276	.11724	211,813	815,204	18.16
55 5	39,633	6,042	.84755	.15245	183,562	603,390	15.22
60 5	33,591	6,781	.79812	.20188	151,456	419,828	12.50
65 5	26,810	7,310	.72733	.27267	116,046	268,372	10.01
70 5	19,500	7,191	.63122	.36878	79155	152,327	7.81
75 5	12,308	6,039	.50934	.49066	45,382	73,172	5.94
80 5	6,269	3,982	.36476	.63524	20,108	27,790	4.43
85 +	2,287	2,287	0.00000	1.00000	7,682	7,682	3.36

TABLE XIV-5 (continued)

ABRIDGED LIFE TABLE, NICARAGUA, 1950
FEMALE

Age x n	l_x	$_n d_x$	$_n p_x$	$_n q_x$	$_n L_x$	T_x	e_x
0 1	100,000	17,218	.82782	.17218	83,987	4,079,535	40.80
1 4	82,782	7,685	.90717	.09283	314,504	3,995,549	48.27
0 5	100,000	24,902	.75098	.24902	398,491	4,079,535	40.80
5 5	75,098	3,629	.95167	.04833	362,867	3,681,044	49.02
10 5	71,468	2,015	.97181	.02819	352,293	3,318,177	46.43
15 5	69,453	2,428	.96505	.03495	341,801	2,965,884	42.70
20 5	67,026	3,080	.95405	.04595	327,724	2,624,083	39.15
25 5	63,946	3,349	.94763	.05237	311,384	2,296,359	35.91
30 5	60,597	3,399	.94390	.05610	294,496	1,984,975	32.76
35 5	57,198	3,434	.93997	.06003	277,421	1,690,479	29.55
40 5	53,764	3,556	.93386	.06614	260,048	1,413,058	26.28
45 5	50,208	3,889	.92254	.07746	241,612	1,153,010	22.96
50 5	46,319	4,447	.90399	.09601	220,879	911,398	19.68
55 5	41,872	5,254	.87453	.12547	196,840	690,519	16.49
60 5	36,618	6,298	.82800	.17200	168,081	493,679	13.48
65 5	30,320	7,307	.75900	.24100	133,937	325,599	10.74
70 5	23,013	7,765	.66257	.33743	95,712	191,662	8.33
75 5	15,248	7,044	.53804	.46196	57,711	95,950	6.29
80 5	8,204	5,012	.38910	.61090	27,053	38,239	4.66
85 +	3,192	3,192	0.00000	1.00000	11,186	11,186	3.50

TABLE XIV-6

ABRIDGED LIFE TABLE, NICARAGUA, 1963
MALE

Age x n	l_x	$_nd_x$	$_np_x$	$_nq_x$	$_nL_x$	T_x	e_x
0 1	100,000	13,802	.86198	.13802	86,961	5,052,498	50.52
1 4	86,198	4,748	.94491	.05509	334,431	4,965,537	57.61
0 5	100,000	18,551	.81449	.18551	421,391	5,052,498	50.52
5 5	81,449	1,914	.97650	.02350	400,116	4,631,107	56.86
10 5	79,535	855	.98926	.01074	395,569	4,230,990	53.20
15 5	78,681	1,266	.98392	.01608	390,797	3,835,421	48.75
20 5	77,415	1,843	.97620	.02380	382,708	3,444,624	44.50
25 5	75,573	2,035	.97307	.02693	372,747	3,061,916	40.52
30 5	73,537	2,112	.97128	.02872	362,490	2,689,170	36.57
35 5	71,426	2,371	.96680	.03320	351,427	2,326,680	32.57
40 5	69,055	2,896	.95807	.04193	338,457	1,975,252	28.60
45 5	66,159	3,715	.94384	.05616	322,109	1,636,795	24.74
50 5	62,443	4,811	.92295	.07705	300,956	1,314,687	21.05
55 5	57,632	6,193	.89254	.10746	273,649	1,013,731	17.59
60 5	51,439	7,831	.84777	.15223	238,739	740,082	14.39
65 5	43,609	9,486	.78247	.21753	195,379	501,343	11.50
70 5	34,123	10,505	.69213	.30787	144,699	305,964	8.97
75 5	23,617	10,020	.57575	.42425	92,139	161,266	6.83
80 5	13,598	7,671	.43584	.56416	46,768	69,127	5.08
85 +	5,926	5,926	0.00000	1.00000	22,359	22,359	3.77

TABLE XIV-6 (continued)

ABRIDGED LIFE TABLE, NICARAGUA, 1963
FEMALE

Age x n	l_x	$_nd_x$	$_np_x$	$_nq_x$	$_nL_x$	T_x	e_x
0 1	100,000	11,964	.88036	.11964	88,773	5,329,354	53.29
1 4	88,036	4,629	.94741	.05259	342,073	5,240,581	59.53
0 5	100,000	16,593	.83407	.16593	430,846	5,329,354	53.29
5 5	83,407	1,938	.97676	.02324	409,914	4,898,508	58.73
10 5	81,469	946	.98839	.01161	405,016	4,488,594	55.10
15 5	80,522	1,311	.98371	.01629	399,807	4,083,578	50.71
20 5	79,211	1,832	.97687	.02313	391,712	3,683,771	46.51
25 5	77,379	2,056	.97343	.02657	381,781	3,292,059	42.54
30 5	75,323	2,132	.97169	.02831	371,326	2,910,278	38.64
35 5	73,190	2,248	.96929	.03071	360,416	2,538,953	34.69
40 5	70,942	2,512	.96459	.03541	348,661	2,178,536	30.71
45 5	68,431	3,048	.95547	.04453	334,970	1,829,876	26.74
50 5	65,383	3,887	.94056	.05944	317,800	1,494,906	22.86
55 5	61,497	5,119	.91677	.08323	295,609	1,177,106	19.14
60 5	56,378	6,895	.87770	.12230	265,974	881,497	15.64
65 5	49,483	9,102	.81606	.18394	226,204	615,523	12.44
70 5	40,381	11,063	.72603	.27397	175,343	389,319	9.64
75 5	29,318	11,468	.60885	.39115	117,439	213,976	7.30
80 5	17,850	9,409	.47289	.52711	63,392	96,537	5.41
85 +	8,441	8,441	0.00000	1.00000	33,144	33,144	3.93

TABLE XIV-7

LIFE EXPECTANCY, NICARAGUA
CENSUS YEARS

Year	Total*	Male	Female
1920	24.3		
1940	34.5	33.9	35.1
1950	40.1	39.3	40.8
1963	51.9	50.5	53.3

*Simple arithmetic average of male and
female.

NOTES

[1]República de Nicaragua, Ministerio de Economía, Dirección
General de Estadística y Censos, Censo General de la República
de Nicaragua, Mayo 1950, Vol XVII, Managua, 1954, p. 17.

[2]República de Nicaragua, Ministerio de Economía, Dirección
General de Estadística y Censos, Censos Nacionales 1963,
Pobliación, Vol. I, p. xi.

[3]A practical example of life table construction by Method B
is given in Appendix II.

XV. PANAMA

Six censuses have been taken in Panama since its indepen-
dence in 1903. However, the age group distribution of the population is given only in the 1930 census and in those following
(decennially). Death statistics, especially for the very early
ages, are incomplete; in fact, so little information is available
of any kind that it would be difficult even to estimate actual
completeness. Thus we do not recommend construction of life
tables using Method A and have utilized Method B.

Fertility in Panama has been relatively constant, with
the possible exception of the 1930's, when there was a slight
decline. However, the variation seems not to have been significant, considering the age structure of the population[1] (see Fig.
XV-1). Net international migration did take place to a certain
extent from 1910 to 1930, but not to an extent which would pro-
hibit the use of Method B. From 1910 to 1920 international immigration was noticeable (relative to the size of the Panamanian
population), but some of the foreign-born seem to have emigrated
in the following decade. Since 1930, the foreign-born enumerated
in the censuses have remained almost constant around 50,000[2]--
with a tendency to decline (only 44,000 were enumerated in the
1960 census[3]). In addition, the average age of the foreign-born
became older between 1950 and 1960--the mean age increased from
45.1 in 1950 to 47.3 in 1960. Therefore, according to census
information, international immigration seems to have been insignificant for the period since 1930. In addition, the emigration
of Panamanians has not been significant. Still, the age distribution, at least in the more advanced adult ages, could have been
affected to some degree by international migration. Fortunately,
the age structure of the native and foreign-born population is
available for 1950 and 1960.

Taking the above factors into account, it is possible to
obtain the proportional age group distribution and the natural
growth rate of the population to construct life tables for Panama
by means of Method B.

PROPORTIONAL AGE GROUP DISTRIBUTION OF THE POPULATION

A graphical cohort analysis of population data for the
years since 1930 is presented on a semilogarithmic scale in
Figure XV-1. The younger age groups of the 1930, 1940, and 1950
censuses seem to be underenumerated when compared with similar

FIGURE XV-1

TEN-YEAR AGE GROUPS BY YEAR OF BIRTH, CENSUS POPULATION,
PANAMA, 1930-1960, MALE

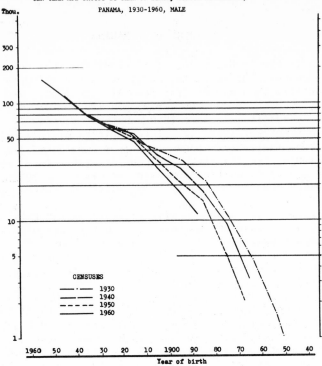

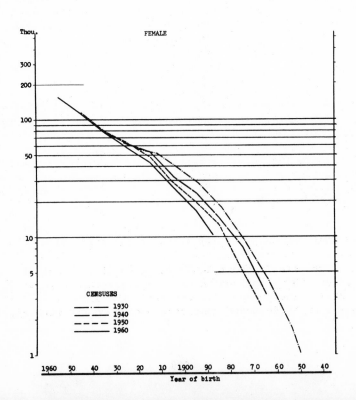

age groups in the 1960 census. Throughout the four censuses, the
enumerated population for males and females belonging to cohorts
born after 1910 does not decline from 1930 to 1950. The number
of cohorts enumerated in 1940, 1950, and 1960 which were born
during the years from 1930 to 1940 remained practically the same
during the twenty-year period. International migration since
1930 has been insignificant and cannot be considered the cause of
this particular age structure. Therefore, there is no doubt that
there was a greater degree of underenumeration in younger ages
than in older ages in the 1930, 1940, and 1950 censuses.[4]

In order to establish the proportional age group distribution 10-59 we considered two factors: the foreign-born population,[5]
and the underenumeration in the young ages. These two factors
made the age structure of the population appear to be a little
older than it actually was.

The age group distribution for each sex in the 1960 census
was modified by slightly reducing the total population enumerated
in the age group 40-59. For the 1950 census, we corrected the
age group distribution in age groups under 20 and over 40. The
younger age groups were increased to compensate for underenumeration; the older age groups were diminished slightly to subtract
the numbers added by the foreign-born population. Corrections in
the 1930 and 1940 age group distributions were made principally
in the young age groups, which were increased according to the
graphical cohort analysis (Fig. XV-1). The corrected age group
distributions were smoothed according to the procedure explained
in Appendix III, and the proportional age group distributions for
each census year were obtained (Table XV-1).

ESTIMATION OF NATURAL GROWTH RATE

Natural growth rates were estimated by taking into account
existing estimates,[6] the intercensal annual geometric growth
rates,[7] and the official growth rates.[8] The estimates of the
growth rates obtained for each census year were: 17.0, 23.0, 27.1,
and 30.2 per thousand for 1930, 1940, 1950, and 1960 respectively.

CONSTRUCTION OF LIFE TABLES

Life tables were constructed using Method B, the proportional age group distribution (Table XV-1), and the estimates of
the natural growth rates given above. The set of $_5L_x$ values from
the United Nations Model Life Tables used in the quotient
$\dfrac{C'(x, x+5)}{_5L_x}$ were: levels 35, 45, 50, and 80 for the years 1930,
1940, 1950, and 1950 respectively. The slopes of the straight

TABLE XV-1

SMOOTHED PROPORTIONAL DISTRIBUTION OF THE POPULATION BY SEX AND FIVE-YEAR AGE GROUPS, AGES 10-59, PANAMA, CENSUS YEARS

Age Groups	1930 Male	1930 Female	1940 Male	1940 Female	1950 Male	1950 Female	1960 Male	1960 Female
Total	1.000000	1.000000	1.000000	1.000000	1.000000	1.000000	1.000000	1.000000
10-59	.668654	.652741	.658122	.653603	.637653	.631755	.622105	.621605
10-14	.114246	.116592	.118707	.120615	.115375	.119057	.118847	.120883
15-19	.101879	.102417	.104070	.105101	.098964	.101948	.099300	.101496
20-24	.089157	.088342	.091231	.091033	.085776	.087731	.082255	.084386
25-29	.078772	.076998	.078939	.078148	.075015	.075451	.070222	.071536
30-34	.069694	.066490	.066455	.065204	.066142	.064280	.060696	.060582
35-39	.060199	.057174	.056278	.054939	.056662	.053995	.052431	.051453
40-44	.051634	.048173	.046602	.045369	.046844	.043435	.045200	.043237
45-49	.043136	.040012	.038771	.037685	.038559	.035428	.038027	.035976
50-54	.034016	.031635	.031825	.030902	.030283	.028053	.030474	.028734
55-59	.026521	.024908	.025244	.024607	.024033	.022377	.024653	.023322

232

lines of adjustment and the growth rates used for each sex are presented in Table XV-2. The life tables for the four years are presented in Tables XV-3 to XV-6,[9] and the summary of life expectancy for each year is given in Table XV-7.

TABLE XV-2

GROWTH RATES USED IN THE CONSTRUCTION OF
LIFE TABLES FOR PANAMA

	Growth Rates			Slopes of the Straight Lines of Adjustment of the $\log_e \dfrac{C'(x,\ x+5)}{_nL_5}$		
Year	Total	Male	Female	Male	Female	Average
1930	.0170	.01580	.01820	.014725	.017623	.016174
1940	.0230	.02208	.02390	.022204	.024054	.023129
1950	.0271	.02523	.02897	.025177	.029128	.027153
1960	.0302	.02860	.03180	.028179	.031330	.029755

TABLE XV-3

ABRIDGED LIFE TABLE, PANAMA, 1930
MALE

Age x n	l_x	$_nd_x$	$_np_x$	$_nq_x$	$_nL_x$	T_x	e_x
0 1	100,000	21,821	.78179	.21821	79,591	3,553,915	35.54
1 4	78,179	8,891	.88628	.11372	293,395	3,474,323	44.44
0 5	100,000	30,712	.69288	.30712	372,986	3,553,915	35.54
5 5	69,288	3,849	.94445	.05555	332,538	3,180,929	45.91
10 5	65,440	1,781	.97278	.02722	322,647	2,848,390	43.53
15 5	63,658	2,175	.96583	.03417	313,541	2,525,744	39.68
20 5	61,483	2,891	.95297	.04703	300,493	2,212,202	35.98
25 5	58,592	3,183	.94568	.05432	285,028	1,911,710	32.63
30 5	55,409	3,349	.93956	.06044	268,815	1,626,682	29.36
35 5	52,060	3,686	.92919	.07081	251,361	1,357,867	26.08
40 5	48,374	4,204	.91310	.08690	231,745	1,106,506	22.87
45 5	44,170	4,803	.89127	.10873	209,220	874,761	19.80
50 5	39,367	5,401	.86279	.13721	183,713	665,541	16.91
55 5	33,966	5,958	.82460	.17540	155,267	481,828	14.19
60 5	28,008	6,370	.77257	.22743	124,324	326,561	11.66
65 5	21,638	6,505	.69938	.30062	91,937	202,237	9.35
70 5	15,134	6,043	.60067	.39933	60,007	110,301	7.29
75 5	9,090	4,766	.47574	.52426	32,492	50,293	5.53
80 5	4,325	2,908	.32757	.67243	13,337	17,801	4.12
85 +	1,417	1,417	0.00000	1.00000	4,464	4,464	3.15

TABLE XV-3 (continued)

ABRIDGED LIFE TABLE, PANAMA, 1930
FEMALE

Age x n	l_x	$_nd_x$	$_np_x$	$_nq_x$	$_nL_x$	T_x	e_x
0 1	100,000	19,945	.80055	.19945	81,494	3,623,368	36.23
1 4	80,055	9,154	.88566	.11434	300,397	3,541,873	44.24
0 5	100,000	29,098	.70902	.29098	381,891	3,623,368	36.23
5 5	70,902	4,198	.94079	.05921	339,705	3,241,476	45.72
10 5	66,704	2,197	.96706	.03294	327,972	2,901,771	43.50
15 5	64,507	2,605	.95961	.04039	316,669	2,573,799	39.90
20 5	61,901	3,316	.94643	.05357	301,548	2,257,130	36.46
25 5	58,585	3,641	.93784	.06216	283,884	1,955,582	33.38
30 5	54,944	3,734	.93204	.06796	265,411	1,671,698	30.43
35 5	51,209	3,771	.92636	.07364	246,621	1,406,287	27.46
40 5	47,438	3,844	.91898	.08102	227,653	1,159,667	24.45
45 5	43,595	4,090	.90618	.09382	207,983	932,014	21.38
50 5	39,505	4,527	.88542	.11458	186,520	724,031	18.33
55 5	34,978	5,137	.85314	.14686	162,508	537,510	15.37
60 5	29,841	5,869	.80332	.19668	135,031	375,002	12.57
65 5	23,972	6,448	.73101	.26899	104,029	239,972	10.01
70 5	17,524	6,454	.63169	.36831	71,259	135,943	7.76
75 5	11,070	5,496	.50353	.49647	40,658	64,683	5.84
80 5	5,574	3,638	.34737	.65263	17,661	24,025	4.31
85 +	1,936	1,936	0.00000	1.00000	6,364	6,364	3.29

TABLE XV-4

ABRIDGED LIFE TABLE, PANAMA, 1940
MALE

Age x n	l_x	$_nd_x$	$_np_x$	$_nq_x$	$_nL_x$	T_x	e_x
0 1	100,000	17,727	.82273	.17727	83,373	4,149,965	41.50
1 4	82,273	6,968	.91530	.08470	313,985	4,066,591	49.43
0 5	100,000	24,695	.75305	.24695	397,359	4,149,965	41.50
5 5	75,305	3,219	.95725	.04275	365,255	3,752,606	49.83
10 5	72,086	1,699	.97644	.02356	356,150	3,387,351	46.99
15 5	70,387	2,099	.97018	.02982	347,306	3,031,201	43.06
20 5	68,288	2,731	.96001	.03999	334,872	2,683,896	39.30
25 5	65,557	2,940	.95516	.04484	320,406	2,349,023	35.83
30 5	62,617	3,018	.95181	.04819	305,628	2,028,618	32.40
35 5	59,600	3,265	.94521	.05479	290,050	1,722,990	28.91
40 5	56,334	3,724	.93389	.06611	272,721	1,432,940	25.44
45 5	52,610	4,381	.91673	.08327	252,566	1,160,219	22.05
50 5	48,229	5,185	.89249	.10751	228,731	907,653	18.82
55 5	43,044	6,082	.85870	.14130	200,603	678,922	15.77
60 5	36,962	6,999	.81064	.18936	167,904	478,319	12.94
65 5	29,963	7,756	.74115	.25885	130,852	310,416	10.36
70 5	22,207	7,851	.64645	.35355	91,169	179,563	8.09
75 5	14,356	6,804	.52605	.47395	53,719	88,395	6.16
80 5	7,552	4,661	.38276	.61724	24,671	34,675	4.59
85 +	2,891	2,891	0.00000	1.00000	10,004	10,004	3.46

TABLE XV-4 (continued)

ABRIDGED LIFE TABLE, PANAMA, 1940
FEMALE

Age x n	l_x	$_nd_x$	$_np_x$	$_nq_x$	$_nL_x$	T_x	e_x
0 1	100,000	15,877	.84123	.15877	85,215	4,326,221	43.26
1 4	84,123	6,978	.91704	.08296	321,402	4,241,006	50.41
0 5	100,000	22,856	.77144	.22856	406,617	4,326,221	43.26
5 5	77,144	3,336	.95675	.04325	374,184	3,919,604	50.81
10 5	73,808	1,897	.97429	.02571	364,301	3,545,421	48.04
15 5	71,910	2,300	.96802	.03198	354,373	3,181,119	44.24
20 5	69,611	2,909	.95821	.04179	341,052	2,826,746	40.61
25 5	66,702	3,148	.95280	.04720	325,653	2,485,694	37.27
30 5	63,554	3,186	.94987	.05013	309,808	2,160,041	33.99
35 5	60,368	3,226	.94656	.05344	293,802	1,850,234	30.65
40 5	57,142	3,379	.94086	.05914	277,408	1,556,432	27.24
45 5	53,762	3,756	.93013	.06987	259,741	1,279,024	23.79
50 5	50,006	4,367	.91268	.08732	239,549	1,019,283	20.38
55 5	45,639	5,262	.88471	.11529	215,726	779,734	17.08
60 5	40,377	6,460	.84001	.15999	186,591	564,007	13.97
65 5	33,918	7,703	.77290	.22710	151,115	377,417	11.13
70 5	26,215	8,440	.67806	.32194	110,222	226,302	8.63
75 5	17,775	7,901	.55548	.44452	68,259	116,080	6.53
80 5	9,874	5,822	.41041	.58959	33,201	47,820	4.84
85 +	4,052	4,052	0.00000	1.00000	14,619	14,619	3.61

TABLE XV-5

ABRIDGED LIFE TABLE, PANAMA, 1950
MALE

Age x n	l_x	$_nd_x$	$_np_x$	$_nq_x$	$_nL_x$	T_x	e_x
0 1	100,000	13,898	.86102	.13898	86,903	4,882,789	48.83
1 4	86,102	5,059	.94124	.05876	333,429	4,795,886	55.70
0 5	100,000	18.957	.81043	.18957	420,332	4,882,789	48.83
5 5	81,043	2,304	.97157	.02843	397,106	4,462,458	55.06
10 5	78,739	1,238	.98428	.01572	390,621	4,065,352	51.63
15 5	77,501	1,629	.97898	.02102	383,971	3,674,731	47.42
20 5	75,872	2,178	.97129	.02871	374,134	3,290,760	43.37
25 5	73,694	2,345	.96818	.03182	362,566	2,916,626	39.58
30 5	71,349	2,397	.96640	.03360	350,819	2,554,060	35.80
35 5	68,952	2,624	.96195	.03805	338,404	2,203,241	31.95
40 5	66,328	3,100	.95326	.04674	324,278	1,864,838	28.12
45 5	63,228	3,851	.93910	.06090	307,064	1,540,560	24.37
50 5	59,377	4,850	.91832	.08168	285,458	1,233,496	20.77
55 5	54,527	6,104	.88806	.11194	258,254	948,038	17.39
60 5	48,423	7,577	.84352	.15648	224,176	689,784	14.24
65 5	40,846	9,045	.77855	.22145	182,540	465,608	11.40
70 5	31,801	9,901	.68867	.31133	134,511	283,068	8.90
75 5	21,900	9,356	.57277	.42723	85,221	148,557	6.78
80 5	12,544	7,110	.43318	.56682	43,040	63,335	5.05
85 +	5,434	5,434	0.00000	1.00000	20,296	20,296	3.74

TABLE XV-5 (continued)

ABRIDGED LIFE TABLE, PANAMA, 1950
FEMALE

Age x n	l_x	$_nd_x$	$_np_x$	$_nq_x$	$_nL_x$	T_x	e_x
0 1	100,000	12,083	.87917	.12083	88,703	5,105,244	51.05
1 4	87,917	5,020	.94291	.05709	340,820	5,016,542	57.06
0 5	100,000	17,102	.82898	.17102	429,522	5,105,244	51.05
5 5	82,898	2,425	.97074	.02926	406,146	4,675,722	56.40
10 5	80,472	1,423	.98231	.01769	398,832	4,269,576	53.06
15 5	79,049	1,764	.97768	.02232	391,287	3,870,744	48.97
20 5	77,285	2,251	.97088	.02912	381,011	3,479,458	45.02
25 5	75,034	2,442	.96746	.03254	369,073	3,098,447	41.29
30 5	72,592	2,488	.96573	.03427	356,763	2,729,374	37.60
35 5	70,104	2,570	.96334	.03666	344,157	2,372,610	33.84
40 5	67,534	2,791	.95868	.04132	330,889	2,028,454	30.04
45 5	64,743	3,263	.94960	.05040	315,945	1,697,565	26.22
50 5	61,480	4,009	.93479	.06521	297,911	1,381,620	22.47
55 5	57,471	5,107	.91114	.08886	275,409	1,083,709	18.86
60 5	52,364	6,686	.87232	.12768	246,278	808,301	15.44
65 5	45,678	8,630	.81107	.18893	208,168	562,023	12.30
70 5	37,048	10,314	.72160	.27840	160,372	353,855	9.55
75 5	26,734	10,559	.60502	.39498	106,753	193,483	7.24
80 5	16,174	8,582	.46938	.53062	57,271	86,730	5.36
85 +	7,592	7,592	0.00000	1.00000	29,459	29,459	3.88

TABLE XV-6

ABRIDGED LIFE TABLE, PANAMA, 1960
MALE

Age x n	l_x	$_nd_x$	$_np_x$	$_nq_x$	$_nL_x$	T_x	e_x
0 1	100,000	8,106	.91894	.08106	92,329	5,975,045	59.75
1 4	91,894	2,726	.97034	.02966	361,641	5,882,716	64.02
0 5	100,000	10,832	.89168	.10832	453,971	5,975,045	59.75
5 5	89,168	1,166	.98692	.01308	441,622	5,521,075	61.92
10 5	88,002	611	.99306	.00694	438,532	5,079,452	57.72
15 5	87,391	908	.98961	.01039	435,053	4,640,921	53.11
20 5	86,483	1,286	.98513	.01487	429,353	4,205,867	48.63
25 5	85,198	1,406	.98350	.01650	422,451	3,776,514	44.33
30 5	83,792	1,468	.98248	.01752	415,359	3,354,064	40.03
35 5	82,324	1,695	.97941	.02059	407,579	2,938,704	35.70
40 5	80,629	2,187	.97287	.02713	398,081	2,531,125	31.39
45 5	78,442	3,023	.96146	.03854	385,286	2,133,044	27.19
50 5	75,419	4,215	.94411	.05589	367,399	1,747,758	23.17
55 5	71,204	5,834	.91807	.08193	342,606	1,380,358	19.39
60 5	65,370	7,947	.87842	.12158	308,481	1,037,752	15.88
65 5	57,422	10,372	.81937	.18063	262,813	729,271	12.70
70 5	47,050	12,447	.73546	.26454	205,266	466,458	9.91
75 5	34,603	12,970	.62519	.37481	140,211	261,192	7.55
80 5	21,634	11,010	.49107	.50893	78,208	120,981	5.59
85 +	10,624	10,624	0.00000	1.00000	42,774	42,774	4.03

TABLE XV-6 (continued)

ABRIDGED LIFE TABLE, PANAMA, 1960
FEMALE

Age x n	l_x	$_nd_x$	$_np_x$	$_nq_x$	$_nL_x$	T_x	e_x
0 1	100,000	6,808	.93192	.06808	93,589	6,317,672	63.18
1 4	93,192	2,491	.97320	.02680	367,339	6,224,084	66.79
0 5	100,000	9,305	.90695	.09305	460,927	6,317,672	63 18
5 5	90,695	1,068	.98822	.01178	449,592	5,856,745	64.58
10 5	89,626	563	.99372	.00628	446,767	5,407,153	60.33
15 5	89,064	802	.99100	.00900	443,604	4,960,386	55.69
20 5	88,262	1,118	.98733	.01267	438,654	4,516,782	51.17
25 5	87,144	1,266	.98548	.01452	432,590	4,078,128	46.80
30 5	85,879	1,352	.98425	.01575	426,069	3,645,538	42.45
35 5	84,526	1,500	.98226	.01774	418,992	3,219,469	38.09
40 5	83,026	1,810	.97819	.02181	410,868	2,800,477	33.73
45 5	81,216	2,378	.97073	.02927	400,572	2,389,609	29.42
50 5	78,838	3,250	.95878	.04122	386,700	1,989,037	25.23
55 5	75,588	4,553	.93977	.06023	367,517	1,602,337	21.20
60 5	71,035	6,554	.90774	.09226	340,324	1,234,820	17.38
65 5	64,481	9,382	.85449	.14551	301,043	894,497	13.87
70 5	55,099	12,494	.77324	.22676	246,279	593,454	10.77
75 5	42,605	14,294	.66450	.33550	177,663	347,175	8.15
80 5	28,311	13,134	.53609	.46391	106,054	169,512	5.99
85 +	15,177	15,177	0.00000	1.00000	63,459	63,459	4.18

TABLE XV-7

LIFE EXPECTANCY, PANAMA,
CENSUS YEARS

Year	Total*	Male	Female
1930	35.9	35.5	36.2
1940	42.4	41.5	43.3
1950	50.2	48.8	51.5
1960	61.5	59.8	63.2

*Simple arithmetic average of male and
 female.

NOTES

[1]The age structure of the population would be more affected by underenumeration and inaccurate reporting of age.

[2]República de Panamá, Contraloría General de la República, Dirección General de Estadística y Censo, Censos Nacionales 1950, Características Generales, Vol. I, Panamá, 1954, p. 66.

[3]República de Panamá, Dirección General de Estadística y Censo, Censos Nacionales 1960, Características Generales, Vol. IV, Panamá, 1963, p. 107.

[4]An overenumeration in ages under 20 in the later censuses is unlikely.

[5]We estimated the effect of the foreign-born population by considering the age group distribution of the population born in Panama. Of course, we bore in mind the fact that the age structure of the native population is affected by the children which foreigners produce while in Panama. This could be a significant factor in the case of 1950 and 1960, when practically all the foreigners were in the ages over 20.

[6]O. Andrew Collver, Birth Rates in Latin America: New Estimates of Historical Trends and Fluctuations (Berkeley: Institute of International Studies, University of California, 1965) [Research Series No. 7], p. 155.

[7]These rates were calculated taking into account the native and foreign-born population in the censuses both with and without the Indian populations, and taking into consideration the underenumeration in the earlier censuses.

[8]We mainly considered growth rates for the later years. See República de Panamá, Contraloría General de la República. Dirección de Estadística y Censo, Estadística Panamá Ano XXII, Estadísticas Vitales 1962, Serie B, Panama, 1964, p. 7.

[9]An example of life tables construction using Method B is given in Appendix II.

XVI. PARAGUAY

For Paraguay population information by age groups is available for the 1886, 1899, 1950, and 1962 censuses, but not for the 1936 census.[1] Death statistics are not complete, and detailed information by age and sex has been published only for recent years. As a consequence, we cannot use Method A to construct life tables. In order to know if it is possible to use Method B, we must analyze fertility and international migration.

There is no indication that fertility has undergone great or permanent changes in the past which could have affected the age structure of the population. A brief change in fertility might have occurred during the Chaco War, but after the period of the war, fertility returned to its previous level. A possible fluctuation in fertility is, in fact, confirmed by observing age structure in the last two censuses (Fig. XVI-1). The irregularity observed in the cohorts born from 1930 to 1939 might be due, in part, to this temporary change in fertility. The change, however, occurs in only one age group, and thus does not affect our study. In addition, international net migration has not been significant. The amount of emigration from Paraguay to Argentina and Brazil is approximately equal to the amount of immigration to Paraguay from these and other countries. Therefore, fertility and international migration conditions allow the utilization of Method B.

PROPORTIONAL AGE DISTRIBUTION OF THE POPULATION

A graphical cohort analysis indicates that Paraguayan censuses, principally those of 1886 and 1889, had irregularities in age group distribution; the analysis also shows that the 1886 census had a low degree of completeness[2] (see Fig. XVI-1). In addition, the age groups of the 1886 and 1899 censuses were not grouped in the usual way.[3] Therefore, it was necessary to regroup the ages for both censuses. As information for individual ages was not available, it was assumed that the proportional distribution of ages within each age group in the 1886 and 1899 censuses in Paraguay did not differ significantly from the proportional distribution in the 1950 census in Bolivia.[4] Once age groups for these years were regrouped in the usual way, the ten-year age group distributions of the four censuses were smoothed and then separated into five-year age groups according to the procedure explained in Appendix III[5] (Table XVI-1).

FIGURE XVI-1

TEN-YEAR AGE GROUPS BY YEAR OF BIRTH, CENSUS POPULATION, PARAGUAY, 1886-1962, MALE

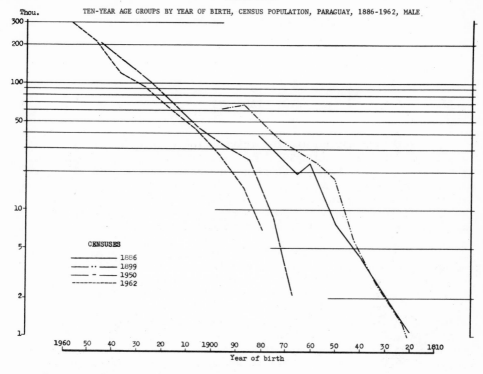

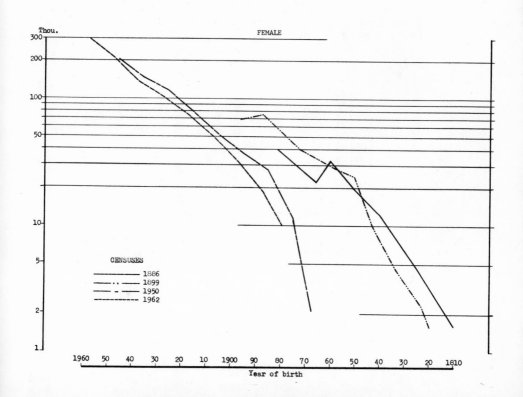

TABLE XVI-1

SMOOTHED PROPORTIONAL DISTRIBUTION OF THE POPULATION BY SEX AND FIVE-YEAR
AGE GROUPS, AGES 10-59, PARAGUAY, CENSUS YEARS

Age Groups	1886		1899		1950		1962	
	Male	Female	Male	Female	Male	Female	Male	Female
Total	1.000000	1.000000	1.000000	1.000000	1.000000	1.000000	1.000000	1.000000
10-59	.640892	.658401	.634521	.652723	.630625	.641593	.609212	.618046
10-14	.112668	.112672	.118981	.119502	.121932	.116343	.124303	.120392
15-19	.101036	.101224	.103578	.104465	.103817	.101679	.103933	.102038
20-24	.088772	.088460	.088148	.089489	.086514	.087498	.084559	.084540
25-29	.077749	.079216	.075662	.076905	.073260	.075720	.070153	.071317
30-34	.068098	.070354	.063176	.064484	.062422	.064788	.057336	.059520
35-39	.057880	.059989	.053870	.055194	.051824	.055161	.047711	.050286
40-44	.046927	.049239	.046199	.047771	.043062	.045686	.036364	.042143
45-49	.037049	.039655	.037198	.040110	.035868	.038135	.032776	.035293
50-54	.028716	.032501	.027451	.030948	.029261	.031165	.026986	.028854
55-59	.021997	.025092	.020257	.023854	.023665	.025418	.022090	.023665

ESTIMATION OF NATURAL GROWTH RATE

To estimate natural growth rates for 1950 and 1962 we used the intercensal annual geometric growth rates of 22.3 and 29.6 per thousand for 1936-1950 and 1950-1962 respectively. The estimates obtained were 25 and 31 per thousand for 1950 and 1962. We estimated the growth rate for 1886 (7.4 per thousand) and for 1899 (12 per thousand) on the basis of the levels of natural growth rates estimated for Mexico, Costa Rica, and Guatemala for approximately the same years.

TABLE XVI-2

GROWTH RATES USED IN THE CONSTRUCTION OF
LIFE TABLES FOR PARAGUAY

	Growth Rates			Slopes of the Straight Lines of Adjustment of the $\log_e \dfrac{C'(x,\ x+5)}{_n L_5}$		
Year	Total	Male	Female	Male	Female	Average
1886	.0074	.00798	.00682	.007012	.007809	.007411
1899	.0120	.01298	.01102	.012058	.012325	.012192
1950	.0250	.02579	.02421	.025301	.023755	.024528
1962	.0310	.03179	.03021	.031440	.029874	.030657

CONSTRUCTION OF LIFE TABLES

Life tables were constructed using Method B, the proportional age group distribution 10-59 (Table XVI-1), and the growth rates estimated above. The United Nations set of $_5L_x$ values used in the quotient $\dfrac{C'(x,\ x+5)}{_5L_x}$ were those belonging to levels 5 for males and 10 for females for 1886, 10 for males and 15 for females for 1899, and 50 and 70 for 1950 and 1962 respectively. The slopes of the straight lines of adjustment and the growth rates used for each sex in the exponent of e (Eq. 5, Chap. I) are presented in Table XVI-2. The life tables are presented in Tables XVI-3 to XVI-6,[6] and a summary of the life expectancy found is given in Table XVI-7.

TABLE XVI-3

ABRIDGED LIFE TABLE, PARAGUAY, 1886
MALE

Age x n	l_x	$_nd_x$	$_np_x$	$_nq_x$	$_nL_x$	T_x	e_x
0 1	100,000	30,870	.69130	.30870	71,341	2,269,379	22.69
1 4	69,130	13,993	.79758	.20242	246,149	2,198,038	31.80
0 5	100,000	44,864	.55136	.44864	317,489	2,269,379	22.69
5 5	55,136	6,051	.89026	.10974	253,717	1,951,890	35.40
10 5	49,086	2,586	.94732	.05268	238,598	1,698,172	34.60
15 5	46,500	2,657	.94285	.05715	226,413	1,459,575	31.39
20 5	43,843	3,244	.92601	.07399	211,382	1,233,162	28.13
25 5	40,598	3,588	.91163	.08837	194,158	1,021,779	25.17
30 5	37,011	3,874	.89533	.10467	175,576	827,621	22.36
35 5	33,137	4,241	.87201	.12799	155,350	652,045	19.68
40 5	28,896	4,590	.84115	.15885	133,204	496,695	17.19
45 5	24,306	4,701	.80657	.19343	109,726	363,492	14.95
50 5	19,604	4,503	.77033	.22967	86,554	253,766	12.94
55 5	15,102	4,097	.72874	.27126	64,962	167,212	11.07
60 5	11,005	3,550	.67739	.32261	45,765	102,250	9.29
65 5	7,455	2,929	.60709	.39291	29,562	56,485	7.58
70 5	4,526	2,221	.50936	.49064	16,582	26,923	5.95
75 5	2,305	1,423	.38279	.61721	7,461	10,342	4.49
80 5	882	677	.23306	.76694	2,405	2,880	3.26
85 +	206	206	0.00000	1.00000	476	476	2.31

TABLE XVI-3 (continued)

ABRIDGED LIFE TABLE, PARAGUAY, 1886
FEMALE

Age x n	l_x	$_nd_x$	$_np_x$	$_nq_x$	$_nL_x$	T_x	e_x
0 1	100,000	26,695	.73305	.26695	75,432	2,460,579	24.61
1 4	73,305	13,615	.81428	.18572	263,794	2,385,147	32.54
0 5	100,000	40,309	.59691	.40309	339,226	2,460,579	24.61
5 5	59,691	6,401	.89277	.10723	276,080	2,121,353	35.54
10 5	53,290	3,265	.93873	.06127	258,011	1,845,273	34.63
15 5	50,025	3,409	.93186	.06814	242,151	1,587,263	31.73
20 5	46,616	3,980	.91462	.08538	223,395	1,345,112	28.86
25 5	42,636	4,252	.90027	.09973	202,622	1,121,717	26.31
30 5	38,384	4,331	.88716	.11282	181,109	919,096	23.94
35 5	34,053	4,287	.87412	.12588	159,470	737,987	21.67
40 5	29,766	4,138	.86098	.13902	138,362	578,517	19.44
45 5	25,628	4,004	.84377	.15623	118,081	440,155	17.17
50 5	21,624	3,921	.81866	.18134	98,271	322,074	14.89
55 5	17,703	3,848	.78261	.21739	78,858	223,803	12.64
60 5	13,855	3,741	.72995	.27005	59,839	144,946	10.46
65 5	10,113	3,479	.65602	.34398	41,638	85,106	8.42
70 5	6,634	2,944	.55624	.44376	25,378	43,469	6.55
75 5	3,690	2,122	.42502	.57498	12,550	18,090	4.90
80 5	1,568	1,167	.25575	.74425	4,496	5,540	3.53
85 +	401	401	0.00000	1.00000	1,044	1,044	2.60

TABLE XVI-4

ABRIDGED LIFE TABLE, PARAGUAY, 1899
MALE

Age x n	l_x	$_nd_x$	$_np_x$	$_nq_x$	$_nL_x$	T_x	e_x
0 1	100,000	28,475	.71525	.28475	73,551	2,535,788	25.36
1 4	71,525	12,816	.82082	.17918	258,289	2,462,237	34.42
0 5	100,000	41,290	.58710	.41290	331,840	2,535,788	25.36
5 5	58,710	5,591	.90476	.09524	273,356	2,203,948	37.54
10 5	53,118	2,470	.95349	.04651	259,119	1,930,592	36.35
15 5	50,648	2,638	.94792	.05208	247,252	1,671,473	33.00
20 5	48,010	3,275	.93178	.06822	232,156	1,424,220	29.66
25 5	44,735	3,618	.91912	.08088	214,744	1,192,064	26.65
30 5	41,117	3,884	.90553	.09447	196,066	977,319	23.77
35 5	37,232	4,252	.88580	.11420	175,807	781,253	20.98
40 5	32,980	4,652	.85894	.14106	153,525	605,447	18.36
45 5	28,328	4,883	.82763	.17237	129,483	451,922	15.95
50 5	23,445	4,854	.79297	.20703	104,999	322,439	13.75
55 5	18,591	4,622	.75137	.24863	81,201	217,439	11.70
60 5	13,969	4,208	.69880	.30120	59,004	136,239	9.75
65 5	9,762	3,644	.62670	.37330	39,321	77,235	7.91
70 5	6,117	2,889	.52782	.47218	22,799	37,914	6.20
75 5	3,229	1,934	.40092	.59908	10,674	15,115	4.68
80 5	1,295	970	.25078	.74922	3,626	4,441	3.43
85 +	325	325	0.00000	1.00000	815	815	2.51

TABLE XVI-4 (continued)

ABRIDGED LIFE TABLE, PARAGUAY, 1899
FEMALE

Age x n	l_x	$_n d_x$	$_n p_x$	$_n q_x$	$_n L_x$	T_x	e_x
0 1	100,000	24,964	.75036	.24964	76,991	2,681,097	26.81
1 4	75,036	12,532	.83298	.16702	273,076	2,604,106	34.70
0 5	100,000	37,496	.62504	.37496	350,067	2,681,097	26.81
5 5	62,504	6,017	.90374	.09626	291,699	2,331,030	37.29
10 5	56,487	3,201	.94333	.05667	274,215	2,039,331	36.10
15 5	53,286	3,416	.93589	.06411	258,467	1,765,116	33.13
20 5	49,870	4,014	.91952	.08048	239,581	1,506,648	30.21
25 5	45,856	4,269	.90691	.09309	218,651	1,267,067	27.63
30 5	41,587	4,315	.89623	.10377	197,147	1,048,417	25.21
35 5	37,272	4,261	.88567	.11433	175,629	851,270	22.84
40 5	33,010	4,141	.87454	.12546	154,608	675,641	20.47
45 5	28,869	4,079	.85871	.14129	134,156	521,033	18.05
50 5	24,790	4,101	.83458	.16542	113,725	386,877	15.61
55 5	20,689	4,157	.79909	.20091	93,109	273,152	13.20
60 5	16,533	4,190	.74656	.25344	72,199	180,042	10.89
65 5	12,343	4,042	.67249	.32751	51,436	107,843	8.74
70 5	8,300	3,548	.57259	.42741	32,195	56,407	6.80
75 5	4,753	2,652	.44198	.55802	16,451	24,212	5.09
80 5	2,101	1,523	.27520	.72480	6,164	7,761	3.69
85 +	578	578	0.00000	1.00000	1,597	1,597	2.76

TABLE XVI-5

ABRIDGED LIFE TABLE, PARAGUAY, 1950
MALE

Age x n	l_x	$_nd_x$	$_np_x$	$_nq_x$	$_nL_x$	T_x	e_x
0 1	100,000	16,354	.83646	.16354	84,622	4,476,836	44.77
1 4	83,646	6,142	.92657	.07343	321,236	4,392,214	52.51
0 5	100,000	22,496	.77504	.22496	405,858	4,476,836	44.77
5 5	77,504	2,701	.96515	.03485	377,853	4,070,978	52.53
10 5	74,803	1,347	.98199	.01801	370,639	3,693,125	49.37
15 5	73,456	1,762	.97601	.02399	363,479	3,322,486	45.23
20 5	71,693	2,388	.96669	.03331	352,755	2,959,007	41.27
25 5	69,305	2,598	.96252	.03748	340,004	2,606,252	37.61
30 5	66,708	2,680	.95982	.04018	326,927	2,266,249	33.97
35 5	64,027	2,942	.95405	.04595	313,007	1,939,322	30.29
40 5	61,085	3,437	.94373	.05627	297,225	1,626,314	26.62
45 5	57,648	4,167	.92771	.07229	278,346	1,329,089	23.06
50 5	53,480	5,097	.90470	.09530	255,303	1,050,743	19.65
55 5	48,384	6,190	.87206	.12794	227,181	795,441	16.44
60 5	42,193	7,382	.82505	.17495	193,300	568,260	13.47
65 5	34,812	8,462	.75691	.24309	153,551	374,959	10.77
70 5	26,349	8,865	.66357	.33643	109,530	221,409	8.40
75 5	17,485	7,966	.54437	.45563	66,472	111,879	6.40
80 5	9,518	5,691	.40207	.59793	31,695	45,407	4.77
85 +	3,827	3,827	0.00000	1.00000	13,711	13,711	3.58

TABLE XVI-5 (continued)

ABRIDGED LIFE TABLE, PARAGUAY, 1950
FEMALE

Age x n	l_x	$_nd_x$	$_np_x$	$_nq_x$	$_nL_x$	T_x	e_x
0 1	100,000	14,531	.85469	.14531	86,432	4,678,151	46.78
1 4	85,469	6,118	.92842	.07158	328,620	4,591,719	53.72
0 5	100,000	20,649	.79351	.20649	415,053	4,678,151	46.78
5 5	79,351	2,799	.96473	.03527	386,888	4,263,098	53.72
10 5	76,553	1,523	.98011	.01989	378,979	3,876,210	50.63
15 5	75,030	1,926	.97433	.02567	370,883	3,497,231	46.61
20 5	73,104	2,513	.96563	.03437	359,492	3,126,347	42.77
25 5	70,591	2,747	.96109	.03891	346,106	2,766,856	39.20
30 5	67,844	2,808	.95861	.04139	332,232	2,420,750	35.68
35 5	65,036	2,887	.95561	.04439	318,015	2,088,518	32.11
40 5	62,149	3,088	.95031	.04969	303,207	1,770,503	28.49
45 5	59,061	3,539	.94009	.05991	286,838	1,467,296	24.84
50 5	55,523	4,252	.92342	.07658	267,489	1,180,459	21.26
55 5	51,271	5,286	.89690	.10310	243,921	912,970	17.81
60 5	45,985	6,709	.85411	.14589	214,187	669,049	14.55
65 5	39,276	8,299	.78870	.21130	176,684	454,862	11.58
70 5	30,977	9,440	.69527	.30473	131,802	278,178	8.98
75 5	21,538	9,167	.57439	.42561	83,990	146,376	6.80
80 5	12,371	7,019	.43261	.56739	42,431	62,386	5.04
85 +	5,352	5,352	0.00000	1.00000	19,955	19,955	3.73

TABLE XVI-6

ABRIDGED LIFE TABLE, PARAGUAY, 1962
MALE

Age x n	l_x	$_nd_x$	$_np_x$	$_nq_x$	$_nL_x$	T_x	e_x
0 1	100,000	11,352	.88648	.11352	89,257	5,424,855	54.25
1 4	88,648	3,824	.95686	.04314	346,277	5,335,598	60.19
0 5	100,000	15,176	.84824	.15176	435,534	5,424,855	54.25
5 5	84,824	1,667	.98034	.01966	418,138	4,989,321	58.82
10 5	83,157	866	.98958	.01042	413,658	4,571,183	54.97
15 5	82,291	1,219	.98519	.01481	408,865	4,157,525	50.52
20 5	81,072	1,690	.97916	.02084	401,323	3,748,661	46.24
25 5	79,382	1,835	.97689	.02311	392,290	3,347,338	42.17
30 5	77,547	1,892	.97560	.02440	383,075	2,955,048	38.11
35 5	75,655	2,123	.97194	.02806	373,174	2,571,973	34.00
40 5	73,532	2,601	.96462	.03538	361,538	2,198,799	29.90
45 5	70,931	3,391	.95219	.04781	346,778	1,837,261	25.90
50 5	67,539	4,517	.93313	.06687	327,208	1,490,484	22.07
55 5	63,023	5,988	.90498	.09502	301,183	1,163,276	18.46
60 5	57,034	7,811	.86305	.13695	266,917	862,093	15.12
65 5	49,224	9,791	.80109	.19891	222,943	595,176	12.09
70 5	39,433	11,269	.71422	.28578	169,679	372,233	9.44
75 5	28,164	11,229	.60129	.39871	112,079	202,553	7.19
80 5	16,934	9,062	.46488	.53512	59,802	90,474	5.34
85 +	7,872	7,872	0.00000	1.00000	30,672	30,672	3.90

TABLE XVI-6 (continued)

ABRIDGED LIFE TABLE, PARAGUAY, 1962
FEMALE

Age x n	l_x	$_nd_x$	$_np_x$	$_nq_x$	$_nL_x$	T_x	e_x
0 1	100,000	9,640	.90360	.09640	90,936	5,724,286	57.24
1 4	90,360	3,647	.95963	.04037	353,534	5,633,351	62.34
0 5	100,000	13,287	.86713	.13287	444,469	5,724,286	57.24
5 5	86,713	1,656	.98090	.01910	427,708	5,279,817	60.89
10 5	85,057	920	.98918	.01082	423,023	4,852,109	57.05
15 5	84,136	1,217	.98553	.01447	418,013	4,429,086	52.64
20 5	82,919	1,626	.98040	.01960	410,713	4,011,073	48.37
25 5	81,293	1,800	.97786	.02214	401,989	3,600,360	44.29
30 5	79,493	1,869	.97649	.02351	392,836	3,198,371	40.23
35 5	77,625	1,987	.97440	.02560	383,244	2,805,534	36.14
40 5	75,637	2,260	.97012	.02988	372,770	2,422,291	32.03
45 5	73,377	2,796	.96189	.03811	360,325	2,049,520	27.93
50 5	70,581	3,628	.94861	.05139	344,430	1,689,195	23.93
55 5	66,954	4,865	.92733	.07267	323,533	1,344,765	20.08
60 5	62,088	6,716	.89184	.10816	295,046	1,021,232	16.45
65 5	55,373	9,158	.83460	.16540	255,723	726,186	13.11
70 5	46,214	11,593	.74916	.25084	203,577	470,463	10.18
75 5	34,622	12,589	.63638	.36362	141,518	266,886	7.71
80 5	22,032	10,917	.50448	.49552	80,398	125,368	5.69
85 +	11,115	11,115	0.00000	1.00000	44,970	44,970	4.05

TABLE XVI-7

LIFE EXPECTANCY, PARAGUAY
CENSUS YEARS

Year	Total*	Male	Female
1886	23.7	22.7	24.6
1899	26.1	25.4	26.8
1950	45.8	44.8	46.8
1962	55.8	54.3	57.2

*Simple arithmetic average of male
and female.

NOTES

[1] Population information was obtained directly from the Dirección General de Estadística y Censos, República de Paraguay.

[2] The survivors enumerated in 1899 were more than those enumerated in the same cohorts 13 years earlier in the 1886 census.

[3] For example, the age groups in 1899 were: 0-5, 6-14, 15-17,
18-35, 36-45, etc.

[4] In spite of the recent date of the Bolivian census, individual
age distribution still shows huge irregularities. Therefore,
among the available individual age distributions, we considered
the Bolivian most appropriate for us to use in regrouping the age
distribution of the Paraguay censuses of 1886 and 1899.

[5] Before smoothing the populations, some age groups were modified because of major irregularities (see Fig. XVI-1). The age
group 20-29 in the 1962 census was increased by 10,000 inhabitants
in each sex. In the 1950 census the age groups over 30 were increased slightly. For 1899 the young age groups were reduced and
the adult age groups increased slightly. The 1886 age distribution (which is most affected by misreporting of age) was modified
according to the 1899 age distribution.

[6] An example of life table construction using Method B is given
in Appendix II.

XVII. PERU

Life tables for Peru have already been constructed and published by the author (see "New Abridged Life Tables for Peru: 1940, 1950-51, and 1961," Demography, Vol. III, No. 1, pp. 218-237). A summary of life expectancy for this country is presented below.

TABLE XVII-1

LIFE EXPECTANCY, PERU
CENSUS YEARS

Year	Total*	Male	Female
1940	36.5	34.6	38.3
1961	48.9	46.9	50.8

*Simple arithmetic average of male and female.

XVIII. VENEZUELA

Since 1873 Venezuela has taken nine national censuses, but age group distribution is available only for the last five. Vital statistics, principally for years before the 1960's are incomplete, and we cannot, therefore, use Method A to construct life tables for the earlier census years.

In the past fertility has been almost constant at a high level; international migration began to become significant after the 1941 census.[1] However, as we fortunately have the age group distribution of the foreign-born for 1950, we could construct life tables using Method B, except for the year 1961, where we applied Method A.

LIFE TABLES FOR 1926, 1936, 1941, AND 1950; CONSTRUCTION BY METHOD B

Census Population

We made a graphical cohort analysis of census information in order to ascertain the general completeness and the completeness of age declaration in each of the four censuses (Fig. XVIII-1). Compared to the 1961 census, these censuses showed some under-enumeration in certain age groups (particularly the younger age groups). Therefore, before smoothing age group distributions for these censuses, we increased ages under twenty years slightly. Because international migration could have affected age distribution in the 1950 census, we considered the age distribution of the foreign-born population. Age group distributions were then smoothed according to the procedure explained in Appendix III. They are presented in Table XVIII-1.

Estimation of Natural Growth Rates

Natural growth rates for census years were estimated by considering geometric intercensal growth rates and existing estimates.[2] Intercensal growth rates were calculated by considering native and total population, taking into account the underenumeration in the young age groups. The estimates for each census year are: 18.0, 19.0, 23.6, and 29.7 for the years 1926, 1936, 1941, and 1950 respectively.

FIGURE XVIII-1

TEN-YEAR AGE GROUPS BY YEAR OF BIRTH, CENSUS POPULATION,
VENEZUELA, 1926-1961, MALE

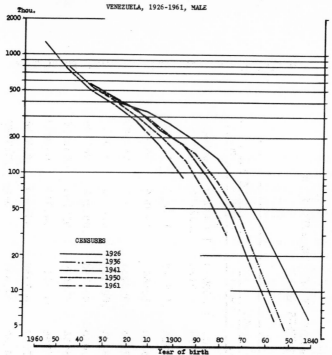

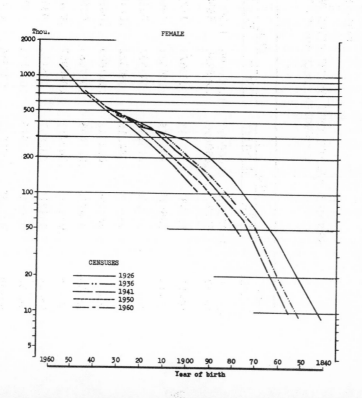

TABLE XVIII-1

SMOOTHED PROPORTIONAL DISTRIBUTION OF THE POPULATION BY SEX AND FIVE-YEAR
AGE GROUPS, AGES 10-59, VENEZUELA, CENSUS YEARS

Age Groups	1926 Male	1926 Female	1936 Male	1936 Female	1941 Male	1941 Female	1950 Male	1950 Female
Total 10-59	1.000000 .677205	1.000000 .680690	1.000000 .668258	1.000000 .669025	1.000000 .653070	1.000000 .658176	1.000000 .632125	1.000000 .635387
10-14	.123931	.117383	.123675	.118990	.118924	.118722	.121222	.119960
15-19	.108979	.106523	.108431	.106438	.105530	.105641	.104006	.103683
20-24	.094400	.095594	.093557	.093937	.092286	.092551	.087522	.087983
25-29	.081679	.084316	.080522	.081679	.079795	.080175	.074530	.075163
30-34	.069456	.072742	.067805	.068923	.067070	.067198	.063109	.063198
35-39	.058716	.061498	.057083	.058059	.056254	.056489	.052595	.053279
40-44	.048473	.049713	.046997	.047364	.045796	.046216	.043914	.044029
45-49	.039211	.039897	.038163	.038752	.037017	.037788	.035660	.036268
50-54	.029825	.030076	.029511	.030703	.028588	.029831	.028090	.028988
55-59	.022535	.022948	.022514	.024180	.021810	.023455	.021477	.022836

CHAPTER XVIII. VENEZUELA

Construction of Life Tables for 1926, 1936, 1941, and 1950

Life tables for these four years were constructed using Method B, the proportional age group distribution (Table XVIII-1), and the estimates of the natural growth rates given above. The United Nations set of $_5L_x$ values used in the quotient $\dfrac{C'(x,\ x+5)}{_5L_x}$ were those of levels 25, 30, 40, and 65 for the years 1926, 1936, 1941, and 1950 respectively. The stopes of the straight lines of adjustment and the growth rates used for each sex are shown in Table XVIII-2. The life tables for these four years are given in Tables XVIII-3 to XVIII-6.[3]

TABLE XVIII-2

GROWTH RATES USED IN THE CONSTRUCTION OF LIFE TABLES FOR VENEZUELA

| Year | Growth Rates | | | Slopes of the Straight Lines of Adjustment of the $\log_e \dfrac{C'(x,\ x+5)}{_nL_5}$ | | |
	Total	Male	Female	Male	Female	Average
1926	.0180	.01811	.01789	.018445	.018231	.018338
1936	.0190	.01947	.01853	.020609	.019616	.020108
1941	.0236	.02386	.02334	.023933	.023409	.023670
1950	.0297	.02980	.02960	.029796	.029605	.029701

LIFE TABLE FOR 1960-1962; CONSTRUCTION BY METHOD A

The life table for this year was constructed using Method A. To apply this method, we needed death statistics by five-year age groups for 1960, 1961, and 1962. Because under-registration of deaths has been common in Venezuela, we made an analysis of the death statistics. We then analyzed the 1961 census population and made an estimate of individual ages 0-4.

NEW LIFE TABLES FOR LATIN AMERICAN POPULATIONS

Analysis of Death Statistics

We estimated the completeness of death registration for the years 1936, 1941, and 1950 by comparing estimates of the gross death rates and the registered death rates.[4] The degree of omission in the death register was 65.8 percent in 1936, 40.9 percent in 1941, and 23.8 percent in 1950. Thus it would not be surprising if in 1961 death registration were still not complete. We estimated the under-registration for 1961 using the following assumptions: (a) Registration of urban deaths for recent years could be accepted as complete; therefore, only deaths in rural areas are under-registered; (b) The improvement of the registration of rural deaths during 1950-1961 was in line with the observed trend of improvement during 1936-1950; (c) There was no differential between urban and rural mortality. (This assumption is not likely but we made it in order to obtain a rough estimation of rural and urban deaths which are not available.)

Using these assumptions, and considering the change in rural-urban population during 1950-1961, we estimated an under-registration of total deaths of 13.2 percent of the registered deaths for 1961.[5]

We also made an analysis of death at age under one year to see whether or not differential omission exists at this particular age. Different ratios were calculated: death at age under one day to under one week, death at age under one day to one-to-seven days, death at under one day to under one month, death at age under one day to one year, and other different ratios considering particular ages at death. Our conclusion was that the registration of death at age under one year seems to have no differential omission when compared to other ages. Perhaps some small differential exists, but because of the lack of available information it is not possible to establish it. Therefore, we assumed that there was an equal degree of completeness in all age groups.

A weighted average of registered deaths in 1960, 1961, and 1962 was taken in order to obtain the average at the census date,[6] and this average was increased by the estimated 13.2 percent of omission (see Table XVIII-7).

Cohort deaths from among those persons born from 1951-1960 (inclusive) were needed to estimate the population of age 0-4 at the census date. The cohort deaths, as usual, were calculated by following the sketch of a Lexis' diagram,[7] once death information was corrected for the estimated underenumeration[8] (Table XVIII-8, col. 4).

CHAPTER XVIII. VENEZUELA

Census Population Statistics

We accepted the age group distribution of the population of the 1961 census, except for the age group 0-4. We estimated these ages by following a procedure similar to the one we used in the case of Chile (Chap. IV).

First, we needed to evaluate birth registration from 1956-1960. We did so by using the native-born enumerated population in the individual ages 3-8 (shifted at January 1, 1961) and their cohort deaths (corrected for omission). Population at young ages is usually underenumerated, but in Venezuela enumeration for ages 3-8 is accurate. Therefore, expected births for the period 1952-1957 were calculated by adding cohort deaths to the enumerated population 3-8 (shifted at January 1, 1961). The expected births were 3.8 percent higher than those registered; we accepted this percentage as possible omission in the birth registration from 1958-1960. By subtracting cohort deaths from the corrected births in 1956-1960, we obtained an estimate of the native population 0-4 by individual ages. The estimated and enumerated native population permits us to know the completeness of enumeration for these ages. Therefore, the same degree of completeness was assumed for the total population (native and foreign-born) at census date. Only ages 0-4 were corrected (Table XVIII-8). The distribution of the population by age and sex used in the life table can be seen in Table XVIII-9.

Construction of the Life Table for 1961

The life table for 1961 was constructed using Method A and death and population distributions from Tables XVIII-7 and XVIII-9. Death and population distributions were not smoothed; however, the force of mortality values (μ_x) were very slightly smoothed. The life table is presented in Table XVIII-10[9] and a summary of the life expectancy for each census year is given in Table XVIII-11.

TABLE XVIII-3

ABRIDGED LIFE TABLE, VENEZUELA, 1926
MALE

Age x n	l_x	$_n d_x$	$_n p_x$	$_n q_x$	$_n L_x$	T_x	e_x
0 1	100,000	23,525	.76475	.23525	78,063	3,164,107	31.64
1 4	76,475	10,085	.86813	.13187	284,052	3,086,044	40.35
0 5	100,000	33,610	.66390	.33610	362,116	3,164,107	31.64
5 5	66,390	4,652	.92993	.07007	315,616	2,801,992	42.20
10 5	61,739	2,345	.96202	.03798	302,680	2,486,376	40.27
15 5	59,394	2,668	.95508	.04492	290,954	2,183,696	36.77
20 5	56,726	3,330	.94130	.05870	275,577	1,892,742	33.37
25 5	53,396	3,580	.93296	.06704	258,040	1,617,165	30.29
30 5	49,816	3,710	.92552	.07448	239,922	1,359,125	27.28
35 5	46,106	3,989	.91348	.08652	220,789	1,119,203	24.27
40 5	42,117	4,403	.89547	.10453	199,879	898,414	21.33
45 5	37,714	4,832	.87188	.12812	176,740	698,536	18.52
50 5	32,882	5,196	.84199	.15801	151,635	521,795	15.87
55 5	27,687	5,462	.80274	.19726	124,911	370,161	13.37
60 5	22,225	5,553	.75017	.24983	97,241	245,250	11.03
65 5	16,673	5,387	.67689	.32311	69,720	148,010	8.88
70 5	11,286	4,759	.57833	.42167	43,935	78,289	6.94
75 5	6,527	3,568	.45329	.54671	22,815	34,354	5.26
80 5	2,959	2,059	.30396	.69604	8,883	11,539	3.90
85 +	899	899	0.00000	1.00000	2,656	2,656	2.95

TABLE XVIII-3 (continued)

ABRIDGED LIFE TABLE, VENEZUELA, 1926
FEMALE

Age x n	l_x	$_nd_x$	$_np_x$	$_nq_x$	$_nL_x$	T_x	e_x
0 1	100,000	21,474	.78526	.21474	80,133	3,275,377	32.75
1 4	78,526	10,272	.86918	.13082	291,900	3,195,245	40.69
0 5	100,000	31,746	.68254	.31746	372,033	3,275,377	32.75
5 5	68,254	4,884	.92845	.07155	324,315	2,903,345	42.54
10 5	63,370	2,640	.95833	.04167	310,147	2,579,030	40.70
15 5	60,730	2,986	.95084	.04916	296,808	2,268,883	37.36
20 5	57,744	3,655	.93671	.06329	279,892	1,972,074	34.15
25 5	54,090	3,953	.92692	.07308	260,620	1,692,182	31.28
30 5	50,137	4,023	.91976	.08024	240,636	1,431,563	28.55
35 5	46,114	4,019	.91285	.08715	220,490	1,190,926	25.83
40 5	42,095	4,020	.90451	.09549	200,439	970,436	23.05
45 5	38,075	4,155	.89087	.10913	180,140	769,997	20.22
50 5	33,920	4,438	.86917	.13083	158,711	589,857	17.39
55 5	29,482	4,838	.83590	.16410	135,623	431,145	14.62
60 5	24,644	5,296	.78511	.21489	110,282	295,523	11.99
65 5	19,348	5,571	.71205	.28795	82,905	185,241	9.57
70 5	13,777	5,342	.61229	.38771	55,191	102,336	7.43
75 5	8,436	4,359	.48324	.51676	30,406	47,145	5.59
80 5	4,076	2,755	.32419	.67581	12,615	16,740	4.11
85 +	1,322	1,322	0.00000	1.00000	4,125	4,125	3.12

TABLE XVIII-4

ABRIDGED LIFE TABLE, VENEZUELA, 1936
MALE

Age x n	l_x	$_nd_x$	$_np_x$	$_nq_x$	$_nL_x$	T_x	e_x
0 1	100,000	22,028	.77972	.22028	79,451	3,329,162	33.29
1 4	77,972	9,437	.87897	.12103	291,477	3,249,711	41.68
0 5	100,000	31,465	.68535	.31465	370,927	3,329,162	33.29
5 5	68,535	4,527	.93395	.06605	327,062	2,958,234	43.16
10 5	64,008	2,430	.96203	.03797	313,840	2,631,172	41.11
15 5	61,578	2,758	.95522	.04478	301,626	2,317,333	37.63
20 5	58,820	3,383	.94248	.05752	285,891	2,015,707	34.27
25 5	55,437	3,589	.93526	.06474	268,192	1,729,816	31.20
30 5	51,848	3,670	.92921	.07079	250,151	1,461,625	28.19
35 5	48,178	3,904	.91897	.08103	231,335	1,211,473	25.15
40 5	44,274	4,293	.90305	.09695	210,933	980,138	22.14
45 5	39,982	4,740	.88146	.11854	188,335	769,205	19.24
50 5	35,242	5,170	.85330	.14670	163,554	580,870	16.48
55 5	30,072	5,548	.81553	.18447	136,707	417,317	13.88
60 5	24,524	5,786	.76407	.23593	108,257	280,610	11.44
65 5	18,738	5,777	.69171	.30829	79,175	172,352	9.20
70 5	12,962	5,261	.59408	.40592	51,108	93,177	7.19
75 5	7,700	4,079	.47032	.52968	27,369	42,069	5.46
80 5	3,622	2,452	.32304	.67696	11,110	14,700	4.06
85 +	1,170	1,170	0.00000	1.00000	3,589	3,589	3.07

TABLE XVIII-4 (continued)

ABRIDGED LIFE TABLE, VENEZUELA, 1936
FEMALE

Age x n	l_x	$_nd_x$	$_np_x$	$_nq_x$	$_nL_x$	T_x	e_x
0 1	100,000	20,104	.79896	.20104	81,387	3,446,747	34.47
1 4	79,896	9,575	.88016	.11984	298,920	3,365,360	42.12
0 5	100,000	29,679	.70321	.29679	380,307	3,446,747	34.47
5 5	70,321	4,717	.93293	.06707	335,494	3,066,440	43.61
10 5	65,605	2,688	.95903	.04097	321,225	2,730,946	41.63
15 5	62,917	3,040	.95168	.04832	307,586	2,409,721	38.30
20 5	59,876	3,677	.93859	.06141	290,473	2,102,134	35.11
25 5	56,200	3,930	.93007	.06993	271,194	1,811,662	32.24
30 5	52,270	3,956	.92432	.07568	251,447	1,540,468	29.47
35 5	48,314	3,928	.91869	.08131	231,711	1,289,021	26.68
40 5	44,385	3,934	.91136	.08864	212,118	1,057,310	23.82
45 5	40,451	4,099	.89868	.10132	192,186	845,192	20.89
50 5	36,353	4,432	.87808	.12192	170,926	653,006	17.96
55 5	31,921	4,913	.84608	.15392	147,689	482,080	15.10
60 5	27,007	5,491	.79668	.20332	121,701	334,391	12.38
65 5	21,516	5,918	.72497	.27503	92,983	212,691	9.89
70 5	15,599	5,826	.62648	.37352	63,166	119,708	7.67
75 5	9,772	4,894	.49919	.50081	35,742	56,542	5.79
80 5	4,878	3,202	.34355	.65645	15,397	20,800	4.26
85 +	1,676	1,676	0.00000	1.00000	5,404	5,404	3.22

TABLE XVIII-5

ABRIDGED LIFE TABLE, VENEZUELA, 1941
MALE

Age x n	l_x	$_nd_x$	$_np_x$	$_nq_x$	$_nL_x$	T_x	e_x
0 1	100,000	19,048	.80952	.19048	82,160	3,916,363	39.16
1 4	80,952	7,657	.90541	.09459	307,205	3,834,203	47.36
0 5	100,000	26,705	.73295	.26705	389,366	3,916,363	39.16
5 5	73,295	3,523	.95194	.04806	354,111	3,526,997	48.12
10 5	69,772	1,828	.97379	.02621	344,234	3,172,886	45.48
15 5	67,944	2,223	.96728	.03272	334,797	2,828,652	41.63
20 5	65,720	2,875	.95625	.04375	321,681	2,493,855	37.95
25 5	62,845	3,099	.95069	.04931	306,456	2,172,174	34.56
30 5	59,746	3,191	.94659	.05341	290,847	1,865,718	31.23
35 5	56,555	3,454	.93893	.06107	274,368	1,574,871	27.85
40 5	53,101	3,920	.92619	.07381	256,069	1,300,503	24.49
45 5	49,182	4,540	.90769	.09231	234,982	1,044,433	21.24
50 5	44,642	5,256	.88226	.11774	210,550	809,452	18.13
55 5	39,386	6,023	.84707	.15293	182,363	598,902	15.21
60 5	33,362	6,750	.79767	.20233	150,380	416,539	12.49
65 5	26,612	7,267	.72691	.27309	115,156	266,159	10.00
70 5	19,345	7.141	.63086	.36914	78,503	151,003	7.81
75 5	12,204	5,992	.50904	.49096	44,983	72,499	5.94
80 5	6,212	3,948	.36450	.63550	19,920	27,517	4.43
85 +	2,264	2,264	0.00000	1.00000	7,597	7,597	3.35

TABLE XVIII-5 (continued)

ABRIDGED LIFE TABLE, VENEZUELA, 1941
FEMALE

Age x n	l_x	$_n d_x$	$_n p_x$	$_n q_x$	$_n L_x$	T_x	e_x
0 1	100,000	17,228	.82772	.17228	83,980	4,066,462	40.66
1 4	82,772	7,712	.90682	.09318	314,410	3,982,482	48.11
0 5	100,000	24,940	.75060	.24940	398,390	4,066,462	40.66
5 5	75,060	3,664	.95119	.04881	362,592	3,668,072	48.87
10 5	71,396	2,048	.97132	.02868	351,848	3,305,480	46.30
15 5	69,348	2,458	.96456	.03544	341,198	2,953,631	42.59
20 5	66,890	3,106	.95357	.04643	326,980	2,612,434	39.06
25 5	63,785	3,371	.94715	.05285	310,520	2,285,454	35.83
30 5	60,414	3,418	.94342	.05658	293,531	1,974,933	32.69
35 5	56,996	3,449	.93949	.06051	276,372	1,681,402	29.50
40 5	53,547	3,567	.93339	.06661	258,935	1,405,030	26.24
45 5	49,980	3,895	.92208	.07792	240,456	1,146,096	22.93
50 5	46,086	4,446	.90354	.09646	219,711	905,640	19.65
55 5	41,640	5,243	.87409	.12591	195,700	685,930	16.47
60 5	36,397	6,275	.82758	.17242	167,023	490,230	13.47
65 5	30,122	7,271	.75862	.24138	133,027	323,206	10.73
70 5	22,851	7,718	.66223	.33777	95,014	190,179	8.32
75 5	15,133	6,995	.53776	.46224	57,261	95,166	6.29
80 5	8,138	4,973	.38885	.61115	26,829	37,905	4.66
85 +	3,164	3,164	0.00000	1.00000	11,076	11,076	3.50

TABLE XVIII-6

ABRIDGED LIFE TABLE, VENEZUELA, 1950
MALE

Age x n	l_x	$_nd_x$	$_np_x$	$_nq_x$	$_nL_x$	T_x	e_x
0 1	100,000	12,629	.87371	.12629	88,081	5,119,946	51.20
1 4	87,371	4,486	.94865	.05135	339,749	5,031,865	57.59
0 5	100,000	17,116	.82884	.17116	427,829	5,119,946	51.20
5 5	82,884	2,054	.97521	.02479	407,210	4,692,117	56.61
10 5	80,830	1,125	.98608	.01392	401,368	4,284,907	53.01
15 5	79,705	1,493	.98126	.01874	395,286	3,883,538	48.72
20 5	78,212	1,998	.97445	.02555	386,265	3,488,253	44.60
25 5	76,214	2,153	.97175	.02825	375,649	3,101,988	40.70
30 5	74,060	2,206	.97021	.02979	364,849	2,726,339	36.81
35 5	71,854	2,426	.96623	.03377	353,403	2,361,489	32.86
40 5	69,428	2,900	.95823	.04177	340,278	2,008,086	28.92
45 5	66,528	3,667	.94488	.05512	324,044	1,667,808	25.07
50 5	62,861	4,708	.92511	.07489	303,264	1,343,765	21.38
55 5	58,153	6,044	.89606	.10394	276,604	1,040,501	17.89
60 5	52,109	7,667	.85286	.14714	242,496	763,898	14.66
65 5	44,442	9,356	.78947	.21053	199,906	521,402	11.73
70 5	35,085	10,483	.70121	.29879	149,665	321,496	9.16
75 5	24,602	10,161	.58698	.41302	96,820	171,831	6.98
80 5	14,441	7,954	.44921	.55079	50,282	75,011	5.19
85 +	6,487	6,487	0.00000	1.00000	24,729	24,729	3.81

TABLE XVIII-6 (continued)

ABRIDGED LIFE TABLE, VENEZUELA, 1950
FEMALE

Age x n	l_x	$_nd_x$	$_np_x$	$_nq_x$	$_nL_x$	T_x	e_x
0 1	100,000	10,860	.89140	.10860	89,824	5,395,395	53.95
1 4	89,140	4,361	.95108	.04892	347,128	5,305,571	59.52
0 5	100,000	15,221	.84779	.15221	436,952	5,395,395	53.95
5 5	84,779	2,075	.97553	.02447	416,712	4,958,443	58.49
10 5	82,705	1,207	.98541	.01459	410,542	4,541,731	54.92
15 5	81,498	1,526	.98128	.01872	404,090	4,131,189	50.69
20 5	79,972	1,972	.97534	.02466	395,128	3,727,099	46.60
25 5	78,000	2,152	.97241	.02759	384,632	3,331,971	42.72
30 5	75,848	2,206	.97091	.02909	373,757	2,947,339	38.86
35 5	73,642	2,304	.96871	.03129	362,524	2,573,582	34.95
40 5	71,338	2,549	.96427	.03573	350,531	2,211,058	30.99
45 5	68,788	3,051	.95565	.04435	336,720	1,860,528	27.05
50 5	65,737	3,838	.94162	.05838	319,656	1,523,808	23.18
55 5	61,900	5,004	.91916	.08084	297,862	1,204,151	19.45
60 5	56,896	6,713	.88200	.11800	268,976	906,289	15.93
65 5	50,182	8,893	.82278	.17722	230,220	637,313	12.70
70 5	41,289	10,927	.73534	.26466	180,313	407,093	9.86
75 5	30,362	11,517	.62066	.37934	122,677	226,780	7.47
80 5	18,844	9,670	.48687	.51313	67,747	104,103	5.52
85 +	9,175	9,175	0.00000	1.00000	36,356	36,356	3.96

TABLE XVIII-7

DEATHS BY SEX AND AGE GROUPS
USED IN THE CONSTRUCTION OF THE LIFE TABLE
VENEZUELA, 1960-1962

Age Group	Male	Female
Total	33,206	29,439
0	11,087	9,141
1	1,837	1,900
2	855	838
3	519	538
4	335	315
0-4	14,633	12,732
5-9	1,041	759
10-14	535	393
15-19	592	468
20-24	876	534
25-29	826	610
30-34	898	671
35-39	922	789
40-44	1,077	793
45-49	1,331	933
50-54	1,510	1,078
55-59	1,477	1,134
60-64	1,957	1,749
65-69	1,364	1,168
70-74	1,339	1,405
75-79	956	1,134
80-84	885	1,323
85 +	987	1,766

TABLE XVIII-8

ESTIMATION OF POPULATION IN AGES 0-4 AT CENSUS DATE, VENEZUELA, 1961

Age at the End of 1960	Year of Birth	Native Population	Cohort Deaths Period 1952-1960	Expected Birth (3)+(4)	Registered Births	Corrected Births(a) (6)x a	Corrected Native Population (7)-(4)	Omission in Native Population $\left(\frac{(8)}{(3)}-1\right)\times100$	Corrected Total Population(b) Census Pop. x $\frac{(8)}{(3)}$
(1)	(2)	(3)	(4)	(5)	(6)	(7)	(8)	(9)	(10)
Male									
0	1960	154,836	8,871	163,707	171,127	177,743	168,872	9.07	170,260
1	1959	143,902	13,245	157,147	165,878	172,291	159,046	10.52	161,232
2	1958	133,252	13,175	146,427	149,208	154,976	141,801	6.42	144,283
3	1957	130,742	16,083	146,825	144,654	150,246	134,163	2.62	136,748
4	1956	124,833	16,782	141,615	142,114	147,608	130,826	4.80	133,611
3-8	1952-57	734,672	101,487	836,159	805,038				
Female									
0	1960	150,027	6,867	156,894	167,072	173,292	166,425	10.93	167,738
1	1959	139,015	11,091	150,106	158,861	164,775	153,684	10.55	155,639
2	1958	128,202	11,512	139,714	142,539	147,846	136,334	6.34	138,696
3	1957	127,703	13,942	141,645	139,426	144,617	130,675	2.33	133,204
4	1956	120,575	15,209	135,784	135,958	141,020	125,811	4.34	128,533
3-8	1952-57	711,093	91,022	802,115	773,325				

$a = \dfrac{\text{Expected Birth (1952-1957)}}{\text{Registered Birth (1952-1957)}}$: Male 1.03866; Female 1.03723

(a) The under-registration of birth was found by using data for the age group 3-8 under assumption of good enumeration of the native population in this age group.

(b) The same underenumeration found for the native population was considered for total population.

TABLE XVIII-9

POPULATION BY SEX AND AGE GROUPS
USED IN THE CONSTRUCTION OF LIFE TABLE
VENEZUELA, 1961

Age Group	Male	Female
Total	3,869,540	3,750,307
0	170,260	167,738
1	161,232	155,639
2	144,283	138,696
3	136,748	133,204
4	133,611	128,533
0-4	746,134	723,810
5-9	591,273	572,047
10-14	458,372	443,509
15-19	340,465	339,171
20-24	311,678	306,733
25-29	283,008	267,874
30-34	264,861	237,836
35-39	210,638	194,534
40-44	174,322	157,264
45-49	146,042	134,760
50-54	112,531	106,242
55-59	84,211	83,098
60-64	62,356	69,358
65-69	36,152	41,570
70-74	21,657	29,358
75-79	12,601	18,348
80-84	7,431	13,301
85 +	5,808	11,494

TABLE XVIII-10

ABRIDGED LIFE TABLE, VENEZUELA, 1961
MALE

Age x n	l_x	$_nd_x$	$_np_x$	$_nq_x$	$_nL_x$	T_x	e_x
0 1	100,000	5,965	.94035	.05965	95,407	6,118,903	61.19
1 1	94,035	1,429	.98480	.01520	93,192	6,023,496	64.06
2 1	92,606	567	.99388	.00612	92,305	5,930,304	64.04
3 1	92,039	349	.99621	.00379	91,858	5,837,999	63.43
4 1	91,690	232	.99747	.00253	91,569	5,746,141	62.67
0 5	100,000	8,542	.91458	.08542	464,331	6,118,903	61.19
5 5	91,458	743	.99188	.00812	455,433	5,654,572	61.83
10 5	90,715	608	.99330	.00670	452,055	5,199,139	57.31
15 5	90,107	797	.99116	.00884	448,543	4,747,084	52.68
20 5	89,310	1,071	.98801	.01199	443,873	4,298,541	48.13
25 5	88,239	1,315	.98510	.01490	437,908	3,854,668	43.68
30 5	86,924	1,575	.98188	.01812	430,683	3,416,760	39.31
35 5	85,349	1,975	.97686	.02314	421,808	2,986,077	34.99
40 5	83,374	2,617	.96861	.03139	410,328	2,564,269	30.76
45 5	80,757	3,587	.95558	.04442	394,818	2,153,941	26.67
50 5	77,170	4,878	.93679	.06321	373,655	1,759,123	22.80
55 5	72,292	6,526	.90973	.09027	345,145	1,385,468	19.16
60 5	65,766	8,550	.86999	.13001	307,455	1,040,323	15.82
65 5	57,216	10,623	.81434	.18566	259,523	732,868	12.81
70 5	46,593	12,301	.73599	.26401	202,213	473,345	10.16
75 5	34,292	12,689	.62997	.37003	139,738	271,132	7.91
80 5	21,603	10,839	.49826	.50174	80,918	131,394	6.08
85 5	10,764	6,998	.34987	.65013	36,325	50,476	4.69
90 +	3,766	3,766	0.00000	1.00000	14,151	14,151	3.58

TABLE XVIII-10 (continued)

ABRIDGED LIFE TABLE, VENEZUELA, 1961
FEMALE

Age x n	l_x	$_nd_x$	$_np_x$	$_nq_x$	$_nL_x$	T_x	e_x
0 1	100,000	5,075	.94925	.05075	96,245	6,468,549	64.69
1 1	94,925	1,400	.98525	.01475	94,099	6,372,304	67.13
2 1	93,525	596	.99363	.00637	93,209	6,278,205	67.13
3 1	92,929	372	.99600	.00400	92,736	6,184,996	66.56
4 1	92,557	223	.99759	.00241	92,441	6,092,260	65.82
0 5	100,000	7,666	.92334	.07666	468,730	6,468,549	64.69
5 5	92,334	611	.99338	.00662	460,143	5,999,819	64.98
10 5	91,723	461	.99497	.00503	457,463	5,539,676	60.40
15 5	91,262	595	.99348	.00652	454,823	5,082,213	55.69
20 5	90,667	815	.99101	.00899	451,298	4,627,390	51.04
25 5	89,852	1,059	.98821	.01179	446,613	4,176,092	46.48
30 5	88,793	1,341	.98490	.01510	440,613	3,729,479	42.00
35 5	87,452	1,673	.98087	.01913	433,078	3,288,866	37.61
40 5	85,779	2,113	.97537	.02463	423,613	2,855,788	33.29
45 5	83,664	2,797	.96657	.03343	411,338	2,432,175	29.07
50 5	80,869	3,858	.95229	.04771	394,700	2,020,837	24.99
55 5	77,011	5,357	.93044	.06956	371,663	1,626,137	21.12
60 5	71,654	7,342	.89754	.10246	339,915	1,254,474	17.51
65 5	64,312	9,641	.85009	.14991	297,458	914,559	14.22
70 5	54,671	11,986	.78076	.21924	243,390	617,101	11.29
75 5	42,685	13,567	.68216	.31784	179,508	373,711	8.76
80 5	29,118	12,996	.55368	.44632	113,100	194,203	6.67
85 5	16,122	9,657	.40100	.59900	56,468	81,103	5.03
90 +	6,465	6,465	0.00000	1.00000	24,635	24,635	3.81

TABLE XVIII-11

LIFE EXPECTANCY, VENEZUELA,
CENSUS YEARS

Year	Total*	Male	Female
1926	32.2	31.6	32.8
1936	33.9	33.3	34.5
1941	39.9	39.2	40.7
1950	52.6	51.2	54.0
1961	62.9	61.2	64.7

*Simple arithmetic average of male and female.

NOTES

[1] The number of foreign-born was under 2% before 1950, 4.1% in 1950 and 7.2% in 1961.

[2] O. Andrew Collver, Birth Rates in Latin America: New Estimates of Historical Trends and Fluctuations (Berkeley: Institute of International Studies, University of California, 1965) [Research Series No. 7], p. 170.

[3] An example of life table construction using Method B is given in Appendix II.

[4] The estimates of the gross mortality rates were obtained by using the life tables for these years constructed according to Method B. The formula used was

$$m = \Sigma \, C(x, x+5) \cdot {}_5m_x$$

[5]Under the above assumptions, registered deaths can be expressed as:

$$aD = D \cdot u + \theta \cdot D \cdot r,$$

where a is the completeness of total deaths, D is the total actual deaths, θ is the completeness of rural deaths, and u and r are the proportions of the urban and rural populations respectively (according to assumption (c), $D \cdot u$ and $D \cdot r$ are urban and rural deaths). This equation can be rewritten as

$$a = u + \theta \cdot r \quad ;$$

thus

$$\theta = \frac{a - u}{r} \quad .$$

The values of a , u, and r are known for 1936, 1941, and 1950. Therefore, we calculated the values of θ for these years at .4420, .5770, and .6311 for 1936, 1941, and 1950 respectively. By observing the trend of θ during these years, we estimated a value of .5880 for 1961. Thus, for this year (by using the estimated θ, a, and r) we calculated a value of a of .8831. This means an omission of 13.2% in the total registered deaths.

[6]The weights were .4445, .3333, and .2222 for 1960, 1961, and 1962 respectively.

[7]See Roland Pressat, L'Analyse Démographique (Paris: Presses Universitaires de France, 1961), Chapters 2 and 3.

[8]Annual under-registration for the period 1951 to 1960 was calculated by interpolating linearly the percentage of under-registration found for 1950 and 1961. The separation factors used in the Lexis' Diagram were 1/2 for ages one and over, and for ages under one the following:

	1951	1952	1953	1954	1955	1956	1957	1958	1959	1960
Male	.2500	.2500	.2387	.2496	.2636	.2429	.2478	.2617	.2386	.2272
Female	.2800	.2800	.2742	.2739	.2912	.2693	.2877	.2920	.2653	.2638

[9]An example of life table construction by Method A is given in Appendix I.

APPENDIX I

EXAMPLE OF METHOD A--THE CASE OF COSTA RICA, 1963

In this section we will give an example of life table construction using Method A according to the theory described in
Chapter I. Our case is Costa Rica, 1963. The five-year age group
distributions of population and deaths, and the individual ages
0-4 needed to apply this method were established during our discussion of Costa Rica in Chapter VI. The necessary figures are taken
from Tables VI-10 and VI-13.

We first calculated central mortality rates ($_nm_x$) for five-
and ten-year age groups and for other irregular groups for ages
under 10 in order to obtain the force of mortality (μ_x) required
in Equation 3 (Chap. 1) and Table I-1. The required regrouping of
population and deaths and the values of $_nm_x$ obtained are presented
in Tables A-I-1 and A-I-2. The values of the force of mortality
(μ_x) obtained with these $_nm_x$ values, using Equation 3 and the coefficients of Table I-1, are presented in Table A-I-3, column 2.
Because neither the population nor the death distributions were
smoothed, we made a graphical smoothing of the μ_x values. The
smoothed values of the force of mortality can be found in Table A-
I-3, column 3.

In order that the survivors be at exactly age x (l_x) from
the μ_x values, we must apply Equations 1 and 2 from Chapter I.
To apply Equation 1 the differences and logarithms of μ_x as well
as the differences of these logarithms are needed. They are given
in Table A-I-4, columns 4, 5, 6, and 7. Calculations were made
for ages up to 65 because age group information for the older age
groups was lacking. We found the values over 65 easily by main-
taining the last value of $\Delta \log_{10} 1000 \mu_x$ (that for 60-65) constant
(Table A-I-4, col. 6). (The assumption involved here is that the
values of μ_x for ages 60-65 follow Gompertz' law ($\mu_x = BC^x$) and
that the same law applies to the older ages.) We then found the
values of $\log_{10} l_x$ using Equation 2, and assigning a value of 5 to
$\log_{10} l_0$ (Table A-I-4, col. 8). By taking antilogarithms of the
values $\log_{10} l_x$, we found the l_x function (Table A-I-4, col. 9) and
from these values, as is usual, we found all the other functions of
the life table, which is presented in Table VI-14.

NEW LIFE TABLES FOR LATIN AMERICAN POPULATIONS

TABLE A-I-1

CENTRAL MORTALITY RATES ($_n m_x$), COSTA RICA, 1963

Age x	Age n	Male P(x,x+n)	Male D(x,x+n)	Male $1000_n m_x$ (3)÷(4)	Female P(x,x+n)	Female D(x,x+n)	Female $1000_n m_x$ (3)÷(4)
(1)	(2)	(3)	(4)	(5)	(3)	(4)	(5)
0	1	30,227	2,699	89.291	29,381	2,110	71.815
0	2	59,175	3,139	53.046	57,479	2,552	44.399
0	3	86,443	3,303	38,210	84,174	2,729	32.421
0	4	112,349	3,402	30.281	109,282	2,827	25.869
1	1	28,948	440	15.200	28,098	442	15.731
1	2	56,216	604	10.744	54,793	619	11.297
1	3	82,122	703	8.560	79,901	717	8.974
2	1	27,268	164	6.014	26,695	177	6.630
2	2	53,174	263	4.946	51,803	275	5.309
2	3	77,929	334	4.286	75,497	339	4.490
3	1	25,906	99	3.822	25,108	98	3.903
3	2	50,661	170	3.356	48,802	162	3.320
3	7	161,154	342	2.122	155,926	307	1.969
4	1	24,755	71	2.868	23,694	64	2.701
4	6	135,248	243	1.797	130,818	209	1.598
5	5	110,493	172	1.557	107,124	145	1.354
10	5	86,185	77	0.893	84,525	56	0.663
10	10	150,199	160	1.065	150,634	110	0.730
10	15	200,777	267	1.330	203,651	178	0.874

CENTRAL MORTALITY RATES ($_nm_x$), COSTA RICA, 1963

Age x	n	P(x,x+n)	P(x,x+2n)	D(x,x+n)	D(x,x+2n)	1000_nm_x (5)÷(3)	$1000_{2n}m_x$ (6)÷(4)
(1)	(2)	(3)	(4)	(5)	(6)	(7)	(8)
				Male			
5	5	110,493	196,678	172	249	1.557	1.266
10	5	86,185	150,199	77	160	0.893	1.065
15	5	64,014	114,592	83	190	1.297	1.658
20	5	50,578	91,949	107	197	2.116	2.142
25	5	41,371	79,918	90	181	2.175	2.265
30	5	38,547	71,917	91	197	2.361	2.739
35	5	33,370	60,299	106	229	3.177	3.798
40	5	26,929	49,721	123	256	4.568	5.149
45	5	22,792	43,798	133	310	5.835	7.078
50	5	21,006	34,410	177	358	8.426	10.404
55	5	13,404	26,287	181	426	13.503	16.206
60	5	12,883	20,245	245	501	19.017	24.747
65	5	7,362	13,435	256	557	34.773	41.459
70	5	6,073		301		49.564	
				Female			
5	5	107,124	191,649	145	201	1.354	1.049
10	5	84,525	150,634	56	110	0.663	0.730
15	5	66,109	119,126	54	122	0.817	1.024
20	5	53,017	96,613	68	140	1.283	1.449
25	5	43,596	82,263	72	154	1.652	1.872
30	5	38,667	72,968	82	179	2.120	2.453
35	5	34,301	61,011	97	198	2.853	3.246
40	5	26,710	49,214	101	219	3.781	4.450
45	5	22,504	43,018	118	257	5.244	5.974
50	5	20,514	33,851	139	280	6.774	8.272
55	5	13,337	25,980	141	360	10.572	13.857
60	5	12,643	20,496	219	430	17.322	20.980
65	5	7,853	13,653	211	462	26.869	33.839
70	5	5,800		251		43.276	

TABLE A-I-3

FORCE OF MORTALITY (x), COSTA RICA, 1963

Age	Male		Female	
	1000 μ_x	Smoothed 1000 μ_x	1000 μ_x	Smoothed 1000 μ_x
(1)	(2)	(3)	(2)	(3)
0	161.447	161.447	124.681	124.681
1	36.519	36.519	32.497	32.497
2	8.947	8.947	9.691	9.691
3	4.664	4.664	4.954	4.954
4	3.174	3.174	3.087	3.087
5	2.685	2.685	2.469	2.469
10	0.996	0.996	0.822	0.797
15	0.973	0.947	0.641	0.703
20	1.741	1.545	1.037	1.067
25	2.207	1.999	1.474	1.448
30	2.211	2.380	1.864	1.852
35	2.682	2.924	2.462	2.432
40	3.849	3.775	3.272	3.272
45	5.123	5.102	4.480	4.480
50	6.915	7.030	5.892	6.120
55	10.739	10.395	8.259	8.998
60	15.822	15.822	13.721	13.721
65	26.249	26.249	21.511	22.558

TABLE A-I-4

VALUES USED FOR DETERMINING l_x , COSTA RICA, 1963

MALE

x	n	1000 μ_x	$\Delta 1000\ \mu_x$	$\log_{10} 1000\ \mu_x$	$\Delta\log_{10} 1000\ \mu_x$	$\log_{10}\ _n P_x$	$\log_{10}\ l_x$	l_x
(1)	(2)	(3)	(4)	(5)	(6)	(7)	(8)	(9)
0	1	161.447	-124.928	2.20803	-0.64551	-0.03650	5.00000	100,000
1	1	36.519	-27.572	1.56252	-0.61084	-0.00851	4.96350	91,939
2	1	8.947	-4.283	0.95168	-0.28292	-0.00286	4.95499	90,155
3	1	4.664	-1.490	0.66876	-0.16715	-0.00168	4.95213	89,563
4	1	3.174	-0.489	0.50161	-0.07267	-0.00127	4.95045	89,217
5	5	2.685	-1.689	0.43068	-0.43068	-0.00370	4.94918	88,957
10	5	0.996	-0.049	-0.00174	-0.02191	-0.00211	4.94548	88,202
15	5	0.947	0.598	-0.02365	0.21258	-0.00265	4.94337	87,775
20	5	1.545	0.454	0.18893	0.11188	-0.00383	4.94072	87,241
25	5	1.999	0.381	0.30081	0.07577	-0.00474	4.93689	86,475
30	5	2.380	0.544	0.37658	0.08940	-0.00574	4.93215	85,536
35	5	2.924	0.851	0.46598	0.11094	-0.00723	4.92641	84,413
40	5	3.775	1.327	0.57692	0.13082	-0.00957	4.91918	83,019
45	5	5.102	1.928	0.70774	0.13922	-0.01306	4.90961	81,210
50	5	7.030	3.365	0.84696	0.16986	-0.01868	4.89655	78,804
55	5	10.395	5.427	1.01682	0.18244	-0.02805	4.87787	75,804
60	5	15.822	10.427	1.19926	0.21985	-0.04473	4.84982	70,765
65	5	26.249	17.298	1.41911	0.21985	-0.07420	4.80509	63,840
70	5	43.547	28.698	1.63896	0.21985	-0.12310	4.73089	53,813
75	5	72.245	47.611	1.85881	0.21985	-0.20423	4.60779	40,531
80	5	119,856	78,987	2.07866	0.21985	-0.33882	4.40356	25,326
85	5	198.843	131.040	2.29851	0.21985	-0.56210	4.06474	11,608
90	w-90	329.883		2.51836			3.50264	3,182

TABLE A-I-4 (continued)

VALUES USED FOR DETERMINING l_x , COSTA RICA, 1963

FEMALE

x	n	$1000\ \mu_x$	$\Delta 1000\ \mu_x$	$\log_{10}1000\ \mu_x$	$\Delta\log_{10}1000\ \mu_x$	$\log_{10}\ _nP_x$	$\log_{10}\ l_x$	l_x
(1)	(2)	(3)	(4)	(5)	(6)	(7)	(8)	(9)
0	1	124.681	-92.184	2.09580	-0.58396	-0.02977	5.00000	100,000
1	1	32.497	-22.806	1.51184	-0.52547	-0.00819	4.97023	93,375
2	1	9.691	-4.737	0.98637	-0.29141	-0.00307	4.96204	91,631
3	1	4.954	-1.867	0.69496	-0.20542	-0.00171	4.95897	90,985
4	1	3.087	-0.618	0.48954	-0.09702	-0.00120	4.95726	90,628
5	5	2.469	-1.672	0.39252	-0.49106	-0.00321	4.95606	90,377
10	5	0.797	-0.094	-0.09854	-0.05450	-0.00163	4.95285	89,712
15	5	0.703	0.364	-0.15304	0.18120	-0.00189	4.95122	89,376
20	5	1.067	0.381	0.02816	0.12261	-0.00293	4.94933	88,988
25	5	1.448	0.404	0.15077	0.11687	-0.00326	4.94640	88,389
30	5	1.862	0.580	0.26764	0.11832	-0.00462	4.94314	87,728
35	5	2.432	0.840	0.38596	0.12885	-0.00615	4.93852	86,800
40	5	3.272	1.208	0.51481	0.13647	-0.00835	4.93237	85,580
45	5	4.480	1.640	0.65128	0.13547	-0.01142	4.92402	83,950
50	5	6.120	2.878	0.78675	0.16740	-0.01621	4.91260	81,771
55	5	8.998	4.723	0.95415	0.18323	-0.02431	4.89639	78,775
60	5	13.721	8.837	1.13738	0.21592	-0.03860	4.87208	74,487
65	5	22.558	14.529	1.35330	0.21592	-0.06346	4.83348	68,152
70	5	37.087	23.886	1.56922	0.21592	-0.10433	4.77002	58,887
75	5	60.973	39.282	1.78514	0.21592	-0.17157	4.66569	46,312
80	5	100.255	64.555	2.00106	0.21592	-0.28195	4.49412	31,198
85	5	164.810	106.145	2.21698	0.21592	-0.46360	4.21217	16,299
90	w-90	270.955		2.43290			3.74857	5,605

APPENDIX II

EXAMPLE OF METHOD B--THE CASE OF HONDURAS, 1940

        In this section we will give a practical example of life
table construction by Method B. Our case is Honduras, 1940. Actually, in our study, we constructed all life tables by this method
using a Data Control 6400 computer, and our final results were tak-
en directly from computer output. Here, however, for the purposes
of presenting an example, we have supplied the intermediate calculations, using fewer significant digits. For this reason, small
discrepancies will be found between the calculations shown and the
final results.

        The smoothing of the proportional age group distribution of
the population by sex will be explained in Appendix III. Thus the
proportional age group distribution ($C'(x,x+5)$) obtained from
Table XII-2 for ages 10-59 was divided by sets of $_5L_x$ values from
the United Nations Model Life Tables.[1] In other words, the ratios
$100 \dfrac{C'(x,x+5)}{_5L_x}$ were calculated for each sex,[2] and Naperian logarithms of these quotients were taken. Then these logarithms were
adjusted by means of a straight line found by the least square
method. In symbols, the adjusted straight line is

$$y = a' - r'(x+2.5) \quad ,$$

where

$$y = \log_e \frac{C(x,x+5)}{_5L_x} \quad ,$$

$$a' = \log_e b \quad ,$$

$$r' = \text{growth rate of the population}$$

$$x = \text{the age}[3].$$

The set of values of $_5L_x$ chosen from the United Nations Model Life
Tables, are those which give the smallest difference between the
slope of the straight line of adjustment and the closest value of
the estimated growth rate for the population. In the case of Honduras, 1940, the $C'(x,x+5)$ (Table A-II-1, col. 2) were divided by

the set of $_5L_x$ values (level 35 from the U.N. Model Life Tables) and multiplied by 100 (Table A-II-1, col. 4). Next, Naperian logarithms of these quotients were obtained (Table A-II-1, col. 5).

For simplicity a change of origin was made in the calculation of the parameters of the straight line to be established by the least square method. The mean age between 10 and 59 was made to equal zero. In other words, for the new variable (z) the age 35 equals zero. In symbols $z = x-35$ and the equation of the straight line can be rewritten as

$$y = a - r'(z+2.5) \quad,$$

where

$$a = \frac{\Sigma\ y}{n}$$

and

$$r' = \frac{\Sigma\ y(z+2.5)}{\Sigma\ (z+2.5)^2} \quad.$$

The values found were, for males, a_m = .80035, r'_m = -.0216619, and, for females, a_f = .78593 and r'_f = -.0224362. The average of the slopes (r) is -.0220326, which is the closest value to the estimated growth rate (22.0) obtained with any set of $_5L_x$ values. With the adjusted straight line we found the values of $\log_e \dfrac{C(x,x+5)}{_5L_x}$ for the age groups 0-4 to 80-84 for z = -35, -30, -25,..., 40, 45. In addition, making z = -37.5, we obtained $\log_e b$ (Table A-II-1, col. 6). Using antilogarithms, we found the quotients $\dfrac{C(x,x+5)}{_5L_x}$ and b (Table A-II-1, col. 7).[4] Multiplying the quotients by the same set of $_5L_x$ values previously used (those from level 35 of the U.N. Tables) and dividing by 100, we obtained C(x,x+5) (Table A-II-1, col. 8). We then applied Equation 5 from Chapter I:

$$b \cdot {_5L_x} - C(x,x+5)\ e^{r(x+2.5)} \quad.$$

We obtained the values of r for each sex on the basis of the estimate of the growth rate for the year 1940 (r = .022). If the average of the slopes r'_m and r'_f is r',[5] then $d = \dfrac{r'_m}{r'}$. Multiplying d by the estimated growth rate for the country (22.0), we obtained the growth rate for both males and females. The values

286

obtained were .02161 for males and .02239 for females. With these estimates of the intrinsic growth rates, we calculated the values $e^{r(x-2.5)}$ (Table A-II-1, col. 9). Multiplying these values by the $C(x,x+5)$ values obtained after the adjustment (Table A-II-1, col. 8), we obtained the b_5L_x values (Table A-II-1, col. 10). By dividing these figures by the correspondent value of b for each sex, we obtained the $5L_x$ values (Table A-II-1, col. 11), after which all other functions could be obtained by any usual method. In this particular case, the method was explained in Chapter I.

Life tables constructed by Method B were checked against life tables constructed by Method A. In certain cases life tables constructed by both of these methods were compared with those constructed by the Reed and Merrell method. These comparisons were made in order to determine (a) whether the level of mortality estimated by Method B corresponded to that calculated by other methods; and (b) whether the pattern of mortality obtained using Method B differed from that obtained using vital statistics.

To check Method B's accuracy in estimating the mortality level, we took the cases of Chile in 1952 and 1960, for which life tables were originally calculated using Method B and A respectively, and this time calculated life tables using the opposite method in each case. We were able to do so successfully because, first, of those countries in which it is possible to apply Method A, Chile has the most reliable death statistics, and second, in 1960 the requirements for the application of Method B are still satisfied. Method B was applied using the 1960 census of the native male population, a growth rate of 24.6 per thousand, and the United Nations Model Life Tables. Method A was applied to the year 1952 using registered deaths and census information. In Chile some omission of deaths would probably be expected for 1952, and according to a graphic cohort analysis, the 1952 census shows some underenumeration (see Fig. IV-1). Hence the omissions would compensate for one another.

Although Chile is a good case for comparison of the mortality patterns determined by Method B and vital statistics, we also considered other cases, such as Costa Rica, 1950, Colombia, 1951, and El Salvador, 1930. In these last three cases it was impossible to apply Method A because of the poor statistics for ages under 5. Once death registration was corrected, the Reed and Merrell method was used. Death registers were corrected assuming that under-registration was proportionally the same in all ages and that it was equal to the difference between the estimated crude death rates (obtained with central mortality rates from life tables constructed by Method B and census information) and the registered death rate. The results are shown in Table A-II-2.

In conclusion, we can say that the levels of mortality estimated using Method B are fairly accurate, judging by the cases of Chile and Costa Rica (in which practically no correction was made). Unfortunately it is more difficult to compare patterns of mortality, principally because of the lack of accurate information. How much the mortality patterns of the life tables constructed using Method B differ from actual mortality patterns cannot be established except in the case of Chile. Mortality patterns obtained from incomplete death registers are affected not only by errors in age reporting but also by differential omission in certain ages, principally in ages under 5.

TABLE A-II-1

VALUES USED FOR DETERMINING $_5L_x$, HONDURAS, 1940

MALE

Age	$C(x,x+5)$	$_5L_x$ (e=37.5)	$100 \dfrac{C(x,x+5)}{_5L_x}$	$\log_e (4)$	Adjusted Column (5)[a]
(1)	(2)	(3)	(4)	(5)	(6)
0					(1.558520)
0-4		3.81293			1.504365
5-9		3.42915			1.396055
10-14	.123144	3.32322	3.7056	1.3098	1.287745
15-19	.105836	3.22362	3.2831	1.1888	1.179435
20-24	.089211	3.08645	2.8904	1.0614	1.071125
25-29	.075996	2.92732	2.5961	.9540	.962815
30-34	.063860	2.76352	2.3108	.8376	.854505
35-39	.053940	2.59028	2.0824	.7335	.746195
40-44	.044935	2.39818	1.8737	.6279	.637885
45-49	.037049	2.17870	1.7005	.5309	.529575
50-54	.029696	1.92908	1.5394	.4314	.421265
55-59	.022878	1.64778	1.3884	.3282	.312955
60-64		1.33688			.204645
65-69		1.00452			.096335
70-74		.66900			-.011975
75-79		.37202			-.120285
80-84		.15842			-.228595
85 +		.04880			

[a]The adjustment was done by the least square method. The least square lines are: $y = .80035 -.021662x$

289

TABLE A-II-1 (continued)

VALUES USED FOR DETERMINING $_5L_x$, HONDURAS, 1940

MALE (continued)

Age	Antilog(6)	Adjusted C(x,x+5) (7)·(3)	$e^{r(x+2.5)}$ (r=.02161)	$b \cdot {_sL_x}$	$_5L_x$
(1)	(7)	(8)	(9)	(10)	(11)
0	(4.751783)				
0-4	4.501294	.1716312	1.055511	.1811584	3.81243
5-9	4.039224	.1385111	1.175948	.1628819	3.42781
10-14	3.624604	.1204536	1.310128	.1578096	3.32106
15-19	3.252536	.1048494	1.459618	.1530401	3.22069
20-24	2.918661	.0900830	1.626166	.1464899	3.08284
25-29	2.619059	.0766682	1.811717	.1389011	2.92314
30-34	2.350211	.0649486	2.018440	.1310948	2.75885
35-39	2.108960	.0546280	2.248751	.1228448	2.58523
40-44	1.892474	.0453849	2.505341	.1137047	2.39289
45-49	1.698210	.0369989	2.791209	.1032717	2.17333
50-54	1.523880	.0293969	3.109699	.0914155	1.92382
55-59	1.367460	.0225327	3.464523	.0780651	1.64286
60-64	1.227089	.0164047	3.859837	.0633195	1.33254
65-69	1.101128	.0110611	4.300258	.0475655	1.00100
70-74	.988096	.0066104	4.790925	.0316699	.66648
75-79	.886668	.0032986	5.337594	.0176065	.37052
80-84	.795651	.0012605	5.946663	.0074957	.15774
85 +		$.0003962^b$	6.731958^c	$.0026672^b$	$.05613^b$

^{b}Estimated value after the calculation of $_5P_{80}$. ^{c}For this open group, x+2.5 = 85+e85+ .

TABLE A-II-1 (continued)

VALUES USED FOR DETERMINING $_5L_x$, HONDURAS, 1940

FEMALE

Age	C(x,x+5)	$_5L_x$ (e=37.5)	$100 \frac{C(x,x+5)}{_5L_x}$	$\log_e(4)$	Adjusted Column (5)[a]
(1)	(2)	(3)	(4)	(5)	(6)
0					(1.571190)
0-4		3.90108			1.515100
5-9		3.50928			1.402920
10-14	.120585	3.39350	3.5534	1.2679	1.290740
15-19	.105487	3.28028	3.2158	1.1681	1.178560
20-24	.090774	3.12962	2.9005	1.0649	1.006380
25-29	.077987	2.95488	2.6393	.9705	.954200
30-34	.065599	2.77410	2.3647	.8607	.842020
35-39	.055092	2.59155	2.1258	.7542	.729840
40-44	.044923	2.40742	1.8660	.6238	.617660
45-49	.036765	2.21530	1.6596	.5066	.505480
50-54	.029405	2.00338	1.4678	.3837	.393300
55-59	.022840	1.76295	1.2956	.2589	.281120
60-64		1.48280			.168940
65-69		1.15978			.056760
70-74		.80985			-.055420
75-79		.47400			-.167600
80-84		.21332			-.279780
85 +		.07323			

[a]The adjustment was done by the least square method. The least square lines are: y = .78593-.022436x.

291

TABLE A-II-1 (continued)

VALUES USED FOR DETERMINING $_5L_x$, HONDURAS, 1940

FEMALE (continued)

Age	Antilog(6)	Adjusted C(x,x+5) (7)·(3)	$e^{r(x+2.5)}$ (r=.02161)	$b \cdot _5L_x$	$_5L_x$
(1)	(7)	(8)	(9)	(10)	(11)
0	(4.812372)				
0-4	4.549876	.1774943	1.057571	.1877128	3.90063
5-9	4.067058	.1427245	1.182848	.1688214	3.50807
10-14	3.635476	.1233699	1.322964	.1632139	3.39155
15-19	3.249691	.1065990	1.479679	.1577323	3.27764
20-24	2.904844	.0909106	1.654957	.1504531	3.12638
25-29	2.596592	.0767262	1.850997	.1420200	2.95114
30-34	2.321051	.0643883	2.070262	.1333007	2.76996
35-39	2.074749	.0537682	2.315499	.1245001	2.58708
40-44	1.854583	.0446476	2.589785	.1156277	2.40272
45-49	1.657781	.0367248	2.896563	.1063751	2.21046
50-54	1.481863	.0296873	3.239681	.0961775	1.99855
55-59	1.324613	.0233523	3.623444	.0846157	1.75829
60-64	1.184049	.0175571	4.052666	.0711531	1.47854
65-69	1.058402	.0122751	4.532733	.0556398	1.15618
70-74	.946088	.0076619	5.069666	.0388432	.80715
75-79	.845692	.0040086	5.670203	.0227296	.47231
80-84	.755950	.0016126	6.341878	.0102269	.21251 [b]
85 +		.0005358 [b]	7.234259 [c]	.0038759 [b]	.08154 [b]

[b] Estimated value after the calculation of $_5P_{80}$.   [c] For this open group, x+2.5 = 85+e_{85}+ .

TABLE A-II-2

COMPARISON OF LIFE TABLES CONSTRUCTED
USING DIFFERENT METHODS

MALE POPULATION

Country and Year	Method	$\overset{o}{e}_o$	1	I_x at Ages		
				5	15	50
Chile 1960	A	54.2	88.542	85,159	83,849	67,557
	B	55.8	90,317	86,544	84,560	69,272
	R.M.*	54.6	88,480	85,716	84,465	67,827
Chile 1952	A	50.3	87,115	83,184	81,371	62,099
	B	50.8	87,349	82,791	79,434	62,152
	R.M.*	50.5	87,083	83,247	81,609	62,121
Colombia 1951	B	47.9	86,050	80,821	76,863	57,764
	R.M.*	47.1	87,380	80,245	77,414	52,073
Costa Rica 1950	B	54.0	88,634	84,760	82,102	67,025
	R.M.*	54.6	90,214	84,934	83,171	68,489
El Salvador 1930	B	26.6	73,229	61,135	52,756	24,922
	R.M.*	27.7	73,749	61,876	53,292	25,714

*Reed and Merrell

NEW LIFE TABLES FOR LATIN AMERICAN POPULATIONS

NOTES

[1] United Nations, Department of Economic and Social Affairs, Methods for Population Projections by Sex and Age, Manual III (ST/SOA/Series A, Population Studies No. 25)(New York, 1956), pp. 78-79.

[2] The values of $_5L_x$ are reduced as if they pertain to $l_0 = 1$ (one). In other words, they are divided by 1000,000.

[3] See Equation 6, Chapter I.

[4] For example, for males, we estimated b in the following way: The straight line of adjustment was $y = .80035 - .0216619 (z+2.5)$. The value of this equation when $z = -37.5$ is 1.558516, and the $\log_e$ of this value is 100 x b. Therefore, taking the antilogarithm, we found that the value of 100 x b = 4.7517668.

[5]
$$r' = \frac{r'_m + r'_f}{2} \quad .$$

[6] L. Reed and M. Merrell, "A Short Method for Constructing an Abridged Life Table," reproduced in U. S. Department of Commerce, Bureau of the Census, Handbook of Statistical Method for Demographers, by A. J. Jaffe, Washington, 1960.

APPENDIX III

SMOOTHING OF THE AGE GROUP DISTRIBUTION

The smoothing of the age group distribution of the population was accomplished in two steps. First we adjusted the ten-year age groups 10-59, using the formula

$$S^*_{x,x+10} = \frac{1}{4}(S_{x-10,x} + 2S_{x,x+10} + S_{x+10,x+20}) , \quad (A\text{-}III\text{-}1)$$

where $S^*_{x,x+10}$ represents the adjusted decennial group, and $S_{x-10,x}$, $S_{x,x+10}$ and $S_{x+10,x+20}$ are the decennial groups from the census. Then, we separated each adjusted ten-year age group into quinquennial age groups, assuming that a second degree function passes through three consecutive central points of decennial groups. By integrating this function between convenient limits, we obtained the five-year age groups.

When the ten-year age group to be separated is the central group of three, the formula to be used is:

$$Q_{x,x+5} = \frac{1}{24}(-S^*_{x-15,x-5} + 11S^*_{x-5,x+5} + 2S^*_{x+5,x+15}). \quad (A\text{-}III\text{-}2)$$

When the decennial group corresponds to an extreme group (the youngest) we use the formula:

$$Q_{x-10,x-5} = \frac{1}{24}(8S^*_{x-15,x-5} + 5S^*_{x-5,x+5} - S^*_{x+5,x+15}). \quad (A\text{-}III\text{-}3)$$

When the decennial group at the oldest extreme is separated, the same coefficients are used, but in inverse order. The other quinquennial group is found from the difference between the decennial group and the estimated quinquennial.

The total population in the smoothed five-year age groups 10-59 was adjusted in accordance with the enumerated population 10-59 in the census. By dividing these smoothed age groups by the total population for each sex, we obtained the proportional distribution to be used in the construction of life tables.

APPENDIX IV

EVALUATION OF LIFE TABLES

In this appendix, we will explain our procedure of evaluating life tables. All calculations were made, as for the life tables themselves, using a Data Control 6400 computer. Our procedure will consist of comparing the estimate of r used in the life table with an independent estimate of r which was obtained from an estimate of the fertility level. If age specific fertility rates--m(x)--for each year for which a life table was constructed are available, then the solution to Lotka's Characteristic Equation would be another estimate of the intrinsic growth rate, that is:

$$\psi_{(x)} = \int_0^\omega e^{r'x} m(x) \, p(x) \, dx = 1 \quad ,$$

which in this case was expressed as:

$$\psi_{(x)} = \sum_{15}^{45} e^{-r'(x+2.5)} \, m(x) \, _5L_x = 1 \quad . \qquad \text{(A-IV-1)}$$

The $_5L_x$ values used were those from constructed life tables where the radix was equal to one.

By solving for the value of r' which satisfies Equation A-IV-1, we can make a comparison between r' and the intrinsic growth rate of the life table from which $_5L_x$ values were taken. Theoretically, if the population for which the life table was constructed can be considered "quasi-stable," if the estimate of the intrinsic growth rate used in the life table is correct, and if the age specific fertility rates used in Equation A-IV-1 are accurate, then both intrinsic growth rates, that used for the life table and the other which is the solution to Equation A-IV-1, should be similar. In practice, however, this similarity is almost impossible to obtain, because x, r, b and the distribution of C'(x,x+5) are estimated. Therefore, it would be desirable to use a confidence interval, the interval within which the intrinsic growth rate used in the life table could vary.

APPENDIX IV

In reality, the quality of demographic statistics in Latin American countries is not good. Registers have improved, but in most cases only recently. Thus, the information needed to calculate age specific fertility rates does not always exist, and when it does the statistics frequently have a low degree of completeness. Therefore, the age specific fertility rates needed in Equation A-IV-1 must be estimated using the only information available--historical estimates of total fertility levels[1] and census information. Here, only female life tables will be evaluated (if they are accepted, male tables will also be accepted). Hence when we speak of age specific fertility rates and crude birth rates, we are referring only to female births and female population.

PROBLEMS TO BE SOLVED

In the calculation of age specific fertility rates, two problems arise: first, how can census errors be avoided--both in general, and in cases of particular underenumeration or age misreporting in certain age groups[2]; second, how can age specific fertility rates be obtained if only estimates of the crude birth rates are available.

Correction of Census Data

Errors in census information, proportional in all age groups, can be avoided by considering the proportional age group distribution. Heaping errors at certain ages can be reduced by smoothing population data (see Appendix III).

The problem of differential completeness in age groups can be solved if we accept the following reasonable assumptions: (a) Population of all Latin American countries for which life tables have been constructed can be assumed to be quasi-stable; therefore, for each case, the proportion of census population in ages 15-49 does not vary significantly from the same proportion of the stable population obtained from the life table and suitable r . (b) The errors in the smoothed proportional five-year age group distribution of ages 15-49 are proportional to the population in each age group. In symbols, if $C''(x,x+4)$ and $C'(x,x+4)$ (for x = 15, 20, ..., 45) are respectively the proportional distribution from actual and enumerated population in ages 15-49, then

$$C''(x,x+4) = aC'(x,x+4) \qquad (x=15,20,25,\ldots,45) \quad,$$

where a , the constant of proportionality, is the reciprocal of the common degree of completeness due to errors. If we accept these two assumptions, the actual proportional five-year age group distribution can be found as follows:

First, the proportion of the population in ages 15-49 in the stable population will be

$$C(15,50) = b \int_{15}^{50} e^{-rx} p(x) \, dx \; , \qquad (A\text{-}IV\text{-}2)$$

or in the discrete case

$$C(15,50) = b \sum_{15}^{45} e^{-r(x+2.5)} \, {}_5L_x \; ,$$

where the ${}_5L_x$ values are from the life tables already constructed where the radix is equal to one.

However, in order to apply Equation A-IV-2 we must first calculate the intrinsic birth rate. This calculation is also made from life table values, using

$$b = \frac{1}{\displaystyle\int_{0}^{\omega} e^{-rx} p(x) \, dx} \qquad (A\text{-}IV\text{-}3)$$

or

$$b = \frac{1}{\displaystyle\sum_{0}^{\omega} e^{-r(x+2.5)} \, {}_5L_x} \; .$$

Once we obtain b we can apply Equation A-IV-2 to find the proportion of population in ages 15-49. This proportion, according to assumption (a), is the expected proportion in the smoothed census distribution. Then, according to assumption (b), we can correct the proportional and smoothed five-year age group distribution from the census, first, by calculating the factor a:

298

$$a = \frac{\sum\limits_{15}^{45} C(x,x+4)}{\sum\limits_{15}^{45} C'(x,x+4)} \quad , \qquad\qquad (A-IV-4)$$

and second, by correcting the smoothed five-year age group distribution from the census by applying (for each group):

$$C''(x,x+4) = a \ C'(x,x+4) \qquad (x=15,20,\ldots,45) \quad .$$

Estimation of Age Specific Fertility Rates

We wanted to estimate age specific fertility rates in a way which would permit their use in any particular case. Fertility levels in Latin American countries--with the exception of Argentina, Cuba, and Uruguay--have been very high. In recent years certain countries have shown some differences in their usual age specific fertility rate patterns. Thus, El Salvador, 1961, and Panama, 1950 show early fertility patterns when compared with other countries. Various countries, such as El Salvador, 1950, Venezuela, 1961, Colombia, 1951, Guatemala, 1950, and Mexico, 1950, present a set of age specific fertility rates which can be considered a late fertility pattern. On the other hand, if we observe Chile, 1952, Mexico, 1960 and Venezuela, 1950, their fertility rates fluctuate between the early and late patterns; we can call this pattern a "normal" fertility pattern. We can conclude from these observations that fertility patterns have not been consistent in all the countries we considered, not even in the same country at different times. Therefore, to estimate age specific fertility rates we must take into account the possibility of any one of the three fertility patterns.

We estimated age specific fertility rates without much difficulty as follows: first, three fertility patterns were obtained by averaging the age specific fertility rates of countries with each type of pattern. Thus it was assumed that for any country at any time, the fertility rate pattern might vary among the three averages. We next had to find the level of each age specific fertility rate pattern. To do so, it was necessary to assume that age specific fertility rate would vary proportionately to the variation of total fertility. Under this assumption-- and because the population used in each case is given in proportion to the total population ($C''(x,x+4)$)--the total number of births is the birth rate.[3] In symbols,

$$b = \int_{a}^{\beta} C(x) \, m(x) \, dx \quad , \qquad \text{(A-IV-5)}$$

or

$$b = \sum_{15}^{45} C''(x,x+4) \, m(x,x+4)$$

Once we accepted an estimate of the crude birth rate, the age specific fertility rates in each of the three fertility patterns could be proportionally adjusted to obtain the accepted estimate of the crude birth rate.

However, one further consideration must be taken into account. Because the crude birth rates are only estimates, there is still a possibility of error. Therefore, it would be better for us to use a confidence interval than the estimated crude birth rates. This interval would consist of 5 percent limits above and below the estimated value.[4] Thus for each case, we used not only three patterns of fertility, but also three levels of crude birth rates--the lower limit interval, the accepted estimate, and the upper limit interval. Hence, nine sets of age specific fertility rates were used in each case.[5] Using these rates, we found the solution to Lotka's Characteristic Equation (Eq. A-IV-1)[6] and estimated nine intrinsic growth rates for each case. Then we compared the intrinsic growth rate used in the life table with those from the characteristic equation. We accepted a life table if the intrinsic growth rate used in its construction fluctuated between the extreme values of the intrinsic growth rates found by solving the characteristic equation, which means that the age distribution of the population, the intrinsic growth and birth rates, and the life table are all in agreement. Therefore, because the proportional age group distribution is derived from census information, the constructed life table represents the actual level of mortality. If the intrinsic growth rates used in the life table exceed those limits given by the intrinsic growth rates which are the solution to Lotka's Characteristic Equation, none of the values used could be correct. A careful analysis is recommended before making any decision as to where the error lies.

In our study, the results of fifty-seven female life tables were satisfactory. In only a few cases, generally those of the earliest dates, were more difficulties found in the estimation of information used in the construction of life tables. After a careful study of all the rejected cases, we made some corrections in intrinsic growth rates and also in proportional age distribution. Then, new life tables with the modified values were constructed, tested, and accepted.

NOTES

[1] The estimates considered are:

O. Andrew Collver, Birth Rates in Latin America: New Estimates of Historical Trends and Fluctuations (Berkeley: Institute of International Studies, University of California, 1965) [Research Series No. 7].

J. R. Rele, Fertility Analysis Through Extension of Stable Population Concepts (Berkeley: Institute of International Studies, University of California, 1967) [Population Monograph Series No. 2].

United Nations, The Population of South America, 1950-1980 (ST/SOA/ Series A, Population Studies No. 21) (New York, 1955), and Human Resources in Central America, Panama, and Mexico, 1950-1980 (ST/TAO/K/LAT/1, E/CN.12/548) (New York, 1960), pp. 28-29.

[2] Underenumeration occurred principally in ages under 10, and sometimes in ages over 55.

[3] Equation 6 (Chapter I) can be obtained from Lotka's Characteristic Equation (Eq. A-IV-I) by replacing $_5L_x$ by its equivalent

$$\frac{1}{b} \ C(x, \ x + 4) \cdot e^{r(x + 2.5)} \quad .$$

[4] If the estimated birth rate is 45 per thousand, then the interval will be from 42.75 to 47.25 per thousand.

[5] It would be appropriate at this stage to mention that our results show that the different patterns of fertility (early, normal, and late) make practically no change in the calculated intrinsic growth rates. The changes are almost completely due to the variation of the level of the age specific fertility rates (from the 5% below to the 5% above the estimated birth rate) for any pattern.

[6] The solution of the characteristic equation was carried out using an iterative secant method. See Ansley J. Coale, "A New Method for Calculating Lotka's r -- The Intrinsic Rate of Growth in a Stable Population," Population Studies, Vol. XI (July, 1957), pp. 92-94.

APPENDIX V

SOME ESTIMATES FOR MEXICO

DIFFERENTIAL OMISSION IN DEATHS UNDER ONE YEAR OLD

In this section we will discuss in detail omission in deaths under one year old. This kind of omission does not affect the total omission figure already estimated in Chapter XIII; however, we will make an attempt to ascertain which part of the total omission belongs to deaths under one year old, and which part to deaths in other age groups.

In Mexico, the completeness of under-one-year-old death figures is seriously affected by the notable under-registration of deaths under one day old. A simple analysis of these deaths gives an immediate impression of incompleteness. For example, the value of the ratio of deaths of age under one day, divided by the daily average of deaths 1-6 days old is for some years lower than one. In addition, the trend of these ratios through time (Table A-V-1)

TABLE A-V-1

TREND OF THE QUOTIENT OF DEATHS AGED $\frac{-1 \text{ day}}{1/6(1 \text{ to } 6 \text{ days})}$

MEXICO, SELECTED YEARS

Period	Male	Female
1936-1938	3.88	3.66
1939-1941	2.35	2.40
1942-1944	.61	.63
1952-1955	.82	.77
1956-1959	1.10	1.13

is peculiar--the decline observed in the 1940's and 1950's is not acceptable, nor is the tendency of the absolute number of deaths under one day (Table A-V-2). The fluctuation of the index in Table A-V-2 should be very smooth, as it is in the case of most of the other countries studied. If fertility does not vary, the index will increase, decrease, or remain constant, according to the changes in mortality. If mortality showed a fast decline, the index would also decline (as in some Latin American countries); or, in countries where there is little change in mortality (where, for example, the level of mortality is already too low), the index can increase.[1]

TABLE A-V-2

DEATHS UNDER AGE ONE DAY
MEXICO, SELECTED YEARS

	1936-1938	1939-1941	1942-1944	1952-1955	1956-1959
		Annual Averages			
Male	4,461	2,426	1,057	1,593	2,189
Female	3,137	1,810	798	1,070	1,597
		Index Numbers (1936-1938=100)			
Male	100	54	24	36	49
Female	100	58	25	34	51

In the case of Mexico, the trend shown in Tables A-V-1 and A-V-2 could be explained not only by a large omission in under-one-day-old death figures, but also by misdeclaration of age. The first possibility is supported by the low values of the ratio (Table A-V-1); the second is supported by the same ratio and the index trend of Table A-V-2.

In order to make a comparison, we calculated certain other ratios for Mexico and various other countries. These ratios are:

$$\text{(A)} \quad \frac{\text{deaths under one day old}}{\text{deaths under one year old}}$$

$$\text{(B)} \quad \frac{\text{deaths under one year old}}{\text{deaths of ages 0-4 years old}}$$

$$\text{(C)} \quad \frac{\text{deaths under one week old}}{\text{deaths under one year old}}$$

and they are given in Tables A-V-3, A-V-4, and A-V-5, respectively.

When compared with other countries, there is no doubt that figures
for Mexico indicate a major irregularity in deaths under one day
old (Table A-V-3); for deaths under one year old and under one
week old, however, the irregularities seem not to be very remarkable. These findings would confirm our previous statement that,
in addition to omission, there was a shift in the declaration of
age in deaths under one day old toward a slightly higher age. Thus
we decided first to estimate the expected deaths of those under
one day old, and second, to estimate how many deaths under one day
were registered as having been later.

Estimation of Deaths Under One Day Old

We estimated deaths under one day old by comparing Mexico
with the other countries listed in Tables A-V-3, A-V-4 and A-V-5.
Among the countries listed, the most similar to Mexico from a demographic point of view are Puerto Rico and Panama. We can observe
some similarities in ratio B between Mexico in 1956-1959, Puerto
Rico in 1946-1948 and Panama in 1948-1950 (Table A-V-4).[2] It
would be possible, therefore, to expect similar values of ratio A
for the same years. However, we can see that ratio A is 35 per
thousand for Mexico in 1956-1959, and 113 and 99 per thousand for
Puerto Rico in 1946-1948 and Panama in 1948-1950 respectively.

We could accept values of 78 for males and 64 for females
in Mexico in 1936-1938 after considering the trends and levels of
ratio A observed in Puerto Rico and Panama and observing that
ratio A tends to change more rapidly than the other ratios presented. Then, by taking into account the trend of ratio B and observing the relation between the ratios presented in Tables A-V-3,
A-V-4, and A-V-5 for Puerto Rico and Panama, we estimated the
values of ratio A for Mexico for each sex at different periods
(Table A-V-6, col. 3).

We next estimated how many actual deaths under one day of
age were registered at other ages. To do so, we assumed that if
in 1936-1938, 78 males and 64 females per thousand of the registered deaths under one year belonged in the under one-day-old
category, we could expect at least the same proportion to have
been registered (2 in any age) during the following years. Therefore, we accepted as differential omission in deaths under one day
of age the difference between the estimated proportion in each
date and that observed in 1936-1938. For example, for the period
1956-1959, we estimated for males a proportion of 120 deaths under
one day per thousand deaths under one year. The difference between this 120 and 78 (the proportion in 1936-1938) gives us the
differential omission of deaths under one day old. Also, 78 minus
31 (the proportion registered in 1956-1959) gives us the number of
deaths under one day per thousand deaths aged under one year which
were registered as belonging to other age groups (47 per thousand
in this case).

TABLE A-V-3

TREND OF THE QUOTIENT OF DEATH AGED $\frac{-1\ day}{-1\ year}$ FOR SELECTED COUNTRIES

(per thousand)

	Mexico	Canada	Chile	Hawaii	New Zealand	Panama	Puerto Rico	South Africa	Sweden	U.S.A.
				Male						
1936-1939	78	179	102	214	271	*	*	150	159	280
1940-1942	36	197	122	316	277	*	*	165	184	302
1943-1945	19	229	132	*	283	*	*	170	212	292
1946-1948	*	246	131	397	300	*	99	205	249	338
1949-1951	*	250	129	396	*	108	113	226b	267	345
1952-1954	26	266	99	422	*	108	134	*	267	352
1955-1957	31	308	88	*	*	112	156	244	299	380
1958-1960	32a	327	*	*	*	124	167a	240a	313	384a
				Female						
1936-1939	65	168	94	224	301	*	*	159	154	270
1940-1942	32	183	115	354	275	*	*	172	194	292
1943-1945	17	212	122	*	287	*	*	176	219	286
1946-1948	*	231	121	382	331	*	93	223	258	330
1949-1951	*	240	122	377	*	97	97	213b	259	337
1952-1954	21	248	87	415	*	97	120	*	275	348
1955-1957	26	298	84	*	*	92	146	239	290	379
1958-1960	32a	326	*	*	*	116	153a	240a	300	383a

* no information   a 1958-1959   b 1949-1950

TABLE A-V-4

TREND OF THE QUOTIENT OF DEATHS AGED $\frac{-1\ year}{0-4\ years}$ FOR SELECTED COUNTRIES

(per thousand)

Year	Mexico	Canada	Chile	Hawaii	New Zealand	Panama	Puerto Rico	South Africa	Sweden	U.S.A.
Male										
1936-1939	524	791	730	783	781	*	572	743	792	792
1940-1942	519	818	725	800	815	602[c]	584	753	822	834
1943-1945	537	835	725	810	792	*	648	766	813	836
1946-1948	*	854	774	839	822	*	650	792	818	864
1949-1951	560	857	776	834	823	633[d]	677	791	801	857
1952-1954	596	858	802	840	812	608	721	824	813	861
1955-1957	614	862	807	*	842	650	794	828	811	872
1958-1960	644[a]	872	*	*	835	652	821[a]	828[a]	822[a]	869
Female										
1936-1939	482	773	711	735	771	*	531	713	788	773
1940-1942	476	780	705	786	790	567[c]	533	713	814	818
1943-1945	491	827	712	794	783	*	603	725	798	822
1946-1948	*	845	743	825	813	*	601	766	813	853
1949-1951	508	847	747	823	815	615[d]	605	782	799	845
1952-1954	545	851	770	821	798	587	666	811	809	849
1955-1957	564	856	777	*	813	592	747	807	829	859
1958-1960	595[a]	859	*	*	819	606	767[a]	825[a]	820[a]	860

* no information   a 1958-1959   b 1949-1950   c 1941-1943   d 1948-1950

TABLE A-V-5

TREND OF THE QUOTIENT OF DEATH AGED $\frac{-1 \text{ week}}{-1 \text{ year}}$ FOR SELECTED COUNTRIES

(per thousand)

Year	Mexico	Canada	Chile	Hawaii	New Zealand	Panama	Puerto Rico	South Africa	Sweden	U.S.A.
Male
1936-1939	197	366	242	354	569	*	*	316	442	476
1940-1942	194	392	219	519	562	*	*	346	466	513
1943-1945	193	414	232	*	563	*	*	370	517	515
1946-1948	*	450	228	604	616	*	249	453	600	606
1949-1951	*	464	222	650	*	255	286	457b	643	616
1952-1954	215	492	220	701	*	287	311	*	654	630
1955-1957	222	539	202	*	613	342	346	545	676	648
1958-1960	228a	556	*	*	622	310	361a	547a	713	645a
Female
1936-1939	170	352	231	329	579	*	*	314	437	452
1940-1942	169	370	211	512	575	*	*	362	465	484
1943-1945	168	384	218	*	573	*	*	353	502	489
1946-1948	*	426	216	604	626	*	218	443	591	579
1949-1951	*	437	207	607	*	240	235	441b	621	585
1952-1954	186	462	201	633	*	253	267	*	630	601
1955-1957	190	506	184	*	580	267	307	517	658	626
1958-1960	196a	541	*	*	620	252	321a	522a	662	626a

* no information   a 1958-1959   b 1949-1950

For the purpose of constructing life tables, we needed an estimate of the deaths under one year. Hence we established the omission in deaths under one year by considering the estimated omission in deaths under one day (Table A-V-6). The omissions for census years were obtained by interpolating and extrapolating the estimates for the periods shown in Table A-V-6.

Now, it is necessary to remember that the omission estimated for deaths under one year old is <u>differential omission</u> in relation to the other ages, and also that it is included in the general under-registration of deaths already estimated in Table XIII-9. Therefore, we calculate the omission in deaths aged under one and those one and over as follows: If a is the omission in total deaths, b is the omission of deaths under one year old, and c is the omission of deaths one year old and over, then

$$aD = bD_{-1} + cD_{1+} \quad , \qquad\qquad (A\text{-}V\text{-}1)$$

where D, D_{-1} and D_{1+} represent respectively total, under one year old, and one year old and over registered deaths. But

$$b = c + d \quad , \qquad\qquad (A\text{-}V\text{-}2)$$

where d is the differential omission of deaths under one year old. Now a, d and the number of registered deaths are known. Therefore, in order to establish b and c, the value of b (Eq. A-V-2) was replaced by c and d in Equation A-V-1; the result obtained was:

$$aD = dD_{-1} + cD \quad ,$$

and subsequently,

$$c = a - d\, \frac{D_{-1}}{D} \quad ,$$

which allows us to estimate c. By placing this value of c in Equation A-V-2, we obtained b and then calculated the percentages of b and c for 1940, 1950, and 1960 (Table A-V-7). For 1930 and 1921 no differential omission was expected.[3] Once we calculated the values of b and c for each census year (Table A-V-8), we found the values for intercensal years by lineal interpolation.

TABLE A-V-6

ESTIMATION OF DIFFERENTIAL OMISSION OF REGISTERED DEATHS UNDER AGE ONE YEAR, MEXICO, 1936-1959

(1)	(2)	(3)	(4)	(5)	(6)	(7)	(8)	(9)
				Male				
1936-38	13.384	78	13.384	13.384	----	171.718	171.718	---
1939-41	9.706	84	14.780	13.724	1.056	175.948	177.004	0.6
1942-44	3.171	90	16.254	14.087	2.167	180.600	182.767	1.2
1952-55	6.371	112	27.656	19.261	8.395	246.933	255.328	3.4
1956-59	8.757	120	29.793	19.365	10.428	248.273	258.701	4.2
				Female				
1936-38	9.413	64	9.413	9.413	----	146.088	146.088	---
1939-41	7.241	70	10.378	9.488	.890	148.253	149.143	0.6
1942-44	2.394	76	11.556	9.732	1.824	152.055	153.879	1.2
1952-55	4.279	98	19.912	13.004	6.908	203.184	210.092	3.4
1956-59	6.390	106	21.868	13.203	8.665	206.300	214.965	4.2

KEY TO COLUMNS

(1) Periods

(2) Registered deaths under age one day

(3) Estimated trend of the quotient of deaths $\frac{\text{under age one day}}{\text{under age one year}} 100$

(4) Estimated deaths under age one day

(5) Registered deaths under age one year by the observed quotient of deaths $\frac{\text{under age one day}}{\text{under age one year}}$ in 1936-1938 (.078 for male and .064 for female)

(6) Differential omission in deaths under age one year (4)-(5)

(7) Registered deaths under age one year

(8) Corrected deaths (by omission) under age one year

(9) Differential omission in deaths under age one as a percent of registered deaths in the same age $100[\frac{(8)}{(7)} - 1]$

TABLE A-V-7

DIFFERENTIAL OMISSION OF DEATHS UNDER AGE ONE YEAR,
MEXICO, CENSUS YEARS
(percent)

Year	Differential Omission for Deaths Under One Year Old
1921	---
1930	---
1940	.6
1950	2.6
1960	4.4

TABLE A-V-8

ESTIMATED UNDER-REGISTRATION AS A PERCENTAGE OF REGISTERED
DEATHS, SELECTED AGES, MEXICO, 1921-1960

Census Years	All Ages	Male Age Under One Year	Male Age One Year and Over	Female Age Under One Year	Female Age One Year and Over
1921	11.90	11.90	11.90	11.90	11.90
1930	11.20	11.20	11.20	11.20	11.20
1940	9.90	10.35	9.75	10.36	9.76
1950	8.50	10.38	7.78	10.47	7.87
1960	5.00	8.04	3.64	8.15	3.75

APPENDIX V

ESTIMATION OF DEATHS BY INDIVIDUAL AGES FROM 1-4 YEARS OLD
FOR 1922-1949

Before making an estimate of deaths by individual ages,
we thought it advisable to make an estimate of the age group 1-5
for the period 1928-1935, for which information is only given for
age group 1-9. We preferred to estimate the age group 1-5 rather
than 1-4 because we considered the trend during 1922-1927, that
is, the trend for the age group 1-5, to be more important for our
estimate than the trend after 1936. The reason for our choice is
explained by a discussion of fertility. It is known that fertility during the period of the Civil War was lower than normal, and
that after that period fertility again reached its usual high
level.[4] Thus, the age distribution of deaths in 1922 and subsequent years could have been affected by these conditions. If the
birth rate increased during 1922 (compared with the previous ten
years) we would expect a high proportion of deaths of age under
one year. In 1923, this high proportion would be in ages under
one and one; and in 1927, the proportion of deaths in ages 0-4 to
those in the age group 0-9 would be expected to be higher than if
fertility had not changed.

Taking into account the influential factor of fertility,
and observing the trend of ages under 1, 1, 2-5, 6-9 and 1-5 during the period 1922-1927, and the trend of ages under 1, 1-9, 1-4
and 5-9 during the period 1936-1942,[5] we made an estimate of the
age group 1-5 for the period 1928-1935 (Table A-V-9). Multiplying
these estimated percentages by the absolute number registered in
that period for ages 1-9, we obtained an estimate of deaths occur-
ing in ages 1-5. We then estimated individual ages 1-4 for 1922-
1949, and the ages 5-9 for some specific years by drawing the
accumulated deaths in each age for which information was available
on a semilogarithmic graph. Reading from the graph the values for
individual ages, we obtained the necessary death figures. We can
use as an example male deaths in 1943. From the cumulative death
figures given in Table A-V-10 for 1943, we obtained Figure A-V-1,
and from that figure we could read the cumulative values shown in
Table A-V-12. By taking differences of the cumulative numbers,
we obtained the deaths for individual ages (Table A-V-11). The
estimates of deaths found in this way were corrected for the calculated omission in ages under and over one year old. Then, our
results were used in the construction of Tables XIII-12 and XIII-13
given in Chapter XIII.

PERCENTAGE DISTRIBUTION OF DEATHS FOR SELECTED
AGE GROUPS, MEXICO, 1922-1942

	Years					
Age	1922	1923	1924	1925	1926	1927
Male						
0-9	100.0	100.0	100.0	100.0	100.0	100.0
0	56.3	56.9	53.9	51.2	52.5	50.1
1-9	43.7	43.1	46.1	48.8	47.5	49.9
1	20.1	20.0	22.1	22.0	19.8	19.0
1-5	37.3	37.5	40.5	42.9	41.6	43.9
2-5	17.2	17.5	18.4	20.9	21.8	24.9
6-9	6.4	5.7	5.6	5.9	5.9	6.0
Female						
0-9	100.0	100.0	100.0	100.0	100.0	100.0
0	52.7	53.0	50.3	47.2	48.8	46.0
1-9	47.3	46.9	49.7	52.7	51.2	54.0
1	22.1	22.0	23.8	23.7	20.7	20.4
1-5	41.1	41.3	43.9	46.5	45.0	47.7
2-5	19.0	19.3	20.1	22.8	24.2	27.3
6-9	6.2	5.6	5.8	6.2	6.2	6.3

TABLE A-V-9 (continued)

PERCENTAGE DISTRIBUTION OF DEATHS FOR SELECTED
AGE GROUPS, MEXICO, 1922-1942

	Years						
Age	1936	1937	1938	1939	1940	1941	1942
Male							
0-9	100.0	100.0	100.0	100.0	100.0	100.0	100.0
0	47.3	46.5	48.6	48.1	47.0	49.0	46.4
1-9	52.7	53.5	51.3	51.9	53.0	51.0	53.6
1-4	43.5	44.1	42.2	42.9	44.0	41.8	43.9
5-9	9.2	9.4	9.4	9.0	9.0	9.2	9.7
Female							
0-9	100.0	100.0	100.0	100.0	100.0	100.0	100.0
0	43.4	42.6	44.6	43.9	42.8	44.4	42.1
1-9	56.6	57.4	55.4	56.1	57.2	55.6	57.9
1-4	47.2	47.8	46.0	46.9	47.9	46.2	48.0
5-9	9.3	9.6	9.3	9.2	9.3	9.4	9.9

PERCENTAGE DISTRIBUTION OF DEATHS FOR SELECTED
AGE GROUPS, MEXICO, 1922-1942

Age	Years							
	1928	1929	1930	1931	1932	1933	1934	1935
	Male							
0-9	100.0	100.0	100.0	100.0	100.0	100.0	100.0	100.0
0	47.1	46.5	46.1	46.6	47.3	45.7	46.8	49.2
1-9	52.9	53.5	53.9	53.4	52.7	54.3	53.2	50.8
1[a]	21.0	20.5	20.8	21.0	21.1	21.4	21.1	21.3
1-5[a]	46.5	47.0	47.2	47.0	46.7	47.5	47.0	45.0
2-5[a]	25.5	26.5	26.4	26.0	25.6	26.1	25.9	23.9
6-9[a]	6.4	6.5	6.7	6.4	6.0	6.8	6.2	5.8
	Female							
0-9	100.0	100.0	100.0	100.0	100.0	100.0	100.0	100.0
0	42.8	24.9	42.0	42.6	43.3	42.1	43.0	45.1
1-9	57.2	57.0	58.0	57.4	56.7	57.9	57.0	54.9
1[a]	22.0	21.5	21.8	22.0	22.1	22.3	22.1	22.3
1-5[a]	50.7	50.5	51.2	50.9	50.6	51.0	50.7	49.0
2-5[a]	28.7	29.0	29.4	28.9	28.5	28.7	28.6	26.7
6-9[a]	6.5	6.6	6.8	6.5	6.1	6.9	6.3	5.9

[a]Estimated

TABLE A-V-10

TOTAL MALE DEATHS AT STATED AGES
MEXICO, 1943

Age	Total Deaths
Under 1	61,592
Under 5	119,366
Under 10	131,861
Under 15	137,377
Under 20	143,522

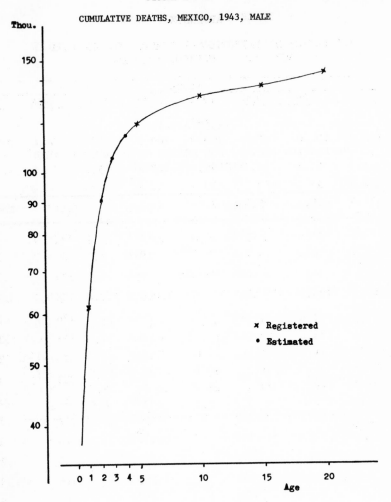

FIGURE A-V-1

CUMULATIVE DEATHS, MEXICO, 1943, MALE

x Registered

• Estimated

TABLE A-V-11

ESTIMATED MALE DEATHS FOR INDIVIDUAL AGES 0-4
MEXICO, 1943

Age	Total Deaths	Age	Deaths at Each Age
Under 1	61,592	0	61,592
Under 2	90,050	1	28,458
Under 3	106,500	2	16,450
Under 4	114,630	3	8,130
Under 5	119,366	4	4,736

314

TABLE A-V-12

SEPARATION FACTORS FOR DEATHS UNDER AGE ONE YEAR
MEXICO, 1922-1961

Year	Male	Female	Year	Male	Female
1922	.344	.346	1942	.331	.338
1923	.344	.346	1943	.330	.338
1924	.343	.346	1944	.329	.337
1925	.342	.345	1945	.328	.337
1926	.342	.345	1946	.326	.336
1927	.341	.344	1947	.325	.335
1928	.341	.344	1948	.324	.335
1929	.340	.344	1949	.323	.334
1930	.339	.343	1950	.319	.337
1931	.339	.343	1951	.317	.335
1932	.328	.343	1952	.318	.330
1933	.337	.342	1953	.319	.337
1934	.337	.342	1954	.316	.327
1935	.336	.341	1955	.312	.335
1936	.335	.341	1956	.301	.321
1937	.335	.340	1957	.314	.334
1938	.334	.340	1958	.307	.331
1939	.333	.340	1959	.302	.322
1940	.332	.339	1960	.299	.320
1941	.332	.339	1961	.296	.317

NEW LIFE TABLES FOR LATIN AMERICAN POPULATIONS

SEPARATION FACTORS FOR ONE YEAR OLD DEATHS

We calculated separation factors using the detailed information on deaths under one year old given in the United Nations
Demographic Yearbook and the Annuarios Estadísticos of Mexico.
These sources do not provide the same information every year.
From 1936-1946 and from 1952-1955, deaths under one year old are
given in the following groups: under one day, one day to one week,
one week to less than one month, one to five months, six months to
less than one year. Information was not available for the period
1942-1950, and after 1955 the groups one to five months and six
months to less than one year were combined in one group of one
month to less than one year. For the years where information was
available, we calculated separation factors using both kinds of
tabulation--one giving the one to five-month age group and six
month to less than one year, and the other, one month to less than
one year. The separation factors calculated from more detailed
information were, of course, smaller than those derived from other
information. The ratios of those factors with detailed information to those without detailed information were approximately .89
for males and .90 for females. Thus for the years for which detailed information was not given, we multiplied the separation factors
obtained by .89 for males and .90 for females. The separation
factors for years before 1950 were smoothed, and for years before
1936, the trend was extrapolated (Table A-V-12).

ESTIMATION OF THE POPULATION 0-4 BY INDIVIDUAL AGES

In order to estimate the age distribution of population
aged 0-4 by individual years we needed the birth figures for the
five-year period before each census year. Registered births[6] for
1935-1940 and 1945-1950 were acceptable, but those of 1925-1930
were not. We therefore made an estimate of the individual age
distribution of population for the ages 0-4 for 1940 and 1950 by
constructing Lexis' diagrams[7] with the registered births and estimated deaths (from Table XIII-13). A summary of the Lexis'
diagrams and the estimates of population at the beginning and at
the end of 1940 and 1950 is given in Tables A-V-13 and A-V-14.

For the purpose of obtaining individual age distribution
for population aged 0-4 in 1930 it was necessary for us to estimate births during the years 1925-1930. There is evidently some
under-registration of births for that period, because the birth
rates obtained from the registers are too low with respect to
those after 1930. We therefore made an estimate of births for the
1925-1930 period using the total population for each year (obtained from geometric interpolation between the 1921 and 1930
censuses) and existing estimates of birth rates.[8] We separated
the total estimated births by sex using a masculinity ratio of

TABLE A-V-13

ESTIMATED POPULATION, AGES 0-4
MEXICO, 1940

Year of Birth	Births	Cohort Deaths		Survivors		Age at Census Date	Survivors at Census Date
		Up to the Beginning of 1940	Up to the End of 1940	At the Beginning of 1940	At the End of 1940		
Male							
1940	450,741		44,220		406,521	0	403,577
1939	445,171	42,240	79,494	402,931	365,677	1	350,962
1938	424,947	77,215	101,269	347,732	323,678	2	324,536
1937	424,463	99,739	112,798	324,724	311,665	3	298,626
1936	407,567	111,803	118,548	295,764	289,019	4	278,162
1935	393,708	117,929		275,779			
Female							
1940	424,730		36,627		388,103	0	384,989
1939	419,910	35,604	69,352	384,306	350,558	1	339,529
1938	404,704	67,596	91,487	337,108	313,217	2	311,897
1937	401,844	90,237	103,552	311,607	298,292	3	284,578
1936	384,158	102,591	109,489	281,567	274,669	4	264,532
1935	370,618	108,311		262,307			

TABLE A-V-14

ESTIMATED POPULATION, AGES 0-4
MEXICO, 1950

Year of Birth	Births	Cohort Deaths		Survivors		Age at Census Date	Survivors at Census Date
		Up to the Beginning of 1950	Up to the End of 1950	At the Beginning of 1950	At the End of 1950		
			Male				
1950	605,675		46,650		559,025	0	542,562
1949	579,273	49,131	82,519	530,142	496,754	1	487,235
1948	561,454	81,399	99,464	480,055	461,990	2	461,848
1947	558,384	96,644	106,679	461,740	451,705	3	427,550
1946	515,863	106,536	112,046	409,327	403,817	4	405,766
1945	521,503	114,267		407,236			
			Female				
1950	569,272		37,503		531,769	0	516,097
1949	544,085	39,811	70,276	504,274	473,809	1	465,712
1948	529,413	69,809	87,929	459,604	441,484	2	437,520
1947	521,432	86,903	97,484	434,529	423,948	3	399,653
1946	478,975	97,649	103,619	381,326	375,356	4	373,855
1945	477,590	104,868		372,722			

1.055 (Table A-V-15). We then constructed a Lexis' diagram, using the estimated deaths from Table XIII-13 (Chap. XIII). In this way, we obtained the estimated population aged 0-4 for 1930 by individual ages (Table A-V-16). We then made a weighted average of the population at both extremes of each year in order to obtain an estimate of the population at census dates.[9] The final results of our estimates are given in Table A-V-17.

TABLE A-V-15

ESTIMATED BIRTHS BY SEX
MEXICO, 1925-1930

Year	Male	Female
1925	360,625	341,801
1926	346,169	328,099
1927	344,311	326,388
1928	370,317	350,987
1929	389,843	369,494
1930	420,892	398,922

For 1921, because of the complete lack of information for the previous five years, we had to estimate the population in a different way. First we estimated the population of the age group 0-4 by sex. We then calculated the population under one year old. Finally, we estimated the proportional age distribution for ages 1-4. We decided to separate the age group 0-4 into categories of under one year of age and ages 1-4 because, by separating out the population under one year of age (affected by the change of fertility in 1921), the proportional distribution for ages 1-4 could be compared with the same distributions in other years.

As the 1921 and 1930 censuses are comparable, in order to estimate the age group 0-4 in 1921, we made a rejuvenation of the 1930 population to 1921, using the reciprocal of the survival ratio from the 1930 life table already constructed. As the intercensal period between these two censuses is 8.5 years, the survival ratio needed was

$$_{8.5}P_{0-4} = \frac{L_{8.5 - 13.5}}{L_{0-4}} .$$

We estimated the $L_{8.5-13.5}$ life table and obtained the following figures:

	Male	Female
$L_{8.5-13.5}$	312,138	315,477 ;

TABLE A-V-16

ESTIMATED POPULATION, AGES 0-4
MEXICO, 1930

Year of Birth	Births	Cohort Deaths		Survivors		Age at Census Date	Survivors at Census Date
		Up to the Beginning of 1930	Up to the End of 1930	At the Beginning of 1930	At the End of 1930		
Male							
1930	420,892		43,139		377,753	0	356,055
1929	389,843	42,226	79,086	347,617	310,757	1	299,027
1928	370,317	75,852	100,663	294,465	269,654	2	255,082
1927	344,311	94,896	109,414	249,415	234,897	3	238,597
1926	346,169	106,133	113,020	240,036	233,149	4	243,744
1925	360,625	112,761		247,864			
Female							
1930	398,922		36,204		362,718	0	341,582
1929	369,494	36,131	69,344	333,363	300,150	1	288,873
1928	350,987	66,500	91,221	284,487	259,766	2	245,811
1927	326,338	85,954	101,019	240,384	225,319	3	226,751
1926	328,099	99,917	107,113	228,182	220,986	4	231,631
1925	341,801	106,033		235,768			

TABLE A-V-17

ESTIMATED POPULATION AT SELECTED AGES, CENSUS DATES
MEXICO, 1930-1950

Age	1930 Male	1930 Female	1940 Male	1940 Female	1950 Male	1950 Female
0	356,055	341,582	403,577	384,989	542,562	402,884
1	299,027	288,873	350,962	339,529	487,235	344,793
2	255,082	245,811	324,536	311,897	461,848	405,508
3	238,597	226,751	298,626	284,578	427,550	415,975
4	243,744	231,631	278,162	264,532	405,766	400,953
	1,392,505	1,334,648	1,655,863	1,585,525	2,324,961	1,970,113

then, as we had the L_{0-4} for each sex, we estimated the $_{8.5}P_{0-4}$ for both sexes:

$$_{8.5}P_{0-4} = .82864 \quad ,$$

and its reciprocal

$$\frac{1}{_{8.5}P_{0-4}} = 1.20705 \quad .$$

The population of the age group 8.5-13.5 in 1930 was estimated from the corrected 1930 census data as 1,740,062 persons. Therefore, we obtained the population aged 0-4 years in 1921 (survivors of which are enumerated as belonging to the age group 8.5-13.5 in 1930) by multiplying:

$$1,740,062 \times 1.20705 = 2,100,342 \quad .$$

This estimate of the total population aged 0-4 years in 1921 was separated into 1,059,108 males and 1,041,234 females, using a sex ratio of approximately 102.

We made an estimate of the population under one year of age, assuming that after the end of the Civil War the birth rate was rising during 1921. The 1921 census was taken at the end of November; therefore, the population under one year of age at the time of the census had already been affected by the increase in fertility. Assuming a birth rate of 46.5[10] during 1921, and applying that rate to the population at the middle of 1921, we estimated 663,000 births for the twelve months prior to the day of the census. In order to consider only the survivors of those births, we estimated a survival ratio of $P_b = \frac{L_0}{l_0}$. The life table for 1930 gives a survival ratio for both sexes of approximately .897. Therefore, for 1921, the value estimated was .885. Multiplying the 663,000 births by the survival ratio .885, we estimated the population under one year of age at 587,000. Assuming a sex ratio of 1.037 for the population,[11] we separated the 587,000 into 298,800 males and 288,200 females.

To estimate the population 1-4 by individual ages, we considered the proportional age distribution for both sexes[12] aged 1-4 for other census years (Table A-V-18). The changes observed in the trend in 1930 could be explained as a consequence of the "normalization" of the fertility level after the "baby boom" subsequent to the Civil War. Therefore, we estimated the proportional age distribution of ages 1-4 for 1921 principally by taking into account the trend during the years 1940-1960 (see Table A-V-18). Then, with the estimated population for 0-4, under one year old, and the proportional age distribution for years 1-4, we established the population for each year of age from 0 to 4 for 1921 (Table A-V-19).

TABLE A-V-18

PROPORTIONAL AGE DISTRIBUTION OF TOTAL POPULATION
AGE 1-4 YEARS, MEXICO, CENSUS YEARS
(percent)

Age	1960	1950	1940	1930	1921*
1-4	100.0	100.0	100.0	100.0	
1	26.6	27.5	28.2	29.0	29.2
2	25.2	26.0	25.9	24.7	25.6
3	24.7	23.9	23.8	23.0	23.4
4	23.5	22.6	22.1	23.3	21.7

TABLE A-V-19

ESTIMATED POPULATION 0-4 YEARS OLD BY INDIVIDUAL AGES
MEXICO, 1921

Age	Male	Female
0-4	1,059,108	1,041,234
0	298,800	288,200
1	222,507	220,552
2	194,914	193,319
3	177,566	175,638
4	165,321	163,525

NOTES

[1] If fertility does not change, it is possible, in an approximate way, to say that the absolute number of deaths under one year will increase, remain constant, or decline if

$$d_t \gtreqless \frac{d_{t-1}}{1+r} \quad ,$$

where d is the mortality rate of under one day with respect to total births, t is the year, and r is the natural growth rate of the population.

[2] For the ratio under one week to under one year, some differences for the same countries and dates appear.

[3] Where total omission is high, lower differential omission would be expected. When death registration improves, the improvement is slower in the under one year old category than in the other ages.

[4] O. Andrew Collver, Birth Rates in Latin America: New Estimates of Historical Trends and Fluctuations (Berkeley: Institute of International Studies, University of California, 1965) [Research Series No. 7], p. 150. Another indicator is the age distribution of the population in censuses after 1921. At all times, the population age distributions present a drop in the age group pertaining to the cohort born during 1910-1920.

[5] The age distribution of death -1, 1-4, 5-9 and 1-9 practically did not change during this period. For example, taking the average of the proportional distribution of these deaths for 1936-1939 and 1940-1942, the following was obtained:

	Proportional Distribution of Deaths			
	1936-1939		1936-1939	
	Male	Female	Male	Female
0-9	100.0	100.0	100.0	100.0
-1	47.6	43.6	47.5	43.1
1-4	43.2	47.0	43.2	47.4
5-9	9.2	9.4	9.3	9.5
1-9	52.4	56.4	52.5	56.9

[6] Mexico, Secretaria de Economía, Direccion General de Estadística, Annuarios Estadistícos.

[7] Roland Pressat, L'Analyse Démographique (Paris: Presses Universitaires de France, 1961).

[8] Collver, op. cit., p. 145.

[9]The weights were given according to the day on which the censuses were taken

Year	Census Date	Weight For Estimated	
		Population at January 1	Population at December 31
1950	June 6	.57	.43
1940	March 6	.82	.18
1930	May 15	.72	.28

[10]From Collver's estimation, op. cit.

[11]Based on the observed sex ratio in 1940 and 1930.

[12]There is practically no difference in this distribution for each sex.